Marginality in the Contemporary British Novel

Continuum Literary Studies Series

Also available in the series:

Active Reading by Ben Knights and Chris Thurgar-Dawson
Beckett's Books by Matthew Feldman
British Fiction in the Sixties by Sebastian Groes
Canonising Hypertext by Astrid Ensslin
Character and Satire in Postwar Fiction by Ian Gregson
Ecstasy and Understanding edited by Adrian Grafe
English Fiction in the 1930s by Chris Hopkins
Fictions of Globalization by James Annesley
Joyce and Company by David Pierce
London Narratives by Lawrence Phillips
Masculinity in Fiction and Film by Brian Baker
The Measureless Past of Joyce, Deleuze and Derrida by Ruben Borg
Modernism and the Postcolonial by Peter Childs
Novels of the Contemporary Extreme edited by Alain-Phillipe Durand and
    Naomi Mandel
Romanticism, Literature and Philosophy by Simon Swift
Seeking Meaning for Goethe's Faust by J. M. van der Laan
Women's Fiction 1945–2000 by Deborah Philips

Forthcoming titles:

Beckett and Phenomenology edited by Matthew Feldman and Ulrika Maude
Contemporary Fiction and Christianity by Andrew Tate
Jonathan Franzen and the End of Postmodernism by Stephen J. Burn
Money, Speculation and Finance in Recent British Fiction by Nicky Marsh

Marginality in the Contemporary British Novel

Nicola Allen

continuum

Continuum International Publishing Group

The Tower Building
11 York Road
London SE1 7NX

80 Maiden Lane
Suite 704, New York
NY 10038

www.continuumbooks.com

British Library Cataloguing-in-Publication Data
A catalogue record for this book is available from the British Library.

ISBN: 978–08264–9706–2 (hardback)

Library of Congress Cataloguing-in-Publication Data
A catalog record of this book is available from the Library of Congress.

Typeset by Newgen Imaging Systems Pvt Ltd, Chennai, India
Printed and bound in Great Britain by Biddles Ltd, Kings Lynn, Norfolk

This book is dedicated with love and thanks
to my grandparents:

Ivy and Dennis Allen

and

Nellie and Douglas Bailey.

Contents

Preface   ix

Acknowledgements   xii

Part I: Critical Concepts and Precursors

1. Critical Concepts   3
2. The Status of the Marginal in Contemporary British Fiction   30

Part II: Marginal Texts and Contexts

3. The Misfit Protagonist   61
4. Revised Histories and Renewed Myths   92
5. Satire and the Grotesque   125

Conclusion   157

Notes   165

Bibliography   169

Index   183

Preface

The following book is concerned with a marked shift in the British novel in the contemporary era towards emphasizing the marginal subject, and examines in detail selected British novels published primarily from the mid-1970s (although certain precursory texts will be alluded to in establishing the significance of marginality in the novel form). The texts under examination in this book are not simply written from the margins or just concerned with marginal characters, but evoke a broader, more ideologically significant sense of the marginal and marginality. Peter Childs acknowledges the significance of such a marginal perspective in the conclusion to *Contemporary Novelists: British Fiction since 1970* (2005), noting that:

> The most valued novels are sometimes those produced outside of the mainstream. The vitality of the genre is not to be witnessed solely in the works routinely celebrated in the press and in the prize awards, but also in the alternative voices that often most strongly encourage the reader to see, in Paul Ricouer's words, 'oneself as another' . . . The novel has perhaps always flourished most at the margin. (Childs, 2005, p. 274)

It is certainly true that some critics perceive the marginal author as offering a fresh perspective, and suggest that thereby such an author can invigorate the form, thus helping the novel to adapt and survive by avoiding stagnation.

Malcolm Bradbury notes in *The Modern British Novel: 1878–2001* (2001) that: 'British fiction in the eighties . . . felt less like the fiction of a communal and agreed culture than the fiction of multiplying cultures, each adding to the sea of stories' (Bradbury, 2001, p. 462). Similarly, Ian Haywood in *Working Class Fiction: From Chartism to Trainspotting* (1997) praises Irvine Welsh's *Trainspotting* (1993) for its departure from the traditional novel, stating that 'The vitality of the writing comes from the rawness of the vernacular language and the debunking of the western Enlightenment tradition' (Haywood, 1997, p. 158). For Haywood *Trainspotting* radicalizes the novel form through the thematic emphasis on the marginal drug-taking subculture of Edinburgh and stylistically through the use of a vernacular Scottish dialect. Haywood acknowledges that it is the dual approach of creating thematic and stylistic innovations that makes *Trainspotting* a seminal novel of marginality; in that it shifts the subject of the novel into a marginal or marginalized world, whilst also presenting the material in a Scottish working class dialect that differs from the usual Standard English, and seems stylistically innovative. The duality that Haywood notes is important to this book as it too engages with novels that address the marginal subject as well as those that present previously marginalized forms, such as the mythic narrative.

This book will develop the contention that the contemporary novel of marginality conveys a belief in the direct or indirect socially transformative powers of narrative. It will develop this contention through an analysis of various aspects outlined in Chapter 1 in terms of three general categories that represent three dominant methods of asserting and representing the marginal subject in the contemporary era. These are: first, the use of the misfit protagonist; second, the evocation of the grotesque subject or subject matter; and lastly, the interrogation of the relationship between fictive and historical forms of narrative that allow for the emergence of both previously under-represented perspectives and formerly marginal narrative forms. These three categories represent a means of exploring the marginalized status of subjects, of groups and of their identities, through the evocation of a set of literary coordinates that have been associated with exposing gaps in liberal humanism's claim to universality and thereby attempt to provide an otherwise missing, marginalized voice.

Throughout each of the chapters I will draw upon a range of theorists in order to substantiate a more cohesive reading of the development of the marginal within contemporary fiction (and, inferentially, culture). In Chapter 2, I will expand upon the concept of the marginal in the contemporary period. I will engage with Colin Wilson in Chapter 3 to provide theoretical interpretations of the role and impetus of the misfit-driven narrative in the contemporary era. Steven Connor and Georg Lukács provide critical perspectives in Chapter 4 for my engagement with the contemporary persistence of the need to create new historical narratives that contain a previously marginalized or silenced perspective on history; and I will utilize Wolfgang Kayser's notion of the roles and functions of the grotesque in art in Chapter 5 in order to assess the contemporary contribution to the field made by authors such as Toby Litt, Will Self and Jeanette Winterson (among many others). Chapter 1 examines the interrogation of the tradition of liberal humanism with which such texts engage in order to challenge its hegemony and efficaciousness. Moreover, this engagement with the concerns of liberal humanism stands as testimony to the fact that a number of authors still regard philosophy as a force to be reckoned with, recognizing its continuing relevance both in the world and for aesthetic forms.

The social theorist and philosopher Georges Bataille provides a philosophical framework for the engagement with the marginal. Bataille is salient in this context because the primary themes of his work converge with those implicitly expressed in many of the novels under examination in this book in that both are concerned with challenges to rationality that nevertheless are committed to a reconstructive notion of meaning and shared universal principles. Bataille himself writes explicitly on the transgressive element within literature in *Literature and Evil* (1973). In addition, the book engages with Rey Chow who suggests in *Ethics after Idealism: Theory-Culture-Ethnicity-Reading* (1998) that the outsider and the 'other' has become a dominant means of depicting protagonists and has thus led to a desire for otherness that has replaced the desire for the classical within literature.

Acknowledgements

I am greatly indebted to Professor Philip Tew who helped to shape the direction of this book and without whose patience, immense knowledge, and support this book would never have been completed. I am further indebted to Dr. Gavin Budge, who has contributed greatly to the project, and I am very grateful for his help in 'polishing' the thesis that eventually became the book. There are many people who have made this book possible. This book is the result of my PhD – a project that would never have occurred had I not received financial assistance from Birmingham City University and therefore I must thank Professor David Roberts for securing financial aid during the last years of the thesis. I would also like to thank the team at Continuum Books for taking on the project and particularly Colleen Coalter for her help.

I must thank my family, particularly my parents and grandparents, for their encouragement and support; both financial and emotional. Clearly I would never have got this far without you and I am grateful for the many sacrifices that you have made for my benefit. I am also indebted to a number of friends and relatives, who offered help in many forms. I must thank in particular Claire Allen, Leone McKenna, Alison Dingle, Wasfi El Shoqairat, Lucy Fraser and Janiece Mullings.

Finally, I thank my partner David Simmons who commented upon, read and re-read the early versions of this book, and who was always encouraging. Your persistent support has been a source of courage. David, I can't fully articulate my debt to you, since this book would not exist without you. Thank you.

Part I

Critical Concepts and Precursors

Chapter 1

Critical Concepts

This chapter will establish definitions for the central ideas referred to in the main body of the book, outlining the usefulness of the work of French philosopher Georges Bataille in an examination of the marginal text. I will argue that the work of Bataille is of importance here because Bataille's primary themes converge with those implicitly expressed in many of the novels under examination in this book in that both are concerned with challenges to rationality that nevertheless are committed to a reconstructive notion of meaning and shared universal principles. It is necessary first, however, to examine the complex relationship that exists between two divergent approaches to the marginal that occur during this period.

The first of these approaches uses the marginal in order to promote a particular polemic, usually linked to idealist, democratizing principles, as Chana Kronfeld suggests in her text *On the Margins of Modernism* (1996): 'writing from a marginal position can – perhaps must – destabilise the norm of the literary and linguistic system by marking the unmarked, charging the neutral, colorizing the colourless, particularising the universal' (Kronfeld, 1996, p. 72). This approach to the marginal regards the process of creating and making popular novels of marginality as a political act, that can help to counter the elitism of the mainstream, and shares the belief that Edward Said expresses in *Culture and Imperialism* (1993) that 'The power to narrate, or to block other narratives from forming and emerging, is very important to culture and imperialism, and constitutes one of the main connections between them' (Said, 1993, p. xiii). Writers of this category attempt to overcome this process at least in part through popularizing the novel of marginality.[1]

The second approach sees writers adopt the marginal as a largely aesthetic device, and is perhaps evident in Graham Swift's advice to aspiring writers: 'My maxim would be for God's sake write about what you don't know! For how else will you bring your imagination into play? How else will you *discover* or *explore* anything?' (Swift, 1990, p. 73), and at least at a topographical level the ethos of those writers that fall into this second category would appear to be largely devoid of any notions that social or moral justice can be achieved through the medium of the novel. W. G. Sebald expresses an aesthetically orientated reason for engaging with the marginal author or the marginal subject in order to make 'better' literature; Sebald states: 'The more homogeneous a society is, the more writers it will produce, but the less good writers' (Sebald, 2003, p. 22). Nevertheless, since both modes in various ways sustain a sense of the powerful quality inherent in such a transformative principle of marginality either ideologically or aesthetically as a means of drawing attention to its 'newness' and its sense of challenge, they both hope to reshape readers' opinions and notions of aesthetic conventions. The latter mode by radicalizing the novel form (one which is essentially concerned with ideas) may ultimately have the effect of allowing people to revise their social and political views, albeit secondarily or tangentially.

Creative writers who utilize the marginal for a social purpose include Bernadine Evaristo, Caryl Phillips, Jeanette Winterson, Will Self and Pat Barker. Such a desire to create a socially transformative text effectively opens the form outward, developing an artistic response to key sociological and ideological currents, of which marginal identity itself is one; thus the 'marginal novel' can be read in terms of Pierre Bourdieu's belief that artistic works are best understood in the context of the societal conditions under which they were produced. These authors often situate themselves as belonging to a minority group (in the case of Will Self perhaps that of the committed intellectual or the lapsed drug abuser) and suggest through their writing that that which has been marginalized often has an immense relevance to the canonical in that the marginal has the capacity to highlight the exclusivity of the mainstream, and demonstrates its failure to account for and integrate a wide enough variety of experiences and peoples to reflect or relate to the community at large, leaving it open to accusations of elitism and irrelevance.

Bourdieu perceives that changes in the literary field are the result of changes in the power relations in the political and social fields; in *The Field of Cultural Production* (1993) he notes that 'change in the space of literary or artistic possibilities is the result of change in the power relation which constitutes the space of positions' (Bourdieu, 1993, p. 32). Authors such as Evaristo attempt to extend the relationship between the text and society. In an interview with Alistair Niven, Evaristo expresses a belief that the text can facilitate as well as reflect change, articulating explicitly her desire that society ought to re-examine British history from different perspectives, hinting that it might take a fictive text (such as her own novel *The Emperor's Babe: A Verse Novel of Londinium, 211 A.D* (2001), which acknowledges Fryer's work) to highlight the lesser known historical re-examinations of British history.

A. N: Do you think people like Peter Fryer and Ron Ramidin, historians of the black experience of Britain, are themselves unacknowledged and should be better known?

B. E: I think so yes, I would say that the majority of the British population have never heard of Peter Fryer and I think that it is important that these books are brought to light and that we re-examine British history from this perspective.

A. N: Was that really your motive in writing this book?

B. E: Yes. (Evaristo, 2004, p. 280)

Authors such as Nicholas Blincoe, Toby Litt, A. S. Byatt, and Jim Crace take a different approach to the marginal, which prioritizes an aesthetic rationale rather than a solely political one. Its very prevalence suggests that the marginal seems to exert an immense influence over the contemporary British novel regardless of which particular approach to the issue that an individual writer adopts.

Alan Sinfield aligns the evocation of the marginal perspective with a growing scepticism concerning the idea that European and North American humanism can lead to a universal culture. He notes:

At first sight, the 'man' of European and north American humanism, in whose name 'good' culture was allegedly produced and has usually been read, seems to include everyone; that is why this seemed the culture for welfare capitalism and left culturalism to proclaim. But in practice 'man' always has a centre and a boundary. The function of the concept after all is to distinguish man from not man, and this means that someone is marginal and someone gets left out. (Sinfield, 1997, p. 300)

This represents a very perceptive reading of the efficaciousness of rendering something as culturally central. Sinfield's very insistence that 'someone is marginal' can be read as a counter to the humanist ideal of a universalizing culture that finds a voice in what Malcolm Bradbury terms the 'traditional' form of the novel. Moreover, Sinfield identifies in this process of making someone marginal a reduction or effacement of subjectivity, thus implicating such a centralizing 'liberal' culture in a dehumanizing process, a denial of rights and agency. Fiction can and has found itself implicated in that process.

In *The Location of Culture* (1994) Homi K. Bhabha suggests that the 'ambivalence' of colonial rule creates a capacity for resistance in the performative 'mimicry' of the colonizer's aesthetic processes. Bhabha discusses authors such as Toni Morrison and Nadine Gordimer, and seeks to locate culture in the marginal, 'liminal' spaces between dominant social formations. In the introduction to *The Location of Culture* Bhabha defines the 'liminal' negotiation of cultural identity across differences of race, class, gender and cultural traditions.

> It is in the emergence of the interstices – the overlap and displacement of domains of difference – that the intersubjective and collective experiences of nationness, community interest, or cultural value are negotiated. How are subjects formed 'in-between', or in excess of, the sum of the 'parts' of difference (usually intoned as race/class/gender, etc.)? How do strategies of representation or empowerment come to be formulated in the competing claims of communities where, despite shared histories of deprivation and discrimination, the exchange of values, meanings and priorities may not always be collaborative and dialogical, but may be profoundly antagonistic, conflictual and even incommensurable? (Bhabha, 1994, p. 2)

For Bhabha cultural identities cannot be attributed to predetermined, ahistorical cultural traits that delineate the principles of ethnicity. 'Colonizer' and 'colonized' should not be regarded as separate and independent entities. Instead, Bhabha suggests that the negotiation of cultural identity involves the continual exchange of cultural performances that in turn produce a mutual representation of cultural difference. As Bhabha argues in the passage below, this 'liminal' space is a 'hybrid' site that witnesses the production – rather than just the reflection – of cultural meaning:

> Terms of cultural engagement, whether antagonistic or affiliative, are produced performatively. The representation of difference must not be hastily read as the reflection of pre-given ethnic or cultural traits set in the fixed tablet of tradition. The social articulation of difference, from the minority perspective, is a complex, on-going negotiation that seeks to authorize cultural hybridities that emerge in moments of historical transformation. (Bhabha, 1994, p. 2)

As Benjamin Graves argues in the contemporary period, Bhabha's liminality model engages culture productively in that it enables a way of rethinking 'the realm of the beyond' (Bhabha, 1994, p. 1) that until now has been understood only in terms of the ambiguous prefix 'post: postmodernism, postcolonialism, postfeminism' (http://www. postcolonialweb.org/poldircource/bhabha/ bhabha2.html). Bhabha's notion of 'liminality' can be likened to marginality because it not only pertains to the space between cultural collectives but between historical periods, between politics and aesthetics.

Graves reminds us that Bhabha's model is useful as it construes the liminal as a position that allows for a meeting point between the centre and the marginal. In a discussion of a museum installation by African-American artist Renee Green, for instance, Bhabha describes the exhibit's post-modern stairwell as a 'liminal space, in-between the designations of identity [that] becomes the process of symbolic interaction, the connective tissue that constructs the difference between upper and lower, black and white' (Bhabha, 1994, p. 4). Bhabha also alludes to different types of marginality; in the quote above, he implies class in the words 'upper and lower', and also discusses race and gender, believing that the liminal is a better working title for those texts that have previously been regarded in terms of post-colonialism and post-modernism etc. This book shares this concern and Chapter 2 discusses the relevance of using the term 'marginal' to find something communicable across socially subordinated groups.

Bhabha's text also introduces a number of potentially serious problems, however, in its translation to the complicated process of collective social transformation. Graves notes that Bhabha's formulation of a liminal space between (rather than supportive of) national constituencies is problematic in that Bhabha's liminal space itself could be said to occupy a privileged, textual, discursive space accessible only to academic intellectuals that fails to properly account for the exiled working classes in the same way that the traditional novel, as defined by Malcolm Bradbury, can be said to exclude marginalized groups.

Bradbury argues that the prime theme of the novel of manners that forms the benchmark of the 'traditional' form of the novel is 'the ethical conduct of man in a society relatively stable and secure' (Bradbury, 1973, p. 32). The general ethos of such a text would largely substantiate the notion that the social and moral worlds are both rationally definable and contiguous since:

[I]t explores dissonances between ethical absolutes or social virtues and the particular individual experience of these, and since it ends with a restoration, that replacement of the social norms, the giving back of sons to fathers and lovers to lovers. (Bradbury, 1973, p. 32)

Thus within Bradbury's concept of a traditional form, although a text may contain moments which delve into the comedic, or the irrational, the novel is still, in essence, easily rationalized and finally construed within traditional notions of a 'rationally definable' world. Marginality results from that centring and moreover, as Kronfeld suggests, there is a history of inverting this process, responding to this act of suppression or exclusion by using the marginal as an exemplary model that can challenge that traditional reliance on rationality. She traces the origins of evoking the marginal to the formation of the modernist canon, noting:

> [. . .] canonical modernisms often cluster around deviant, atypical examples. Modernism at large is obsessed with the marginal as exemplary, in its choice of stylistic and intertextual models, in its selection of paragons, and in its thematics. (Kronfeld, 1996, p. 71)

Kronfeld believes that the marginal can be regarded as a powerful force within modernist art, which she believes expresses marginality through stylistic and thematic innovations. The use of the marginal as an exemplary model did not decline with the end of the 'golden age of modernism' (Kronfeld locates this end point as the closing stages of the 1930s) however, but instead continues into the contemporary era and has been appropriated by many different authors. Examples of authors who represent the marginal in their novels range from modernist Virginia Woolf to John Fowles, each of whom represents the servants alongside the more usual 'central' characters in *Mrs Dalloway* (1925) and *The French Lieutenant's Woman* (1969) respectively, encompasses Zadie Smith in *White Teeth* (2000) and Hanif Kureishi in *The Buddha of Suburbia* (1990) and *The Black Album* (1995), both of whom investigate cultural hybridity and the positive and negative effects that the 'doubly marginalised' status that feeling 'half' affiliated to two or more cultures can create and extends to Graham Joyce and Will Self who create fantastic non-realist means of 'marginalising' their characters to allow for an investigation into the human need to 'belong' in texts such as *The Limits of Enchantment* (2005) and *Great Apes* (1997). This aesthetic rebalancing has been achieved at least in part by means of a return to a 'belief' in the importance of narrative (rather than deconstructive or stylistic forms). Richard Kearney expresses the impulse towards narrative forms that he regards as being at the heart of human experience.

> Every human experience is a life in search of a narrative. This is not simply because it strives to discover a pattern to cope with the experience of

chaos and confusion. It is also because each human life is always already an implicit story. Our very finitude constitutes us as beings who, to put it baldly, are born at the beginning and die at the end. (Kearney, 2001, p. 21)

The links between the two phenomena of a return to narrative and the shift towards expressing the marginal subject within the novel have remained largely untheorized, a failing that this book attempts to address by exploring the changing dynamic between marginality and narrative in the British novel between 1975 and 2005. This 30-year period is essential in this process since it witnesses a re-emergent emphasis upon the importance of narrative forms in the novel during a period characterized by a concomitant and widespread critical belief in the perceived failure of both post-modernism and liberal humanism to create texts that truly democratize the form of the novel, or its aesthetic-cultural significance. David Harvey asserts that 'the rhetoric of postmodernism is dangerous for it avoids confronting the realities of political economy and the circumstances of global power' (Harvey, 1989, p. 117). The contemporary shift into marginal space and subjectivities attempts to avoid the trap that Harvey asserts, and this novel of marginality aims precisely to engage with and confront the reader with 'the realities of political economy and the circumstances of global power' by employing experimental stylistic and thematic innovations, yet not succumbing to a Lyotardian deconstruction of 'meaning'.[2]

Whilst not succumbing to the total deconstruction of 'meaning' contemporary writers and readers are still wary of an overreliance on the 'rational explanation' to account for experiences that cannot be fully accounted for through the rational processes of science and the enlightenment style of criticism. Something remains in the contemporary era of Northrop Frye's assertion that

[. . .] the positive value-judgement is founded on a direct experience which is central to criticism yet forever excluded from it. Criticism can account for it only in critical terminology, and that terminology can never recapture or include the original experience. The original experience is like the direct vision of colour, or the direct sensation of heat or cold, that physics 'explains' in what, from the point of view of experience itself, is a quite irrelevant way. (Frye, 1957, p. 27)

Frye's dissatisfaction with the gap between 'experience' and rational explanation perhaps explains the public willingness to accept; as Marguerite Alexander notes 'that fictional explorations of madness, neurosis, hysteria, breakdown, might yield "truths" about the human condition of equal value to those that the novel has traditionally offered' (Alexander, 1990, p. 85). Thus, it is no longer unusual for a text to make it problematic to easily distinguish between what is 'real' and what is not; as Salman Rushdie highlights in his novel *The Satanic Verses* (1987) when Gibreel considers his adolescent experiences in Mumbai.

> Sometimes when he looked around him, especially in the afternoon heat when the air turned glutinous, the visible world, its features and inhabitants and things, seemed to be sticking up through the atmosphere like a profusion of hot icebergs, and he had the idea that everything continued down below the surface of the soupy air: people, motor cars, dogs, movie billboards, trees, nine-tenths of their reality concealed from his eyes. (Rushdie, 1988, p. 21)

Angela Carter similarly evokes a world beyond the grasp of the rational conscious mind in *Nights at the Circus* (1984) when Beauty appears to withdraw from the world because of her exploitation.

> She sleeps. And now she wakes each day a little less. And, each day, takes less and less nourishment, as if grudging the least moment of wakefulness, for, from the movements under her eyelids, and the somnolent gestures of her hands and feet, it seems as if her dreams grow more urgent and more intense, as if the life she leads in the closed world of dreams is now about to possess her utterly, as if her small, increasingly reluctant wakenings were an interruption of some more vital existence, so she is loath to spend even those few necessary moments of wakefulness with us, wakings strange as her sleepings. Her marvellous fate – a sleep more lifelike than the living, a dream which consumes the world . . . (Carter, 1985, p. 86)

Carter and Rushdie both present a feeling or a sense of something, which can be said to be real but which lies outside of the process of rationalization that so characterizes the progress of action in a more traditionally realist text; a process which Bernard Bergonzi argues has been largely deconstructed as a product of a particular nineteenth-century realist standpoint which prizes only a limited version of the rational (Bradbury, 2001, p. 3). If the rational has been questioned nevertheless Philip Tew asserts the continuance of 'meaning and external reference' in the fictional text:

> Although postmodernism depends upon emphasising a reflexive, closed system of language reference and a crisis of knowledge, as most novelists

know at least intuitively, meaning and external reference both persist. (Tew, 2004, p. 6)

Bataille writes explicitly on the transgressive element within literature in *Literature and Evil* (1973). Bataille's text seeks to challenge Jean Paul Sartre's assertion that 'literature is innocent' with the contradictory thesis that literature is complicit with evil as a means of reaching a fuller level of communication with the reader. Bataille analyses a selection of major authors (Bronte, Kafka and De Sade) in order to suggest that literature functions as a kind of safety valve for releasing some of the forces repressed by culture.

The application of Bataille to literature is not without precedent, yet it is surprisingly rare given the thematic similarity between the work of the French philosopher and many contemporary British authors. Bataille's exploration of, the potentially positive facets of the 'irrational' in *Unfinished Systems of Nonknowledge* (2001), homogeneity's need for deviance, his atheist mysticism (which aligns him with the work of authors such as Jim Crace and Angela Carter) and his own contributions and development of the notion of a literature of transgression seem to find an echo in writers such as Will Self, Irvine Welsh, Graham Joyce, Jeanette Winterson and Toby Litt. One noticeable exception to this absence of scholarly utilization of Bataille is evident in *The Contemporary British Novel* (2004), in which Tew frequently alludes to a 'Bataillean' framework as a means of analysing the thematic and ideological concerns of the contemporary literary scene. Tew's references to Bataille suggest that contemporary writers share an approach that seeks to utilize that which has been demarcated as marginal in order to enable a critical re-evaluation of the ideology of the mainstream.

Bataille's writing 'actively contests systematic codes of academic inscription and takes thought to the limit of comprehension' (Botting, 1998, p. 1) in order to show that it may be (or is) possible to reach beyond those limits. This strategy finds aesthetic parallels in many of the works under consideration in this book. Fred Botting and Scott Wilson suggest that

[E]ncounters with horror, violent disgust, that miraculously transform into experiences of laughter, intoxication, ecstasy, constitute, for Bataille, inner experiences that overwhelm any sense of the distinction between interiority or exteriority. At the limit of knowledge, unknowing is activated, a process in which subjectivity is torn apart, unworked at the core of physical and mental being. (Botting, 1998, p. 2)

Bataille calls for literature to play a part in allowing humans to see beyond the familiar ways of understanding the world as he perceives that the act of reading a novel can be regarded as a form of protest against anonymity, allowing us to put 'a human face' on strangers.

> In order to perceive the meaning of a novel, it is necessary to go to the window and watch *strangers* go by. Letting go of our profound indifference for everyone we don't know is the most complete protest against the face adopted by humanity as a species of anonymous passers-by. (Bataille, 2001, p. 199)

This ability of the novel to humanize characters for the reader is particularly important in the contemporary era given the pervasiveness of twentieth-century existentialist notions of anonymity and incongruity; Timothy Mo's protagonist, Adolph Ng, suggests in *The Redundancy of Courage* (1992) that

> [. . .] the world of television, of universities, of advertising, of instant communications, made me what I am. It made me a citizen of the great world and it made me a misfit forever. (Mo, 1992, p. 24)

Similarly Hanif Kureishi's protagonist in *Intimacy* (1998) notes his lack of connection to family, friends and colleagues:

> Perhaps I should be impressed by the fact that I haven't attached myself to things, that I am loose and free enough to walk away in the morning. But what am I free for? Surely the ultimate freedom is to choose to dispense with freedom. (Kureishi, 1998, p. 13)

A key way in which contemporary novelists have expressed the idea of anonymity is through seizing upon the figure of the migrant as a representative of such feelings. Zadie Smith's millennial novel *White Teeth* (2000) states that

> [T]his has been the century of strangers, brown, yellow and white. This has been the century of the great immigrant experiment. It is only this late in the day that you can walk into a playground and find Issac Leung by the fish pond, Danny Rahman in the football cage, Quang O'Rourke bouncing a basketball, and Irie Jones humming a tune. Children with first and last names on a direct collision course. Names that secrete within them mass exodus, cramped boats and planes, cold arrivals, medical checks. (Smith, 2000, p. 326)

Linked to Smith's notion of the twentieth century being *the* century of strangers is her evocation of the power of the fear of the unknown; she links this directly with the fear of losing one's identity when she engages in what appears to be an authorial comment or intervention.

> It is only this late in the day, and possibly only in Willesden, that you can find best friends Sita and Sharon, constantly mistaken for each other because Sita is white (her mother liked the name) and Sharon is Pakistani (her mother thought it best – less trouble). Yet, despite all the mixing up, despite the fact that we have finally slipped into each other's lives with reasonable comfort (like a man returning to his lover's bed after a midnight walk), despite all this, it is hard to admit that there is no one more English than the Indian, no more Indian than the English. There are still young white men who are *angry* about that; who will roll out at closing time into the poorly lit streets with a kitchen knife wrapped in a tight fist. (Smith, 2000, pp. 326–7)

Smith draws attention implicitly to the unknowable quality of this culturally and linguistically hybridized process of naming, suggesting that it is the fear of the unknown that creates the threat of violence. The mixing of names suggests the artificiality of the barriers between races in the first place, and Smith insists that 'it is hard to admit that there is no one more English than the Indian, more Indian than the English'. Smith suggests that the destruction of these artificial barriers leads into the unknown, and causes violence and anger, but that the process is also inevitable. Bataille's notion of the 'unknowable' suggests that humans are instinctively drawn towards that which cannot be determined and so controlled by the exterior political and social world.

The unknowable is a temporary state, often found within acts such as laughter, for such laughter signifies the acceptance or confrontation of the unknown, which Smith recognizes in her text, commenting 'it makes an immigrant laugh to hear the fears of the nationalist, scared of infection, penetration, miscegenation, when this is small fry, *peanuts*, compared to what the immigrant fears – dissolution, *disappearance* . . .' (Smith, 2000, p. 327). In his work Bataille privileges the unknowable and the uncontrollable; he notes:

> It makes us laugh to pass very abruptly . . . from a world in which each thing is given its stability, . . . to a world in which we perceive that this

assurance is deceptive . . . We see that finally, given the exercise of knowledge, the world is likewise situated completely out of reach of this exercise, and even that not only the world but the being that we are, is out of reach. (Bataille, 2001, p. 135)

A Bataillean approach suggests it is possible to discern that within the context of an experimental, or parodic genre, it is feasible to detect a tone that is ambivalent towards any reliance upon a perception of 'a degree of relative stability in . . . the idea of reality; the nature of the fictional form; and the kind of relationship that might predictably exist between them' (Bradbury, 2001, p. 3). Bataille focuses upon the act of laughter as he suggests that it is this act in particular that possesses the ability to alert the individual to the potentialities of finding meaning in the irrational: 'if laughter is the effect of nonknowledge, . . . we do not accept the idea that we know nothing when we laugh' (Bataille, 2001, p. 144). Bataille proposes that the act of laughter provides a break from the reality principle through which truths are revealed concerning the relative nature of that belief system.

Bataillean laughter encourages the individual to find a profundity in the irrational which leads to a more extensive re-evaluation of ostensibly definitive and restrictive 'closed system [s] of logic' (Bataille, 2001, p. 144). This more critical approach to the homogeneity of the rational creates a space for the possible re-interpretation and introduction of that that would normally be considered as too deviant or heterogeneous, allowing the marginalized to be heard. In *The Satanic Verses* (1988) Rushdie uses the power of laughter and parody to subvert the grand narratives of religion and culture that were dominant in Britain (and across much of the world) in the late 1980s.

Bilal continues to address the darkness. 'Death to the tyranny of the Empress Ayesha, of calendars, of America, of time! We seek the eternity, the timelessness, of God. His still waters, not her flowing wines.' Burn the books and trust the Book; shred the papers and hear the Word, as it was revealed by the Angel Gibreel to the Messenger Mahound and explicated by your interpreter and Imam, 'Ameen,' Bilal said, concluding the night's proceedings. While, in his sanctum, the Imam sends a message of his own; and summons, conjures up, the archangel, Gibreel. (Rushdie, 1988, p. 211)

In an interview, Caryl Phillips demonstrates the appeal to an author of creating a sense that there are links between different marginalized communities and groups. Marginalization and racism are central themes in Phillips' *Crossing the River* (1995) and significantly one of the narrators of the novel is female. When asked whether he felt comfortable about assuming a female (as another marginalized) voice in his novel, Phillips responds thus:

> Women's position on the edge of society – both central in society, but also marginalized by men – seems to me, in some way, to mirror the rather tenuous and oscillating relationship that all sorts of people, in this case, specifically, black people, have in society, and maybe there is some kind of undercurrent of communicable empathy that's going on. (Davison, 1994, p. 77)

Phillips creates 'communicable empathy' between those excluded by gender and those by race in order to create a sense of parity between the two positions and perhaps thereby to combine forces and bring the marginal story to the centre. Phillips assertion of the need to identify and affirm the 'communicable' empathy between marginalized groups refrains from engaging with the more usual 'ghettoising' of authors and texts into post-colonial, feminist, or working-class 'types' (by understanding texts solely through an examination of ethnicity, class or gender) and instead insists on a broader category of the marginalized that deals with the common experiences of those who have traditionally been, or still are, excluded from the mainstream.

Crossing the River delivers what at first appears to be a post-modern deconstruction of the text in order to account for previously marginalized and untold experiences, yet Phillips stops short of fulfilling a Lyotardian breakdown of structure and meaning in the narrative. *Crossing the River* is deliberately structured *differently* as opposed to lacking structure. Phillips proceeds to give voice to a multitude of otherwise traditionally marginalized perspectives in *Crossing the River* as the text switches narrator several times, from the narrative of a black slave during the American civil war to that of a white British woman during the Second World War.

One purpose of such polyphony within the novel is to bring into question the traditional European emphasis on an Aristotelian concept of linear mimetic narrative.[3] Phillips chooses not to rely on a traditional linear narrative to deliver the 'message' of his text. As mentioned above, in *Crossing the River* the story is told by many different 'voices' and spans over a century. The concluding section takes the form of a diary but again the text defies the notion of linear narrative by offering no fixed chronological sequence; the diary begins in June 1942, but the second entry takes the reader back three years to June 1939.

Phillips' book does not however, defy linear narrative to the extent that 'meaning' itself is sacrificed for Lyotardian post-modern purpose. The story of the novel does have an identifiable beginning, when the father of three children Nash, Martha and Travis sells them into slavery. The novel develops into an exploration of the story of the second child, Martha, and the book ends with a thematic continuance from the initial parting of parent and child in that, although the characters are different, the novel concludes with the reunion of a mother and son in the twentieth century. Phillips' novel suggests that the realignment of the novel form to account for the marginal perspective often comprises the inversion of well-established didactic narrative themes, but that these adaptations retain some basic principles of narrative that are *almost* Aristotelian.

In order to demonstrate how the marginal text exposes the apparent gaps in liberal humanism's claim to universality to which both theorists and creative writers have responded, it is first necessary to define the term itself and its potential limitations in terms of the novel and aesthetic culture. 'Liberal humanism', can be most accurately understood as a literary critical response or reading that assumes a certain mimetic transparency of realist or naturalistic texts (and therefore of language) and whose influence persists most particularly in those who avoid theory-based criticism and indeed in their belief that it is possible to abstain from theory at all in interpreting and accounting for fictionality. Such liberal humanism is based upon and is derived from certain cultural beliefs (or assumptions) about textuality. First that literature is timeless – liberal humanism holds that all literature speaks to what is constant in human nature. Therefore for the proponents of such an aesthetic sense the multitude of theoretical approaches currently on offer would seem to simply form a distraction from the ultimately timeless and universal aspects of human nature to which literature should appeal. Second, liberal humanists believe that the 'meaning' of the text is inherent in the work itself; therefore the application of theoretical approaches again simply detracts from the inherent 'message' of the text.

A third tenet of liberal humanism is the belief that literature should be studied with close analysis of the text; a result of this belief is that if adhered to strictly, Marxist or feminist theorists cannot also be liberal humanists, as their bias would at least implicitly interfere with studying the text as a coherent entity. Fourth, liberal humanism holds that all people are inherently stable and intentional in a way unaffected by social conditions when producing such an aesthetic object within what is essentially a transhistorical tradition, with the implication that therefore literature ought to be analysed in terms of the person who produced it and not the environmental conditions under which it was created.

The final liberal humanist bias that is of concern for the marginal text's interaction with the theme is the liberal humanist notion that the purpose of literature is the enhancement of one's inner or spiritual life. Thus it ought not to be used primarily in a political (ideological) way; to politicize literature is to become a propagandist not an artist, and lastly that content stems from form and never the other way around.[4] Clearly, the majority of critics find this position untenable, but surprisingly it is still influential in at least a covert manner in the resistance to reading fiction as basically ideologically framed and suggestive. This book takes the interpretative position that fiction is ideologically situated. Lukács informs this position and revisits the notion that fiction should be regarded as a product of the ideology that it writes about, against and within, in both *The Historical Novel* (1938) and *Studies in European Realism* (1950); in the former Lukács notes: 'Artistic form, as the concentrated and heightened reflection of the important features of objective reality, both regulative and individual, can never be treated purely as such, in isolation' (Lukács, 1938, p. 332). In *Studies in European Realism* Lukács suggests that

> [R]ealists such as Balzac or Tolstoy in their final posing of questions always take the most burning problems of the community for their starting point; their pathos as writers is always stimulated by those sufferings of the people which are the most acute at the time; it is these sufferings that determine the objects and direction of their love and hate and through these emotions determine what they see in their poetic visions and how they see it. (Lukács, 1950, p. 12)

Lukács highlights his belief that writers such as Tolstoy and Balzac should be regarded in terms of an adjacent understanding of the ways in which they interact with their surrounding communities. This book contends that contemporary British fiction is not immune to the same ongoing impulses that led Balzac and Tolstoy to create fiction that is both impelled and mediated by their understanding of their social situation.

This book proposes that the novel of marginality, and specifically, the taxonomies of the misfit protagonist, the mythopoeic or revisionist historical novel and the grotesque form, all represent means of exposing the very specific gaps in the ideology of liberal humanism (for its avowal of an apparent neutrality is highly ideological and politicized) but most importantly without promoting a straightforward return to traditional realism in several ways. The primary means by which the novel concerning the marginal subject rejects the universalizing ideology of liberal humanism is through the use of a revisionist approach to the historical novel, which immediately prioritizes a politicized historical narrative that highlights the 'message' of the novel but crucially seeks a social understanding of the text that is bound up with, rather than exterior to, the society and culture that produced it. Such a novel is effectively extended in two primary ways: through its relevance and referentiality; and through a deployment of archetypal elements. Moreover the inclination is typically toward a plurality and relativistic position. The revisionist novel in particular does this as a means of revising cultural understandings of a particular period, and would therefore seem to posit itself in opposition to the liberal humanist notion outlined above, that literature should not promote a specific (as opposed to universal) 'political' message in place of concentrating on addressing itself to the spiritual advancement of humanity itself.

The use of the misfit character or the grotesque subject or subject matter would also seem to suggest that all people are not inherently stable, and instead prioritizes an understanding of narrative that is itself driven by an engagement with the environmental, social and historical factors that have led to marginalization in the first place. Further, novelists such as Zadie Smith are perhaps best understood in terms of providing an interaction with theoretical stances that are explored in their own novels; Smith's interaction with issues of genetic science has been read by Dominic Head as a fictional counter position to Donna Harraway's interpretation of the relationship between genetic science and racism. Similarly Pat Barker does not simply redress what she regards as a lack of historical documentation regarding marginalized groups such as women, the working class or homosexual experiences of war, but rather interacts with the way in which history itself is recorded and constructed and so doing seems close to espousing a theoretical position herself (that of a new historicist reading of the past through the personal and the fragmentary).

While superficially it would appear that the marginal is appropriated by a range of writers with the social purpose of beginning to articulate the concerns of those largely denied a voice in 'high-brow' or serious literature, there is a deeper and broader engagement. In this light, this book attempts to present a more complex picture of the precise ways in which writers, writing both from the mainstream and from various minorities in cultural terms, utilize the marginal to both formulate and express an aesthetic, which enables them to create what might seem often apparently quite diverse effects. Some writers, for example, Bernadine Evaristo[5] and Jeanette Winterson,[6] appear to believe in, and attempt to use, the marginal novel as a socially democratizing force. Other writers such as Nicholas Blincoe and Matt Thorne, editors of *All Hail the New Puritans* (2000), a collection of short stories that attempts to remove elaborate devices of rhetoric and instead to prioritize the principles of direct storytelling: 'Primarily storytellers, we are dedicated to the narrative form' (Blincoe and Thorne, 2001, p. viii), appropriate the marginal as a means to an end in achieving their own desires for a return to a more narrative-focused type of fiction. Despite these diverse viewpoints or dispositions, both camps might still be seen as characterized by a belief in the efficaciousness of narrative, and in its ongoing relevance, very much a rejection of the notions that prevailed a generation earlier concerning the death of the author and the text.

This book examines the tensions that arise from these different appropriations of the marginal, which although by no means in direct opposition to one another, seem to be in conflict due to the polemical aspect of the former in comparison to the latter's more solipsistic focus upon aesthetics. In order to initiate such a reading, this chapter proceeds to establish the means by which a selection of British authors allude to a multiplicity of artistic genres and engagements in their fiction, and in so doing attempt to democratize the novel form. Although this approach is seen by critics such as Alison Lee as primarily in terms of articulating a post-modernist aesthetic, my book will contest Lee's suggestion that such a re-emphasis on the narratival is restricted to post-modernism alone, in that such fiction

> [. . .] concerns itself with questioning margins and boundaries valorised by the dominant cultural authority. [. . .] one of postmodernism's most important concerns is to decentre the humanist notion of 'individuality', of a coherent essence of self which exists outside ideology. (Lee, 1990, p. xi)

I disagree with the implication in Lee's suggestion that it is solely post-modernism that achieves this questioning of the 'margins and boundaries valorized by the dominant cultural authority'; indeed the work of writers such as Blincoe, Evaristo, Zadie Smith, Jim Crace, Jonathan Coe, Nick Hornby, Toby Litt, Will Self and Adam Thorpe appears to reject a post-modern decentring of the individual in favour of a preoccupation with the humanist self (albeit seen as contestable and prone to interrogation). It can be inferred that these authors, rather than commenting upon the humanist notion of 'individuality' through diverging from the kind of traditional novel that Bradbury identifies above, are in fact ensuring that each of their distinct divergences from the realist mode be viewed directly in relation to the political impetus behind the novel rather than in aesthetic terms at all.

Lee's concept of democratizing the form through post-modern techniques is too aesthetically oriented and neglects to take into account the
social (rather than textual) influences behind many novels that deal with
marginality through distancing themselves from realism. Indeed, in a time
in which 'in politics the reality and myth of Margaret Thatcher and an
attendant concept of history were dominant' (Lane, 2003, p. 11) the elected
descriptive modes of these novels are ultimately bound to their subject
matter. The relation of the novel of marginality to reality is expressed in
Andrej Gąsiorek's analysis of *Midnight's Children* when he suggests that to
rely solely upon 'flat realist prose would be to deny the diversity, dynamism
and political confusion of [Britain] at that time' (Gąsiorek, 1995, p. 167).
Gąsiorek notes:

> Rushdie's verbal pyrotechnics, I suggest, attempt to do justice to the peri-
> od's often unreal atmosphere rather than to make some universal claim
> about the intrinsically fantastic nature of all history. Rushdie's narrative
> mode does not seek to do away with the distinction between fantasy and
> reality but shows how strange and unstable was the political reality of the
> time. (Gąsiorek, 1995, p. 167)

It is possible to discern a double refusal of connectedness and extension,
which is part of a more general refusal of the novel as a genre, and, embod-
ied within that, of the implied continuity between the form of the realist
novel and the form of social life itself. These texts neither entirely abandon
nor entirely remain within the form of the traditional realist novel (Connor,
1996, p. 94). Instead they evoke and create something of a hybrid form,
akin to magical realism but not entirely identical to it, since in these British
texts the 'magical' elements are ultimately removable from the realist
aspects of the text so that the two are not finally embedded in each other.
In fact the points of exaggeration of unreality derive more from a sense of
the radical spectacle undermining the authorized one propounded by Guy
Debord and the Situationists. They might be seen as quasi-situationist texts.
In *The Society of the Spectacle* (1967) Debord says of the traditional social
narrative that he seeks to disrupt, '[B]y means of the spectacle the ruling
order discourses endlessly upon itself in an uninterrupted monologue of
self-praise' (Debord, 1967, p. 19). In literature, marginality can disrupt and
challenge the endless repetition of such hegemonic aesthetic discourses of
self-representation, those of conventional social and textual forms, while its
adoption reveals those very forms. The purpose of radicalizing the textual

spectacle (as in magic realism) always seems to be to directly influence and change the situation of the actual world, to create a jolt back into that real-life world and to therefore comment upon its specifics, its actuality. Marc Wardle notes that

> [. . .] man becomes non-existent within the mode of production of the 'spectacle'. Reality remains an unattainable illusion to the blind soul of man. In essence, as Debord implies, the 'innovative' nature of man 'isolates' him from his reality. (Wardle, 2002, p. 26)

In order to create a meaningful effect there must be something that exists beyond the spectacle, such that a distinction can in fact be made between the spectacle and the underlying 'real' conditions. Indeed there is a sense in which the spirit of the carnivalesque is so present within Angela Carter's *Wise Children* that the text almost demands that the reader undertake a critique of the novel itself, and thus implies that there is something beyond the spectacle of the carnival that must be recognized in the reading. Nora's affirmation that she said 'maybe' to life, rather than the unequivocal yes of her sister is a plea to the reader to stay sceptical, to ask questions of the text. In order to address this return to an assertion of the importance of the individual in Chapter 3, I examine the role that the misfit character plays in contemporary novels, suggesting that such a figure enables the author to present a particular political viewpoint without appearing either too partisan or polemical.

Contemporary critics are increasingly aware of not only the marginal as a characterization or authorial position, but seem conscious of its wider potential as a social discourse. John Brannigan evokes a sense that the novel can be a socially conscious and committed artefact because of its potential to promote the fictions of marginalized peoples when he concludes his survey of modern English fiction, *Orwell to the Present: Literature in England, 1945 – 2000* (2003) with an optimistic wish that literature may be capable of becoming 'available as a voice for the silenced, and as an imaginative space for dissidence, critique and reinvention' (Brannigan, 2003, p. 204). Brannigan's proposal that literature can provide a voice for the silenced is pertinent as it suggests that he regards literature as a useful social tool that can provide a means for the marginalized and the dispossessed to gain a voice in society. He implies that this will lead to the creation of an idealist, imaginative space in which truly democratic social critique can take place. While Brannigan's idealism might well seem naive to the archetypal post-modern literary critic, nevertheless it undoubtedly echoes a wider belief in the literary form that seems to exist amongst many contemporary writers as practitioners who think about the wider impact of their work.

Branningan's definition of 'the silenced' seems very specifically to refer to those who are seen as peripheral, often grotesque and comic, and outside of the mainstream. Contemporary British fiction has resonated with a cultural re-figuration. Such silence is not only literal; it also concerns the previous dynamics of certain marginalities that are among those currently in the process of acquiring aesthetic, ideological and socio-historic significances. Childs observes the extent to which the marginal position is significant in the construction of literary identities and suggests that twentieth-century writers have perceived themselves as occupying marginal positions in society: 'The exiles and émigrés of modernism included few writers who did not feel marginalized: Woolf by her sex, Lawrence by his class, Forster by his sexuality, many others by their nationality' (Childs, 2005, p. 274). Such writers came to occupy elevated social positions by the ends of their careers, but the significance of marginality deriving from one's gender and sexual orientation on the part of such authors is prescient, although their efforts were somewhat limited in terms of any larger impulse towards prioritizing other, socially marginalized groups or individuals who are economically and subjectively dispossessed.

The tendency for those of an once-marginalized position who gain cultural centrality to begin to attempt to control the marginal space is documented by Kronfeld, who notes that with the publication of works by 'historically marginalized authors, [. . .] literary historiography appears to be entering a more inclusive phase' (Kronfeld, 1996, p. 226). Kronfeld believes that this creates a 'seductively misleading impression' (Kronfeld, 1996, p. 226), which suggests that the literary canon has become more open and inclusive, when in reality the inclusion of such authors represents only the first step into opening the canon. Kronfeld contends that this can lead to those newly included authors maintaining, rather than deconstructing the barriers to an increasing inclusivity.

The problem for Kronfeld resides in the social and cultural power dynamics that affect the literary canon as much as any other realm of social interaction. Kronfeld notes that on occasion those that have been permitted into the centre from the margins conspire to maintain their cultural dominance even to the disadvantage of other marginal groups.

Discussions of marginality face an almost unavoidable temptation to treat the 'minor' condition of a literature or a writer as an achievement, a nothing which is something, a status attainable only by an elite, consisting of the 'marginally correct' [. . .] those in the know, by setting the terms of the discussion, deny the margin's right to its own marginality, perhaps the only property that truly belongs to it. As long as exclusionary practices figure so dominantly in canon formation, the process of revising or reforming the literary canon runs the risk of duplicating or re-circulating the domination it has set out to subvert. (Kronfeld, 1996, pp. 225–6)

There is a discernable move to change this situation that occurs early in the contemporary period, when, in another wave of experimental fiction writers such as John Fowles in *The French Lieutenant's Woman* (1969) begin to detail the lives of the previously undocumented, rather than rely on their own status as marginal or otherwise. Fowles' novel depicts the servants of a Victorian household as dignified individuals deserving equality, and in doing so in a deliberately socially and ideologically aware fashion, Fowles highlights the lack of the authentic and dignified development of marginal characters in previous generations of the novel.

Like Fowles, Jonathan Coe creates a text that decentres the traditional biography of the great and the good by including perspectives that the reader would perhaps expect to remain untold. Coe documents the otherwise marginal or untold story of the documenter in *What a Carve Up!* (1994), when Michael realizes that his role as a biographer of the Winshaw family may not remain as marginal as he first thought. Michael's plight concerning the nature of his involvement and possible 'guilt' in creating the ruthless success of the Winshaws again depends upon recognizing the tentative nature of the notion of truth within this novel. Acquiring real truth entails the ability to remain unfulfilled by what appears to be an explanation. Moreover Michael himself comes to the verge of suggesting that progress will only be truly made towards achieving real truth within British politics and economic policy if society as a whole can break its reliance upon the presumption that truth and falsity are both fixed poles and contain no act of interpretation on the part of those at the margins. Thus as long as the public remain 'detached' and 'disinterested' (Coe, 1995, p. 427) the Winshaws will control the mode of description, as Rushdie's immigration officers do over the immigrants that they make into demons.

Michael remains unable to establish solid fact or truth, yet truth is still available to him as an ideal in his dreams, which speak to him of events that will later occur. Indeed the novel is premised on the notion that something other than politically defined 'fact' and 'truth' should govern our understanding of reality and truth as it opens by telling us that if we dream we should listen to our dreams. It is the death-dealing, topsy-turvy world of the carnival that allows Michael the power of description once and for all as he is enlisted to write the biography of the Winshaws, but once given this power of description Michael leaves behind the lure of the 'irrational' and seemingly goes in search of something more solid. The fictional revelation of the grounds of such a spectacle creates a jolt back to a sense of a more complex and radicalized reality in these texts, particularly as the fantastical elements are always designed to speak of a targeted, specific political or historical moment that has hitherto been expressed in terms of partial iconography rather than with any true attempt at adherence to varied or otherwise marginalized viewpoints and truths.

The shift towards the marginal in the novels of contemporary writers results in what might be described as a marginal revisionism. This process of re-evaluation is evident in the proliferation of two kinds of contemporary fictional narratives. The first is the appropriation of marginalized sensibilities, which is manifested in terms of a change in perspective that prioritizes those very characters that have traditionally been deemed to occupy a marginal position and in so doing reorients the narrative perspective and focalization. In the case of *The Wide Sargasso Sea* (1966) Jean Rhys adapts and rewrites a previous fiction: Charlotte Brontë's *Jane Eyre* (1847), in order to give a voice to Rochester's first 'mad' wife: whom Rhys renames Antoinette. Rhys' novel represents one of the most popular and influential instances of this shift into prioritizing the marginal perspective deploying intertextual techniques to remind the reader of the inadequacies of the original text. The popularity of the novel was to rescue Rhys from the relative obscurity into which she had lapsed since her novels fell out of favour in the 1940s and suggests the potential market for novels that explicitly seek to realign and democratize older narrative forms.

While Rhys and Fowles respectively rewrite previous fictions or revisit (and alter) previous styles in order to relocate what was marginal into a more central position the contemporary novel has also witnessed a more general attempt to realign and retell the narratives of history, a second kind or category of relevant contemporary fiction. In particular, this historical revisionism seeks to incorporate previously 'untold' narratives. Pat Barker's *Regeneration* (1991) is an example of this approach in which the novelist imagines untold histories whilst simultaneously deconstructing the very practice of creating historical narratives.

In *The English Novel in History: 1950–1995* (1996) Connor analyses the novel both itself as an historical artefact and as challenge to authorized historicity, suggesting that narrative should be seen as

[. . .] the form by which cultures make themselves subjects of history (in both passive and active senses, as the makers of history and those acted on by history). With the awareness of the multiple lines of consequence in the contemporary world has come the possibility of a plurality of forms of agency in or ways of being the subject of history. [. . .] where the role of narrative might once have been to call its audience into the position of the subject of history, narrative in the post-war world has been much more sceptically or modestly concerned to investigate the conditions of possibility under which history may be narratable at all. (Connor, 1996, p. 133)

Connor proposes that the revisionism of the contemporary novel is part of an ongoing investigation into the limits of narrating history and that such a role is the preoccupation of a large part of the contemporary canon. This book goes further than Connor to suggest that in recent years through the recuperation and acknowledgement of the subjective quality of all 'types' of history in texts such as *The Gift of Stones* (1988) which deals with mythic history and *Oranges Are Not The Only Fruit* (1985) which is concerned with personal histories, authors have again begun to make ambitious claims concerning the socially transformative powers of narrative as revealing intuitive truths about the historical past and the role of history in terms of personal apprehensions of the world. Graham Swift details this theme in his novel *Waterland* (1983) which Tew describes as being 'variously [. . .] a sedimented family history, official and unofficial classroom narratives, a confessional and rites of passage, and an expression of the current exigencies of Thatcherism' (Tew, 2004, p. 143).

Haywood, Alison Lee and Connor situate specific incarnations of the marginal subject or the marginal author (such as the feminist text, the postcolonial text, and the working-class text) within and against mainstream literary culture. Dominic Head and Tew examine the social and philosophical repercussions of the inclusion of authors considered by many to represent a marginal stance into a canonical body of literature (such as the working-class author, the female author, the immigrant author etc.) although both reach different conclusions as to the way that the contemporary preoccupation with the novel of marginality should be considered. Head maintains an approach to the contemporary novel that eschews what he regards as

> [. . .] the theoretical preoccupations that have become dominant in the academy since 1980 – and that may be overtly alluded to in the work of a Carter, a Rushdie, or a Winterson – [but which he believes] had no relevance to the novelists of the 1950s and earlier 1960s. (Head, 2002, p. 1)

In contrast to Head, Tew maintains the importance and validity of a theoretical approach to understanding the interaction between marginal groups such as immigrant writers, working-class writers etc. Regarding theoretical readings as a means of democratizing the field by introducing social theorists and philosophers in order to understand the cultural politics at the heart of fiction, Tew demonstrates the reasons for his insistence on the validity of a theoretical approach in his explanation of the application of Roy Bhaskar's philosophy when he notes:

> In my experience snobbishness and elitism are alive and well in Britain even among the apparently 'radical' element of the intellectual and political classes. Roy Bhaskar charts as a historical response the exclusion of the working classes from the philosophical discourse of modernity. (Tew, 2004, p. xiii)

For Tew a theoretical approach, such as an application of Roy Bhaskar, allows the literary critic to overcome what he regards as a middle class critical hegemony.

The results that an appropriation of liberal, post-colonial and postmodern interpretive tropes can have are also explored in Rey Chow's *Ethics after Idealism: Theory-Culture-Ethnicity-Reading* (1998). She argues that in the contemporary period such interpretive schemas have taken on what are essentially Fascistic aspects, as they have effectively come to dominate literary criticism to the extent that they often deny the validity of all other readings. Chow's radical re-evaluation of the marginal informs my own approach to the subject. Of particular importance is her suggestion that the exclusion of the possibility of alternative interpretations has led to a new kind of elitism. For Chow, the dominance of liberal, post-colonial, and postmodern readings have worked to limit the way in which critics are able to receive texts regardless of the merits or otherwise of individual applications of these theories.

In the white liberal enthusiasm for 'peoples of color' that is currently
sweeping through North American academic circles, something of the
fascism we witnessed in earlier decades has made its return in a new guise.
The basis for this fascism is, once again, the identification with an ide-
alised other placed in the position of unquestionable authority. . . .
Fascism happens when people willingly suspend disbelief in fraudulence.
(Chow, 1998, p. 29)

Chow's words here demonstrate her belief that the West (particularly
North American academia) has lost its ability to critique liberalism and has
succumbed to a kind of Fascistic stance which means that other methods
are seen as not only less valid but to be excluded from the academy. Chow
calls for a more truly pluralistic interpretative schema which would allow:
'feminism, cultural pluralism and multidisciplinary approaches' (Chow,
1998, p. 29) to exist alongside more traditional readings, believing that only
in doing this will true equality between marginalized and mainstream narratives be achieved.

For Chow the notion that the new can exist alongside the old, creating a
plurality of readings represents the pinnacle of critical success. This belief
in the need for plurality finds an echo in the work of many authors such as
Salman Rushdie (who famously called for 'newness' in the novel form),
Zadie Smith, Jeanette Winterson, Jim Crace, Will Self, Adam Thorpe and
Toby Litt, who often create novels that seek to engage in a self-referential
way with older narratives (rather than seeking to replace older versions of
the same story); Self by reworking Oscar Wilde's *A Picture of Dorian Gray*
(1890/91) in *Dorian* (2002); Winterson by evoking the books of the Old
Testament, in *Oranges Are Not The Only Fruit* (1985); Crace by retelling the
story of Christ in *Quarantine* (1997). Crace's *The Gift of Stones* (1988) and
Winterson's *Oranges Are Not the Only Fruit* also express a dual approach in
that the novels imply both the importance of narrative and to some extent
the ambivalence of its present status; moreover neither texts can be said
to be fully or comprehensively post-modern, nor reductively mimetic and
conventional. In the fictional stone age village of Crace's novel the character
of the storyteller's daughter seems to personify the dual status of narrative
in that she occupies both the traditional position of narrator, detailing the
past, but significantly through the novel it is this otherwise 'old fashioned'
narrator who also tells of a point of change at which a storyteller (in the
form of her adoptive father) will also shape the future: 'The stories that
he'd told were now our past. His new task was to invent a future for us all'
(Crace, 2003, p. 169). Through hinting that it is the storyteller who is the

only 'stoney'[7] not to be made redundant by the discovery of a new metallic material; the storytellers 'craft' is the only one to survive to the end of the novel. Crace provides a link between the ancient act of storytelling and the status of narrative in the twenty-first century, which seems to affirm a faith in the power of human desire for narrative (through the act of reading this novel the reader themselves demonstrates that storytelling is a craft that is still alive).

Winterson provides a summary of the nuances of her faith in narrative when she states in the introduction to the 1996 edition of her novel:

> Fiction needs its specifics, its anchors. It needs also to pass beyond them. It needs to be weighed down with characters we can touch and know, it needs also to fly right through them into a larger, universal space. This paradox makes work readable and durable, from its impossible tension, something harmonious is born. (. . .) once you can talk about what troubles you, you are some way towards handling it. I know from my postbag that *Oranges* has given a voice to many people's unspoken burdens. And when you have found your voice, you can be heard. (Winterson, 1996, p. xiv)

Winterson summarizes a complex means of understanding the way in which contemporary British authors seem to construe the marginal narratives that they create, incorporating elements of the post-modern tradition but ultimately insisting upon a balance that incorporates a more traditional understanding of narrative. Saliently Winterson tells her readers that *Oranges* has given a voice to those who previously felt that they were denied one, that its success can in part be attributed to the fact that it managed to be both radical, '*Oranges* is a threatening novel' (Winterson, 1996, p. xiii), and consoling, '*Oranges* is a comforting novel' (Winterson, 1996, p. xiii). This balance is crucial to Winterson's suggestions regarding the success of the novel as a form.

The margin has become more widely appropriated in the contemporary era but perhaps risks becoming merely a controlled spectacle, rather than an active disrupter of social hierarchies. This has particular relevance for the modern British novel, as Andrzej Gąsiorek notes: '[. . .] history and politics lie close to the fore in postwar writers' accounts of reality because they are central to any society's understanding of itself and thus become hotly contested terrains' (Gąsiorek, 1995, p. 191). Indeed, from Salman Rushdie's rewriting of the grand narratives of the politics of race and religion in a post-colonial, modern context, and Angela Carter's rewriting of the myths of sexuality and gender politics, to Jonathan Coe's insistence upon the importance of dreams to the human psyche in maintaining a defence against an almost omnipotent New Right politics in *What A Carve Up!*, and Ian McEwan's manipulation of the depiction of time in order to expose the inadequacies of the linear narrative to fully account for the human experience, the strategy of rewriting and revisiting the myths, narratives and histories that have governed interpretations of every aspect of life in order to reveal 'that established authority and truth are relative', and to offer an alternative interpretive schema, has become almost a staple in the modern British novel.

Chapter 2

The Status of the Marginal in Contemporary British Fiction

This chapter will explore further both the critical and aesthetic dimensions of marginality, and specifically how this interrelates with both traditional and more radicalized notions of the real. In addition, it will seek to define in a literary-critical context various notions of 'marginality' and seek to chart and examine the manner in which those at the social periphery of contemporary British society have been represented far more centrally in aesthetic terms than in previous literary periods, a movement that helps both situate and characterize the contemporary depiction and utilization of marginality within the novel form.

The marginal encompasses both the marginal theme (such as those concerning minority groups or individuals), and the marginal genre (such as magic realism and the carnivalesque novel). In order to assess the impact of the marginal on the contemporary scene it is first necessary to situate textually such representations of marginality, reality and the carnivalesque, and to examine the expression and the importance of these concepts thematically and aesthetically.

'The marginal novel' (particularly in its contemporary setting) is essentially a problematic term. Although ostensibly 'the margin' refers to a space occupied and peopled by communities who live on the fringes of society and describes those who are not permitted for some reason to express their authentic voice within mainstream discourse. As soon as that voice gains even a little representation in the novel form its claim to being truly marginal would seem to become strained. It could be argued that the margin retains its marginal qualities as long as the injustices committed against the groups it can be taken to represent are not addressed seriously within mainstream discourse, either aesthetically or socially. Once the particularity of the margin is recognized and accepted by the mainstream, the margin becomes an inherent part of that larger community, its radicality is reduced and its formal innovativeness undercut. Essentially it remains contextual not just aesthetically, but ideologically and socially. It cannot be divorced from its larger relevance. Hence, it should be accepted that the centre at least to a certain extent, defines the state of being marginal, and therefore paradoxically it is the centre that licenses and controls whoever has access to the unique voice that such a position affords.

The margin must be therefore that which is implicitly excluded from the centre. The marginal is thus often described in terms of groups whose cultural practices are not represented or supported by the state, and who have limited representation at the level of parliament and other social institutions. The margin is therefore defined in terms of negation (i.e. what it isn't) rather than by its positive qualities (i.e. what it is). This is the reason that marginal politics is so concerned with depicting reality in terms of binary oppositions. The obvious logical extension of such thinking would be to suggest that the marginal subject is inclined to define itself via a process of negative dialectic. But consistently this is not so within the marginal novel, rather the marginal novel consistently seeks to problematize and complicate the relationship between the margin and the centre, suggesting perhaps an urge to move beyond the age of binary dialectics.

Bernadine Evaristo's *The Emperors Babe* (2001) forms an example of a text that seeks to problematize the popular conception that the arrival of the *Empire Windrush* in 1948 represents the 'beginning' of multi-cultural Britain. Evaristo's novel reminds the reader of earlier multi-ethnic incarnations of Britain, through setting her novel at the court of a Roman emperor and details the exploits of his lover, a young black woman living in London (Londinium) before the birth of Christ.

An easy misunderstanding would be to assume that the marginal subject must believe that s/he conveys a genuine self, and that this is at the root of the marginal work, since belief in a truly authentic identity would appear to be crucial for the realization of the self as a genuine autonomous agent. Accordingly, one can experience a pure awareness of oneself. This notion was articulated by Descartes' *cogito*: 'I think therefore I am.' In phenomenological terms, it is the pure and lucid 'awareness' of me thinking which removes any doubt concerning me 'being in the world', at least as a thinking entity. Phenomenology attempts to describe how the world is constituted and experienced through conscious acts and what is given to us in immediate experience without being mediated by preconceptions and theoretical notions. According to phenomenology, one's self-awareness can depict an unmediated authentic form of knowledge.[1] Within the marginal text however a more complex relationship with the notion of the authentic self is being played out.

The marginal novel is engaged in an open dialogue about the nature of a marginal identity and interacts with the notion that the nature of any identity is being questioned and complicated in the contemporary age. The crisis of identity referred to above is most often expressed by critics and theorists in terms of Martin Heidegger's belief that 'being in the world' might be slightly more complicated than his mentor, Husserl had suggested. Within his critical reading of Husserl, Heidegger suggests that unmediated awareness is actually hard to conceive. If this is the case, there is no longer room to talk about identity in terms of a genuine expression of 'a real self' and thus the very notion of marginalized identity comes under attack almost as soon as it begins to gain a voice. As theorists and philosophers such as Heidegger have claimed that unmediated self-awareness is in fact not available to any of us, the notion of asserting an identity within a novel becomes forever complicated, and the difficulty of this experience is not lessened when we move into the realm of the non-realist text, since for Heidegger, even when we touch the sublime or come across an inexpressible unmediated experience, as soon as we aim to share it even simply within ourselves, we are already surrendering to language. Hence, looking into oneself can never reveal an authentic identity.

This has serious repercussions for the fiction of a marginalized self, since to some extent this category had until the advent of such a theory relied upon the notion that it was mediating a 'true and complete' self that could be said to represent a particular marginalized position. As we come to view identity as a meaningless term, however we (as a culture) have moved towards an understanding of self-perception that sees the self as a dynamic mechanism.

Perhaps the most obvious textual examples of texts that have been regarded as offering a glimpse of the 'splintered' marginal 'self' in terms of contemporary British fiction are the novels of Salman Rushdie and Hanif Kureishi, both of whom will be discussed in more detail in subsequent chapters. Rushdie and Kureishi have both created texts that have been regarded in terms of a post-modern fracturing, Rushdie famously by Marguerite Alexander, in *Flights from Realism: Themes and Strategies in Post-modern British and American Fiction* (1990). This dynamic mechanism, however, is increasingly understood in terms other than simply the post-modern, and one major alternative influence upon the development and proliferation of novels that assert a marginal status may have come from early post-colonial theories. These post-colonial theories begin to examine the conflicted, sometimes contrary nature of the elements that compose an individual psyche, whilst still expressing a modernist concern with the nature of 'being'. Critics such as Edward Said epitomize this notion of an implicit ontology. Said in *The World, the Text, and the Critic* (1979) extracts from Frantz Fanon's *The Wretched of the Earth* (1963) a compelling image of the relation between the margin and the centre that presents a picture of the colonized human being as a 'fractured being' whose feelings towards the colonizer can be regarded in some instances as a fusion of desire with hostility:

> The zone where the natives live is not complementary to the zone inhabited by the settlers . . . The settlers' town is a strongly-built town, all made of stone and steel. It is a brightly-lit town; the streets are covered with asphalt, and the garbage-cans swallow all the leavings, unseen, unknown, and hardly thought about. . . . The settlers' town is a well-fed town; its belly is always full of good things. The settlers' town is a town of white people, of foreigners.
>
> The town belonging to the colonized people, or at least the native town, the Negro village, the medina, the reservation, is a place of ill fame, peopled by men of evil repute. They are born there, it matters little where or how. It is a world without spaciousness; men live there on top of each other, and their huts are built on top of the other. The native town is a hungry town, starved of bread, of meat, of shoes, of coal, of light. The native town is a crouching village, a town on its knees, a town wallowing in the mire. . . . The look that the native turns on the settlers town is a look of lust, a look of envy; it expresses his dreams of possession – all manner of possession: to sit at the settler's table, to sleep in the settler's bed, with his wife if possible. The colonized man is an envious man. (Said, 1993, p. 49)

Fanon's colonized/colonizer relations can be extended and seem to typify the relations of all forms of marginalization to the centre: a fusion of desire with hostility, of identification with alienation that embodies contradictory elements but does not ultimately distract from the notion that a discernable and discrete marginal identity can be exerted. One direct result of the theoretical and cultural shift into the post-colonial has been that the marginal self has to some extent become a fractured and parodic self just in the same way that the centred self has, but nevertheless remains assertable in terms of the ontological. This approach perhaps reaches its climax in Rushdie's *The Satanic Verses* (1988).

Rushdie states in an introduction to the novel that 'imagination is one of the keys to our humanity' (Rushdie, 1988, p. xi). Rushdie prizes the fact that humans have the ability to sense the world around them in a different way to that of simply visible and tangible reason, and that they do at times revel in this ability. Rushdie suggests that it is a radical act for an individual to subvert their usual pattern of reasoning and to exist in a realm other than the rational. Importantly it is the rational state of mind that has been left behind, not the 'self' (or 'id'). George Bataille also suggests that choosing to move beyond rationality can be construed as a radical act.

> I think that knowledge enslaves us, that at the base of all knowledge there is a servility, the acceptation of a way of life wherein each moment has a meaning only in relation to another or others that will follow it. (Bataille, 2001, p. 129)

For Bataille, when an individual chooses to lay aside that rationality this act can also be construed as an act of laying aside the servility that accompanies the rational, since

> [K]nowledge limits itself to what happens and all knowledge is extinguished if we envision what does not happen. [. . .] if I now speak about what does not happen, I introduce the unknown, the unknowable into the discourse, the meaning of which was to substantiate the known for the unknown.
> All that I can know about the unknown is that I pass from the known to the unknown. That is the margin abandoned to discourse. (Bataille, 2001, p. 217)

Rushdie's novel celebrates the notion that the marginal subject might finally be as complex and diverse as the mainstream individual is permitted to be.

> It has been a night of masks. Walking the debauched Jahilian streets, his heart full of bile, Hamza has seen men and women in the guise of eagles, jackals, horses, gryphons, salamanders, wart-hogs, rocs; welling up from the murk of the alleys have come two-headed amphisbaenae and the winged bulls known as Assyrian sphinxes. Djinns, houris, demons populate the city this night of phantasmagoria and lust. (Rushdie, 1988, p. 117)

It must also be noted that despite the insistence in Rushdie's text that there is something other than the rational world that must be accessed in order to fully experience the world, it stops short of a complete deconstruction of grand narratives. Indeed rather than being truly Lyotardian such texts often implicitly present a particular version of liberalism that prizes difference as the answer, therefore validating a grand narrative of pluralism rather than a pluralism of ideology itself.

Emmanuel Levinas's philosophy of ethics was also published in the 1960s, with the aim of going beyond the ethically neutral tradition of ontology. His first major work on the topic, *Totality and Infinity* (1961), can trace its influences from figures such as Franz Rosenzweig and Martin Buber, and in line with this dialogical philosophical tradition *Totality and Infinity* seeks to accomplish a departure from the ethically neutral through an analysis of the 'face-to-face' relation with the Other. The work is largely focussed upon Levinas' belief that the Other is not knowable in itself, but that direct (or 'face-to-face') contact with the Other calls into question and challenges the complacency of the self through the individual's reaction to, and interaction with, the Other.

The fact that we find the appearance of novels dealing with otherwise marginalized subjects coinciding with the publication of Levinas' ethical philosophy is perhaps not surprising. The essentially ethical representation of the marginal within the contemporary British novel offers a vital means to any author of rewriting the problematic nature of narrative in a supposedly post-modern age. This is especially timely given the recurrence and momentum of the traditional critical debate concerning the genre as a vehicle for ethical understanding.

The predominance of the marginal subject in the contemporary British novel can also be traced to the fact that in the post-1975 era there has been a general move towards highlighting the relativity of mainstream positions (which are no longer regarded simply as natural). This has in turn led to mainstream positions losing the power to create a novel that seems to speak to the entire nation. Thus the novel that appears to speak from the margins seems in comparison to be both more acceptable (allowing the author to avoid confronting the issue of universality) and less problematic. Several critics, from several different fields have been responsible for this trend. Georg Lukács' suggestion in *History and Class Consciousness* (1923) that consciousness depends upon class position and similarly Pierre Bourdieu's belief that different classes have different forms of consciousness (Bourdieu, 1993, p. 91) represent two examples of critics who have helped to destabilize the cultural hegemony of the mainstream (the white middle classes in terms of literature). Later in his preface to the new edition of the book (1967), Lukács wrote:

[O]bjectification is indeed a phenomenon that cannot be eliminated from human life in society. If we bear in mind that every externalisation of an object in practice (and hence, too, in work) is an objectification that every human expression including speech objectifies human thoughts and feelings, then it is clear that we are dealing with a universal mode of commerce between men. (Lukács, 1967, p. i)

Lukács' work of the 1930s set the tone for Marxist criticism for three decades. Although Lukács was a supporter of the official Soviet aesthetic doctrine of social realism, he did not accept it wholeheartedly, but developed his own version known as 'critical realism'. Realism was not for Lukács a style but instead could be construed as the desired basis for every piece of literature (see *Probleme des Realismus*). Many of the novels included in this book can in fact be read as direct descendents of or responses to the political and social impetus that forms an inherent part of the marginal text, that reached its apex in seminal early (in terms of contemporary fiction) incarnations of the marginal text such as Sillitoe's *Saturday Night Sunday Morning*, (1958), *The Loneliness of the Long Distance Runner* (1959) and Dunn's *Up the Junction* (1963) Haywood suggests that working class marginalized fiction has made a lasting contribution to the creation of a more experimental style that has penetrated mainstream fiction without leaving behind the socio-political impetuses that informed its conception.

> The most productive context for enjoying and interpreting working class fiction is within a labour movement and political tradition; the collective struggle for equal representation in the political, social and literary spheres. This does not mean that a working-class novel or short story must always reveal a high degree of class consciousness, but class factors will always be a material influence on a working-class text's production and reception, and therefore, ultimately on its aesthetic dimensions. (Haywood, 1997, p. 3)

Haywood's assertion that working class novels should be read alongside an appreciation of working class history can be extended to suggest that the marginal novel is most profitably regarded in terms of the backdrop of the history of the marginal novel – in a polemical sense – this insistence upon prioritizing a polemical reading of such novels reasserts the social impetus behind the genesis of many marginal texts.

One example (though not discussed by Haywood) where such a reading is profitable is Jonathan Coe's novel *What A Carve Up!* in which the caricatured Winshaw family, representing the capitalist elite at the centre of a corrupt and failing Britain, find themselves in a space in which the marginalized (due to his failure as a novelist and social ineptness) young writer Michael Owen has to attempt to render their lives into a narrative in the form of a family biography. Michael finds himself unable to write the biography as he has previously found himself unable to create any more novels. Michael has become socially isolated and therefore finds himself unable to create fiction. The novel suggests that there is an unbreakable link between the social and the novel, and further provides evidence that there has been a reassertion of the belief in the necessity for narratives that provide, 'veridical accounts of the world . . . if various forms of oppression are to be opposed by rational critique and if the transformation of society is not to recede from view as a political desideratum' (Gąsiorek, 1995, p. 193). Ultimately Haywood's assertion that there are certain aesthetic dimensions that a working class text should have can also be used to argue that there are certain dimensions that if used will ensure that a novel will be received in such a way. Philosopher and critic, Pierre Bourdieu isolates the pivotal role that culture plays in creating a sense of the marginal.

Bourdieu situates artistic works within the social conditions of their production, circulation and consumption, analysing the structure of the cultural field itself, alongside its position within the broader social structures of power. Bourdieu argues that 'because they are based on a relation to culture which is necessarily also a relation to the 'economy' and the market' institutions producing and marketing cultural goods, whether in painting, literature, theatre or cinema, tend to be organized into structurally and functionally homologous systems which also stand in a relation of structural homology with the field of the fractions of the dominant class (from which the greater part of their clientele is drawn). As such it becomes clear that the 'dominant class' controls the production and consumption of the marginal novel; as such, the marginal novel is at risk of providing nothing more than 'tourism' for the dominant reading class. As Tew notes:

> [P]ostcolonial is more appropriate a term for the crisis of identity among the privileged middle classes that sustained the empire culturally, economically and intellectually, even providing a critique of its inappropriateness and absorbing its ethnic identities, much as contemporary postcolonial discourse does, while leaving the essential structures untouched. (Tew, 2004, p. 20)

The acknowledgement of the possible flaws in the appropriation of some aspects of post-colonial theory has not led to a decline in the production of novels that have been understood and promoted in terms of the marginal; however, many publishers still use the perception of a marginal-ized status of the author to present a work to the reading public. Head notes this trend in his essay 'Zadie Smith's *White Teeth*: multiculturalism for the millennium' when he notes of Zadie Smith.

> On the jacket of the first hardback edition of *White Teeth* (2000) the pho-tograph of Zadie Smith is intended to give out several unmistakable signals. This bespectacled and studious writer, the publisher is telling us, has achieved a level of maturity of vision that is unusual for someone in her twenties. But we also note, if only subliminally, the Afro hairstyle, and the complexion that betokens a mixed race identity.
>
> These details become worth remarking upon with the publication of the paperback edition a year later. Now the author has lost her glasses and sports long, straight, dark hair – [. . .] Smith now has an Asian look, and this demonstrates an indeterminate ethnicity. (Head, 2003, p. 106)

Head's words highlight that there might be a positive effect on sales if an author can be aligned or even realigned with what are now interchangeable groups within the broader category of the marginal. Head also highlights the fact that a marginalized status is still noteworthy, 'if only subliminally' and this suggests that marginalized status for an author is still a complex issue. Being 'marked out' by race suggests a lamentable lack of penetration into the dominant reading group of ethnic minority groups, and also hints that at least in Smith's case her ethnicity is being 'used' as a selling point. Attaching her to a particular set of ideas through changing the way she appears ethnically suggests that there are still very strong associations with race in the minds of the publishers. Smith's work is to be interpreted in line with these associations. Ironically, although this is an idea that *White Teeth* itself complicates, the promotion of the book seems to have been presented along much more 'traditional' lines.

For an author who occupies a marginal status it can be difficult to pro-duce a work of fiction that will be interpreted outside of that position. With the continuing influence of theories of post-colonialism, feminism, etc. writers can risk being limited in terms of how their work will be interpreted. The prevalence and recent popularity of such theories has meant that pub-lishers have often highlighted the marginalized status of their authors, Smith and Kureishi in terms of race, Winterson in terms of sexuality, Welsh in terms of 'Scottishness', Frank McCourt in terms of 'working classness' etc. Many novels have been promoted in terms of the view into a marginal-ized world that they allow.

Significantly both Haywood and Sinfield conclude their texts at the point of the end of conservative rule and the election of a 'New Labour' government in 1997, and both cite the decline of liberal humanism and the decline of realism as influences upon the contemporary British novel. Haywood, however, asserts the influence that working class fiction has had upon the form of the novel, suggesting that working class authors (from all ethnic and both gender groups) have moulded the novel into a tool that can now express a wider range of experiences and voices (in a dialogic sense). As previously recorded in the preface Haywood notes of *Trainspotting* that 'the vitality of the writing comes from the rawness of the vernacular language and the debunking of the western Enlightenment tradition' (Haywood, 1997, p. 158). Sinfield suggests that the rise of 'new right' politics and the decline of both socialism and the welfare state have led to a culture that relies upon social division and the exclusion of marginalized groups even within the supposedly inclusive narrative of post-modernity. Sinfield notes:

> [. . .] blacks and 'scroungers' bear much of the brunt of such scapegoating in modern Britain, and powerful discourses are mobilized around them in order to handle unemployment, violence and disaffection. . . . the homosexual community is an obvious target (. . .) the arrival of aids delighted the gutter press, which made clause 28 possible (at least it disproves the complacent postmodernist view that all cultures are now equal). (Sinfield, 1997, pp. 300–7)

Haywood states his hope that *Working Class Fiction: From Chartism to Trainspotting* (1997) will provide 'some encouragement to any working class authors who still feel that they are denied "a literature of their own"' (Haywood, 1997, p. 160). Sinfield similarly expresses his belief in the importance of the marginal or the subcultural novel.

> Their outlaw status may exert a fascination for the dominant, focussing fantasises of freedom, vitality, even squalor. So they form points from which its repressions become apparent, its silences audible. (Sinfield, 1997, p. 303)

Sinfield's insistence that the subcultural novel draws attention to the otherwise silent repressions of the dominant mean that any representation of the marginal within the contemporary British novel can offer a vital means by which the problematic nature of the social and political functions of narrative in a supposedly post-modern age can be rewritten. As Sinfield posits a convincing argument about the importance of subcultural texts upon the notion that narrative can be a potentially radical tool in creating a socially transformative text, it is not only the post-modern detraction from narrative that allows for the marginalized voice. Georges Bataille seems particularly relevant here. Bataille stands against the post-modern deconstruction of language, since he first acknowledges the banality of such a position: 'It is a banality to claim that there is a fundamental difficulty in human communication' (Bataille, 2001, p. 5), and second opposes the deconstruction of discourse directly when he states that '[. . .] poetry cannot effectively deny the affirmation of coherent discourse' (Bataille, 2001, p. 222).

It could surely be argued then that the deliberate representation of something that has been deemed 'deviancy' can be utilized as something that is avant-garde and risqué by any movement that wishes to disrupt the dominant ideology. By evoking such contentious representations of the marginal subject matter any author who does so immediately posits his art on one side of the process of discourse; the side of protest, without overtly even mentioning a political agenda; simply because of the fact that the discursive practices of the power of the state have entered even the most intimate aspect of the daily life of those living under its reach.

Dominic Head notes in *The Cambridge Introduction to Modern British Fiction 1950–2000* (2002) that

> [T]he state of affairs in society as a whole hinges on the larger middle class group, which thus emerges as the crucial (and culpable) term in the post-industrial equation. The nature of what it means to be 'middle-class' is transformed in the post-war years, generating a crisis of identity no less problematic than that which surrounds the working-class experience, and post-war novelists have not left the contradictions of middle-class experience unremarked. (Head, 2002, p. 75)

Head's analysis of the continued predominance of the middle classes in literary circles suggests an exclusionary nature to the contemporary novel, which is particularly interesting since it is the crises of the middle class that can be perceived to have formed the very roots of much of contemporary British fiction. Indeed it may not be too far removed from the truth to suggest that such fiction has become obsessed with the different crises (of identity, of morality, of ideology) of the middle classes to the exclusion of all else. The narrow focus of the contemporary novel results in a narcissistic body of work omitting (or only touching upon) the concerns of many of those within society, particularly the working class. Philip Tew suggests that it is important to note that in the contemporary era 'most aesthetic issues remain political ones' (Tew, 2004, p. 66). Tew critiques Head's work, suggesting that it ignores some of the larger class-based issues surrounding the novel.

> Head's analysis neglects three major elements: a middle class identity is concerned with a position of relative privilege and hegemonic power; the continuity of privilege in British culture; and the capacity for many key writers to pick obsessively over their own middle-class identities to the exclusion of almost everything else. (Tew, 2004, p. 67)

Tew suggests that the crisis affecting the middle classes was in fact greatly limited in terms of creating an actual change in the perception of a middle-class right to cultural dominance, and therefore was less problematic than the crisis affecting the working class in the same period, Tew reminds us that

> [T]he post 1970s generation of writers while seeking to reconfigure a legitimate middle-class identity, distancing their cultural identity from the hegemony or elitism of the past, are not immune to assuming the superiority of their critical perceptions to which supposedly 'radical' novelists of the post-war era were prone. (Tew, 2004, p. 69)

While such a critical debate implies the existence of incongruities in discussion centred on class in the novel it is important to note how malleable and radical many perceived the culture in the post-1975 era to be, for critics such as Malcolm Bradbury this has affected the way that class distinctions affect culture, as Bradbury suggests:

> [. . .] it ['culture'] no longer represented a classic canon or a definable national tradition, or a set of elite judgements and values. (. . .) culture was youth style, fashion, rap, body-piercing, nudity, designer labels, supermodels, gourmet eating, alternative therapies, organic vegetables, sports and fitness. In the universities, courses in English became courses in Cultural or Media Studies or Feminism, or Gay Iconography. (Bradbury, 2001, p. 512)

Bradbury notes how courses in classical English literature (perhaps *the* only 'classical' subject to survive in most institutions into the contemporary era) began to ostensibly incorporate aspects of the previously marginal. Yet on closer analysis these marginal areas of study are moulded to fit a middle-class-centred approach, such that feminist and gay literature gained a foothold on such courses, typifying a growing acceptance of those lifestyles that had been previously marginalized but existed firmly within the middle classes (women and gay people); and were therefore regarded as being suitable for further inspection. Those categories that remained outside of the middle classes, such as the more 'working class' graphic novel and those black and Asian authors whose work fell outside of a post-colonial context, still remained largely excluded.

Furthermore an increasing hybridization of culture from something entirely classical to something incorporating elements of both the classical and the more populist resulted in a move away from class as a perceived social marker, both because such hybridization brought with it a blurring and subsequent obscuring of categories but also because the markers of working class culture were extended and appropriated by the middle classes. This blurring of class markers can in fact facilitate the marginalization of the working class as they no longer posses a distinct voice through which to speak. Even a cursory glance at Childs' *Contemporary Novelists* highlights that there is still an absence of writers defined and celebrated as 'working class' (while Jeanette Winterson and Irvine Welsh appear, their work is often scrutinized as examples of lesbian or Scottish writers respectively).

It seems that with regards to fiction that is predominantly discussed in academia, class can still be considered as a difficult or taboo subject. For although many of the writers that I discuss in this study have to some extent moved successfully from a position of marginalization to one of centrality the absence of working class figures, including sympathetic working class characters, indicates that the working class constitutes a significant marginalized and under-represented (almost at times to the point of being unrepresented) group failed by both liberal humanism and its descendant, post-modernism.

While the contemporary appropriation of the marginal often aims to democratize the novel by representing those in society perceived to have been denied a 'voice', some writers have attempted to establish a causal relationship between the marginal and the ethical. The marginal becomes an intrinsically positive force in the work of writers such as Nick Hornby, Bernadine Evaristo and Caryl Philips, who often depict the marginal character as a 'better', more moral person than those who inhabit the mainstream.

This authorial approach to the marginal protagonist is referred to in critical analysis of post-colonial writers, where the appearance of a previously marginalized perspective is regarded as having a moral impetus with the implicit purpose of aiming to put right a social wrong. In *The English Novel in History: 1950–1995* (1996) Connor takes such an approach, and situates the modern English novel against a historical background of social change. For Connor the developments of texts that promote previously marginalized perspectives are seen as having a social function. Connor takes an approach that has echoes of Bradbury's view that the post-colonial text will provide an important way in which the novel will gain new perspectives and thus create a purpose for the novel that will promote a moral message and thereby make the novel socially relevant once more, preventing staleness and provinciality leading the form into self-destruction.

While Connor's analysis attempts to support the role of the minority novelist it inadvertently burdens texts produced from a minority culture with the demand that they should all be primarily innovative and refreshing to the form. Indeed by branding the marginal author as an innovator Connor thereby places a greater emphasis on how the marginal novel does not fit into established canons, and thereby implicitly limits the kind of text that an author working from the margins can produce. Authors such as Zadie Smith and Kureishi have invigorated the form but surely they have also written texts that can be regarded as coming from within the traditional English canon. Kureishi constructs *The Black Album* (1995) for instance like a traditional *bildungsroman*, and Smith constructs her latest novel *On Beauty* (2005) as a homage to E. M. Forster.

The critical attention that alternative or marginalized stories have received from critics such as Bradbury and Connor, who regard the marginal as a possible place for the salvation of contemporary British fiction to occur has led to an open discussion amongst contemporary authors about how such a task can be accomplished within the novel. A. L. Kennedy acknowledges her belief that representing marginalized or alternative perspectives in the modern novel is both complex and problematic. Kennedy construes the role of the author in this morally motivated task solely in terms of his/her ability to create a sense of the personal within the text. For Kennedy identification remains the key to the way the novelist can interact with social themes of marginalization. Hence Kennedy (1995) reaches the following standpoint:

> Let's get practical and perhaps even moral. I don't believe I have the right to lecture you on what I am, or what you are. I wouldn't accost a friend or someone I respect (and I always try to respect my reader) with my pet theory on any kind of -ism or -ness. If I tried to, you wouldn't listen to me, you wouldn't read on. If I can't engage your attention, keep you

interested, make that contract of mutual respect and define the truth we will be working with, then I fail as a writer. In other words, if I do not say what I want to the limit of my ability, I rob myself of any chance I might have to develop my craft and I fail as a writer. If you don't read me, I fail as a writer. I don't get to say anything, or if I do, you won't be listening. So person-to-person is the only way I know to make fiction work. It solves a complicated problem, very simply.

So does this mean I think we are all – readers and writers – helpless, isolated individuals, driven by subconscious clockwork? No. That truth I was talking about, that world I will always be trying to define well enough for you as a reader to move in and believe – that's where identification comes in.

And with identification? There we find the moral, political, sexual etc. meat of any piece of work. (Kennedy, 1995, p. 101)

Kennedy's reading of narrative seems to hint at an almost Lyotardian assertion that narrative is inherently self-reflexive; that narrative will comment upon its own relationship with the 'moral, political, sexual' themes that it engages with. Kennedy's opinion is reflected in the work of many contemporary authors such as Martin Amis and Hanif Kureishi. Novels such as Amis' *Money: A Suicide Note* (1984) and Kureishi's *The Black Album* (1995) detail the growing crisis of liberalism and refuse to offer any easy answers regarding the effects on liberalism when it is confronted with an innately illiberal ideal (such as religious fundamentalism or hedonistic capitalism). When Hat gets severely burnt whilst holding a home made 'bomb' at the climax of *The Black Album* this finally facilitates Shahid's transformation from an outsider who is undecided about his stance to becoming a proponent of liberalism. The explosion is the moment that he rejects the fundamentalism of his friends Hat and Chad and chooses instead life with Deedee. Kureishi's novel provides moments of dialogue between the ideologies of liberalism and fundamentalism (and liberalism and hedonism), which serve to present the perceived threat to liberalism posed by alternative ideologies, such as the religious fundamentalism of the book burning episodes at the college. Ultimately the novel upholds and promotes a cautious, considered liberalism through depicting an adherence to the ideology as Shahid's only real choice, when Riaz suggests that Shahid:

'Just believe the truth! These intellectuals tie themselves up in knots. Look at Dr Brownlow. Who would want to be such a clever, tormented fool?

In the end there is the leap of faith and trust in God. But there is something in what you say, too.'

Shahid looked keenly at Riaz. 'There is?'

'You know how some people love to say we are undemocratic. Why shouldn't we fully discuss this entire thing?'

Shahid said, 'Surely we should talk it over without prejudice.'

'Why not? Will you speak to the interested brothers and sisters about a time and place?' Shahid nodded. 'We must do it soon. Why not tomorrow morning? And please, will you write a draft of an article about Western arrogance with regard to our right not to be insulted?'

'After the discussion,' Shahid said. (Kureishi, 1995, p. 176)

Shahid essentially represents an externalized position that lends him an advantage; in being slightly removed from the fundamentalist, liberal, and hedonistic ideologies that he encounters whilst in London he can comment upon them. Kureishi's representation of the marginal characters in *The Black Album* offers one means by which the problematic nature of the social and political functions of narrative in a supposedly post-modern age can be rewritten.

Alan Sinfield has delineated the importance of the marginal or the subcultural novel thus:

First . . . a subculture promotes its own stories and renders them plausible by making them work in that bit of the world where the subculture is effective. It creates a distinctive circle of reality, partly alternative to the dominant. In your subculture you can feel that Black is beautiful, gay is good. At the same time, and this is the second reason why they may unsettle the prevailing order, subcultures are by no means independent of the dominant. On the contrary, they are formed partly by and partly in reaction to it. They redeploy its cherished values, downgrading, inverting or reapplying them, and thereby demonstrate their incoherence. Their outlaw status may exert a fascination for the dominant, focussing fantasises of freedom, vitality, even squalor. So they form points from which its repressions become apparent, its silences audible. (Sinfield, 1997, p. 303)

Sinfield's theory seems also to explain the shifts in the symbols used to represent the margins in contemporary British fiction. Thus as the 1970s saw gender and racial tensions come to the fore in social terms, so too the emergence of voices from these groups begin to gain greater symbolic significance. Feminist, Nigerian-born writer Buchi Emecheta articulated as early as 1968 the emergence of a new concept of the marginal in Britain, evoking class, race and gender as changing and important cultural classifications, that can be used to divide (through the symbols of race, colour and gender) those who would otherwise be strong enough to affect change if only they would stand together, an approach that authors such as Evaristo and Phillips are still interested in utilizing within their novels. Emecheta notes:

> In Britain, the immigrant poor are living out, more sharply than any other identifiable group, the whole range of general social deprivation: in the decaying centres of cities, in overcrowded schools, in bad housing, in the low wages of unskilled work. Yet this experience, which is in fact a concentration of a general problem of the society, and which is imposed, in similar ways, on other groups of the unsettled poor, is displaced, internally and externally, by the false consciousness of skin colour. (Emecheta, 1968, p. 167)

Sukhdev Sandhu sees Hanif Kureishi as a case in point of a literature which speaks to the 'mainstream' British culture as well as to the potentially marginalized group of young disaffected Muslim males, and thus creates a sense of common ground that seeks to equalize, rather than make a feature of British Asian lives.

> If there is one figure who is responsible for dragging Asians in England into the spotlight it is Hanif Kureishi. . . . He has presented their lives to mainstream audiences with unrivalled wit and candour. Not only did he show that their lives were worthy of attention, but he did so in a manner that eschewed worthiness. (Sandhu, 2003, p. 230)

This equalizing desire pervades Kureishi's work, most noticeably in his depiction of London through the sights, sounds, and smells created from the varied cooking of its various marginal groups, which sit alongside each other rather than competing with one another. Kureishi depicts London as being a collection of different marginalized groups rather than a homogenous entity. In *The Black Album* it is the margins that make London the sensory experience that makes it so easily recognizable to the visitor.

> [. . .] the college had allocated a bed-sitting room in a house beside a Chinese restaurant in Kilburn, north-west London. The many rooms in the six-floor building were filled with Africans, Irish people, Pakistanis and even a few English students. The various tenants played music,

smoked dope and filled the dingy corridors with the smell of bargain aftershave and boiled goat, which odour amongst others, caused the wallpaper to droop from the walls like ancient scrolls. At all hours, though favouring the night, the occupants disputed in several languages, castigated their dogs, praised their birds and played the trumpet. (Kureishi, 1995, p. 1)

These new sights, smells and sounds were to form what the critic Elaine Yee Lin Ho terms 'significant literary landmarks' in contemporary British fiction (Ho, 2000, pp. 1–2). Indeed from the early popularity of writers such as V. S. Naipaul, Sam Selvon and Buchi Emecheta to the emergence of Salman Rushdie, Kazuo Ishiguro, Arundhati Roy and Timothy Mo in the second half of the twentieth century, it is not difficult to discern 'a current of change which was gathering momentum' (Kureishi, 1995, p. 2).

In the 1990s Lyotard took this spirit of change to the level of genre, and famously formulated and proposed that we see the relationship between realism and reality in a completely different way to the traditional assumption that reality informs the realist text. He suggests that it is realist art forms that prescribe and dictate how we construe reality rather than reality dictating realist art (Lyotard, 1997, p. 91). This has obvious historical and political repercussions since if 'reality demands to be interpreted, but it does not licence the free play of just any vocabulary' (Gąsiorek, 1995, p. 192), then the question of which and more importantly whose vocabulary is allowed and which is forbidden immediately begs to be asked, and it is this question with which many contemporary writers are engaged. It is the interrogation of this point that links the political and social contexts outlined above with the preceding interrogation of the three directions that many contemporary British novelists appear to be taking the novel: the misfit novel, the grotesque form and the revisionist historical novel.

In *Allegories of Telling: Self-Referential Narrative in Contemporary British Fiction* (2003) Lynn Wells explains the problems that an attempt to return to realism would entail; Wells defines 'realism' in terms that are worth repeating here:

Realism's basic premise is confidence in art's ability to reflect or imitate the external world . . . dating from Aristotle's *Poetics*, or localized as a period in nineteenth century European aesthetics, widely associated with liberal humanist principles and art's responsibility to depict the social realities of certain groups, notably the lower classes. (Wells, 2003, pp. 10–11)

Wells suggests that among the problems with this concept is the fact that literary realism in the terms outlined above 'does not exist except as a critical fabrication' (Wells, 2003, p. 11). Alison Lee and Linda Hutcheon share Wells' notion that the term realism has become problematic to the extent that it cannot be said to exist except as a critical fabrication. This critical engagement with the issue of post-modernity and reality has not escaped many of the authors whose work is examined in this book. Indeed, Ian McEwan expresses frustration with the limitations of the debate surrounding the uses and limitations of realist and post-modern tropes within fiction. He suggests that it may be more profitable now to turn to a third way, which he seeks to instigate by beginning the search for a literature that creates a sense of identification, that speaks of those things that, tangible or not, govern the very nuances of everyday life. There need not necessarily be an incontrovertible divide between creating this sense of identification and experimentalism (often involving non-realist elements) within the novel.

> The formal experimentation of the late sixties and early seventies came to nothing largely because the stuff was inaccessible and too often unrewarding – no pleasure in the text. [. . .] Experimentation in its broadest and most viable sense should have less to do with formal factors like busting up your syntax and scrambling your page order, and more to do with content – the representation of states of mind and the society that forms them. (McEwan, 1978, p. 51)

McEwan believes that previous attempts to experiment with form were unsatisfactory because they failed to engage their audience sufficiently, were 'inaccessible' and 'unrewarding'. McEwan has nothing against experimentalism itself, but is concerned with a less formal, more thematic style of experimentalism that would be concerned with radicalizing and innovating in terms of subject and content. Lee Yin Ho argues that such a thematic or content-driven experimentalism could come from writers, such as Rushdie, Mo and Ishiguro who whilst writing within Britain have a second cultural heritage available to them, and can therefore 'creat[e] an alternative fiction fuelled by the dynamics of their own trans-national and cross-cultural provenance' (Ho, 2000, pp. 1–2). As such, these writers push otherwise invisible minorities into mainstream fiction within Britain, aiming to invert the perceived 'normal' relationship between the margins and the centre, and in so doing either coincidentally or intentionally invigorate, renew and simply increase the scope of, the British novel.

McEwan is not alone in expressing his frustration with what he regards as the limits of the post-modern deconstruction of narrative.

[A]nd there can surely be no more mileage to be had from demonstrating yet again through self-enclosed 'fictions' that reality is words and words are lies. There is no need to be strangled by that particular loop – the artifice of fiction can be taken for granted. (McEwan, 1978, p. 51)

As Gąsiorek notes, there is a discernable attempt to 'move on' from simply stating that narrative is a lie. Gąsiorek notes this tendency amongst historians:

Many historians recognize the predominantly textual nature of what constitutes the historical record, but see this as the necessary ground of research into history, not as an insuperable obstacle to knowledge of the past (Gąsiorek, 1995, p. 148).

Many of the writers that utilize the marginal in their novels also often portray a desire for a return to narrative, aware of but not halted by the limitations that can be levelled against the form (see Chapter 4). The desire for a return to narrative has roots that can be traced back to the serious scrutiny that affected the novel during the 1960s. The critical deriding of the usefulness of narrative involved a marked debunking of the inherited forms, realism being amongst the first to come under attack. Literary critics responded to the social and political questions arising concerning race, gender, class and sexuality by asking whether the supposedly timeless universal human truths found in literature really were so timeless and universal, or rather, whether they weren't just as bound to race, class, gender, sexuality and culture as everything else in the world.[2]

Jago Morrison reminds the reader in his text *Contemporary Fiction* (2003), that from the middle of the 1960s, the frequent apocalyptic prophecies concerning the death of the novel that had plagued the form since the end of the Second World War reached something of a climax. Morrison recounts how figures such as John Barth and Marshall McLuhan suggested that the novel might have reached its limits, that the force of modernist writers such as Joyce and Woolf had perhaps taken the novel to the limits of its form. Set against the rise of electronic media such as televisions and personal computers, Barth and McLuhan thought that the novel as recreation had little hope for survival as a dominant cultural force. (Morrison, 2003, pp. 3–5)

Morrison notes the so-called 'theory boom' that occurred in the 1970s compounded the problem of survival as one of many different ways of presenting a story as it brought many of the liberal humanist assumptions that had previously underpinned the value system expressed in the novel form into question (Bradbury, 2001, p. 376). The attack on liberal humanism that such theories posed can be summed up thus, first the idea that things previously thought of as constant, including the notion of our own identity (gender identity, national identity, etc.), are not stable and fixed, but rather are fluid, changing and unstable. Theorists also discarded the idea of objectivity, as a belief that language actually creates and structures our perceptions of 'reality' came to predominate. Furthermore critical readings that relied upon notions of ambiguity, fluid meaning and multiple meaning gained ground at the expense of liberal humanist readings of literature.

Morrison rightly suggests that the dissolution of the dominance of rationality at the symbolic level had a profound and lasting effect upon the novel. Indeed as early as 1962 McLuhan argued that the novel itself was becoming socially peripheral, as humanity was entering a post-literate age, the novel therefore with its linear formality, and association with elitism, was doomed (McLuhan, 1962). As Morrison notes 'McLuhan's prophesy quickly gained momentum, leaving the novelist, in John Barth's eyes as nothing more than a "print oriented bastard"' (Morrison, 2003, p. 3).

Morrison reminds us that figures such as Malcolm Bradbury have, with the benefit of hindsight, interpreted the 1960s differently from McLuhan, believing that rather than witnessing the disappearance of the novel, and indeed the author, the 1960s saw a variety of new treatments of the form, with various aspects of the novel coming under scrutiny and drawn anew from a different set of coordinates, Bradbury notes that

> [T]he remarkable quality of the mainstream British novel in the Sixties was its rising self-consciousness; indeed we could fairly say a rediscovery of the novel was in the process of occurring. Realism came in for examination in Wilson and Fowles, character and vision in Murdoch, plot in Spark, language and play in Burgess. (Bradbury, 2001, p. 376)

Not all of his peers share Barth's views however. Iris Murdoch, writing almost concurrently with Barth, asserts the persistence of textual narrative in the contemporary era.

> Reality is not a given whole . . . we are not isolated free choosers, monarchs of all we survey, but benighted creatures sunk in a reality whose

nature we are constantly and overwhelmingly tempted to deform by fantasy. (Murdoch, 1961, p. 20)

Thus by expressing a critical and authorial belief that 'reality' at some level must be represented, it is, Murdoch suggests, the failure of the quest of fiction so far to adequately possess such a reality and thus render it for the reader. Murdoch, as a moral realist, holds that there are 'moral truths' which exist, ready for us to recognize; and that exist independently from our ability to understand them. In a 1956 paper, 'Dreams and Self-Knowledge' (Conradi, 1997, p. 92) Murdoch discusses the nature of 'moral Goodness'. Murdoch positions herself on the side of *Vision* against *Choice*. Murdoch's juxtaposition of the terms is aimed at clarifying her Platonic perspective of post-Kantian moral philosophy, and focuses her critique of the positions held by G. E. Moore, and of the various blends of Kantianism, utilitarianism, behaviourism and existentialism prevalent among her language-analyst contemporaries.

Given Murdoch's understanding of narrative as an attempt to render reality but one that is always in danger of succumbing to fantasy it is perhaps not surprising that changing cultural conditions bring about several changes in the types of narrative produced since as notions of what constitute reality shift so too do the art forms that attempt to render it. This reading would imply also that there is a direct relationship between the social situation of contemporary Britain and the changing form that novels of the era will take.

As the notion that it is possible to assert a universal reality principle begins to break down significantly Murdoch uses the example of 'people who are not philosophers' (Conradi, 1997, p. 65) to suggest that a practical morality for the way we live our everyday lives is rooted in a notion of 'a larger structure of reality':

Surely many people, who are not philosophers and who cannot be accused of using faulty arguments since they use no arguments, do think of their morality in just this way? They think of it as continuous with some sort of larger structure of reality, whether this be a religious structure, or social or historical one. (Conradi, 1997, p. 65)

This return to the use of the everyday, rather than the highly philosophical for an understanding of the truth seems akin to Lukács' notion that it is within the literature of the proletariat that the truth can be found. As such when an author evokes a proletarian, or minority setting for his/her novel they seem, according to Murdoch and Lukács, to be able to demonstrate better a moral position that can be identified with.

This shift in the aesthetics of the 'moral' was accompanied in the 1960s and 1970s by a shift in the focus of the novel. Christopher Lasch argues that the 1970s witnesses an increasing acceptance of what have come to be known as post-modern methods and practices, and an increasing concern with individual growth and personal development. The publication of *The Female Eunuch* in 1970 and the founding of the Booker Prize, which included commonwealth fiction also led to something of a change in the literary landscape within Britain. Bradbury argues that for the first time, otherwise marginalized literature, such as the fiction of the post-imperial age, and the feminist novel, grew massively in significance almost simultaneously: 'The subjects of fiction were widening, the tradition growing a good deal more free and various' (Bradbury, 2001, p. 381).

The period from the start of the 1960s to the end of the 1970s witnessed just such a change in form as a growth in the Marcusian, the Trotskyite, even the anarchist novel saw the marginalized subject gain prominence, and sought to disrupt 'the public authority of moral norms', novels such as Allan Sillitoe's *Saturday Night, Sunday Morning* (1958), Stan Barstow's *Ask Me Tomorrow* (1962), and David Storey's *Saville* (1979). This new kind of 'state of the nation' novel successfully popularized the working class character, but the growing popularity of previously silenced or marginalized characters left many novelists unhappy with what they saw as the lack of any adjacent social or cultural realignment.

Margaret Drabble's novel *The Ice Age* (1977) forms an early mordant attack on the betrayal of the social principles heralded in the 1970s, illustrating how the centres of social and financial power in Britain remained almost universally untouched by the social revolution that was supposed to be giving voice to the masses within literature. David Lodge's novel *Nice Work* (1989) also laments how little the social hierarchy has changed. The protagonist of *Nice Work* laments the mutual distance that is maintained between the predominantly white students and the young black gardener at a university campus:

> There is no overt arrogance on the students' part, or evident resentment on the young gardener's, just a kind of mutual, instinctive avoidance of contact. Physically contiguous, they inhabit separate worlds. It seems a very British way of handling differences of class and race. Remembering her Utopian vision of the campus invaded by the Pringles workforce, Robyn smiles ruefully to herself. There is a long way to go. (Lodge, 1989, p. 384)

The socially conscious modes used by writers such as Lodge, Barstow, Sillitoe, Drabble and Storey however, do allow for different types of expression than the 'traditional novel of manners' form that according to Malcolm Bradbury has a much narrower focus. Bradbury argues in *Possibilities: Essays on the State of the Novel* (1973) that the prime theme of the novel of manners that forms the benchmark of the more 'traditional' form of the Novel is 'the ethical conduct of man in a society relatively stable and secure' (Bradbury, 1973, p. 32). The general ethos of such a text would largely substantiate the notion that the social and moral worlds are both rationally definable and contiguous since

> [I]t explores dissonances between ethical absolutes or social virtues and the particular individual experience of these and since it ends with a restoration, that replacement of the social norms, the giving back of sons to fathers and lovers to lovers. (Bradbury, 1973, p. 32)

The necessary restoration at the end of such a novel is usually only facilitated by the laws of fiscal inheritance or economically fruitful marriage, opportunities from which marginalized groups were often excluded. Thus within a more traditional form, although a text may contain moments which delve into the world of the marginalized in society, the world of the novel is still, in essence, easily rationalized and finally construed within traditional notions of an economically mobile and ultimately very narrow (because it is solely a) middle class perspective. Bradbury suggests that the traditional novel is limited because it cannot escape the economic 'facts of life'. Often in the contemporary setting however narrative has become removed altogether from facts, and what is promoted instead is narrative's ability to convey feelings. Evidence of this kind of interpretation of the novel can be found in Zadie Smith's response to James Wood's criticism of what he discerns to be the proliferation of 'hysterical realism'.[3] He suggests that 9/11 will make readers want a return to novels that detail feeling rather than dramatic events, as he thinks the reader will no longer require drama in novels and that an increase in terrorism and war will make such a form unviable in the future. Smith on the other hand responds in an article entitled 'This is how it feels to me' that the hysteria Wood discerns is not hysterics at all but, rather essentially, accurately conveys the feelings of the author about the world through the text. (Smith, 'This is how it feels to me', 2001)

Wood suggests that the attacks on the World Trade Center in September 2001 should alter the way writers interact with the world.

It ought to be harder, now, either to bounce around in the false zaniness of hysterical realism or to trudge along in the easy fidelity of social realism. Both genres look a little busted. That may allow a space for the aesthetic, for the contemplative, for novels that tell us not 'how the world works' but 'how somebody felt about something' – indeed, how a lot of different people felt about a lot of different things (these are commonly called novels about human beings). A space may now open, one hopes, for the kind of novel that shows us that human consciousness is the truest Stendhalian mirror, reflecting helplessly the newly dark lights of the age. (Wood, 2001)

In this statement Wood seems to betray an old prejudice against a perspective that he sees as overblown simply because it does not represent his own version of 'reality'. He refers to his desire for a new world in which feeling is prioritized in the novel, calling for 'novels that tell us not "how the world works but how someone felt about something"' but his use of the word aesthetic seems to betray his real desire which is for a return to a more introspective subject. Interestingly, he refers to 'novels about human beings', as if only an introspective narrative position can facilitate this feeling of humanity in the novel.

Smith adroitly points out that just because her novels do not evoke feelings recognizable to Wood, does not mean that they do not speak to others. This is a key point in terms of any interrogation of the marginal subject since there is a sense in which the battle for representation has yet to fully address the fact that it can seem like a novel that represents a marginal subject is only of worth in terms of political and social medicine. The reading of the marginal text as 'medicine' can lead to such texts being regarded as a social tool but being denied access to the realm of the 'great literature' of feeling.

The return to narrative can involve a return to classical and/or mythical narratives. Various writers have incorporated into their fiction either overtly or covertly a re-evaluation of the importance of narrative to the human psyche, a position that seems to be akin to Eleazar M. Meletinsky's analysis of the process of myth.

The question of implicit mythification in the literature of realism is complex. First, the conscious selection of a realistic genre and the cognitive orientation this entails do not preclude the use of traditional and modern elements of thought. Second, the elements that link the nineteenth century novel to archaic traditions are not necessarily survivals, even in the Jungian sense. (Meletinsky, 2000, p. 264)

It is in this context of the mythopoeic potential of the novel that in Chapter 4 I turn my attention to a still emerging group of novels, that present a self-reflective attitude to narrative, be it mythic or historic, but whose prime engagement seems to be with a definite (at times perhaps, seemingly naive) assertion of the importance of a multiplicity of narratives both complimentary and oppositional. In this sense an evocation of the Romantic Movement might well be discerned in their work, since writers such as Pat Barker, Thorpe and Byatt are less concerned with definable historical accuracy (Barker in fact highlights the problematic and relative nature of creating 'historical truth' within a novel) but instead recognize the advantage of having shared narratives of the past, and thus set about creating narratives that detail previously silenced perspectives (the fifteenth-century illiterate peasant, the gay First World War soldier etc.). In creating a sense of the importance of history as a narrative that binds a community together, rather than as a purveyor of identifiable 'truth' these authors essentially often negate the difference between history and myth. The approach taken by such authors seems akin to Meletinsky's notion of the Romantic concept of the inter-relationship between history and myth. Meletinsky notes that: 'The Romantics did not see myth and history as opposed [to one another]' (Meletinsky, 2000, p. 273).

However, as discussed in Chapter 4, the contemporary reconciliation perhaps assumes a less authoritative notion of history and the historiographic.

In *The Historical Novel* (1962) written in 1936–37, Lukács uses Sir Walter Scott's novels to demonstrate what he believes represents an archetypal example of historical consciousness in literature. Lukács does not consider Scott a romantic but a great realist, who depicted the conflict of classes. Indeed Lukács' contribution to the field of literary studies is perhaps most noted for his work on realism, although he distanced himself from some of the tenets of 'social realism', Lukács maintained an advocacy of realism in aesthetics which has been criticized by Theodor Adorno. Adorno accuses Lukács of narrowly prioritizing nineteenth-century realist fiction, particularly Balzac, and then demanding that this form be replicated throughout fiction regardless of historical context. Adorno argues against what he sees as Lukács' too narrow definition of 'realism':

Today the primacy of the object and aesthetic realism are almost absolutely opposed to each other, and indeed when measured by the standard of realism: Beckett is more realistic than the socialist realists who counterfeit reality by their very principle. If they took reality seriously enough they would eventually realize what Lukács condemned when during the days of his imprisonment in Romania he is reported to have said that he had finally realized that Kafka was a realist writer.' (Adorno, 1997)

Adorno essentially promotes a notion of 'realism' that would broaden the category to enable it to encompass a range of texts that did not display mimetic qualities but did seem to speak to some part of the human psyche that recognized such texts as true representations of human society. Beckett and Kafka would be obvious examples of this kind of method. In theatre such a method would perhaps be subsumed under the heading of theatre of the absurd, but critics of the novel have it seems become rather obsessed instead with notions of the post-modern to the exclusion of all other interpretations of a novel that exhibits these qualities. Bertolt Brecht criticized Lukács as early as the 1930s for his failure to take into account historical contextualization.

This debate seems to foreshadow the current and ongoing debate concerning the uses and limitations of the post-modern novel, given that it has been argued that this form has particular relevance for the marginal position in that figures such as Jean Francois Lyotard and Julia Kristeva have argued that the advent of the post-modern period has had a particularly positive impact in terms of allowing the emergence of art concerned with previously underrepresented figures and groups. In her book *Revolution in Poetic Language* (1974) Kristeva claims that the language of avant-garde literature can create a space for the marginal text (and potentially marginal identities) to flourish. Similarly Edward James argues that the post-modern proliferation of the deconstruction of grand narratives and the adjacent development of otherwise subjugated genres such as science fiction would lead to a greater ability to see through the ideologies behind genre distinctions that marginalize certain voices and certain texts. He notes that 'A genre requires a consciousness of appropriate conventions, a certain aesthetic, and even a certain ideology, as well as readers who have particular expectations' (James, 1994, p. 51). As such the assumption of what is and is not expected within a genre is encoded with ideological discourses. Writing *consciously* within a particular genre can therefore complicate the status of supposedly unchanging or given 'truths' operating within the understanding of the nature of narrative itself, and expose and question some of the concepts behind the expectations and the boundaries which form a genre. Thus it might ultimately overcome some of those boundaries and move beyond such expectations. The post-modern mode may have initiated alongside the politics of identity a breaking down of authorized voices, but subsequently writers attempt to redeem much of the novelistic tradition and its formal gestures not simply in an ironic fashion, but more as an engagement with a plurality beyond the limitations of the post-modern orthodoxies. Rather, as Lynn Wells asserts

> [T]he British novel continues to evolve, in defiance of the ever-changing pronouncements of its obsolescence. By theorising, in and though the act of storytelling, the ability of contemporary narrative to transcend metafictional self-absorption, the texts of Fowles, Carter, Swift, Byatt and Rushdie have called attention to some of the pressing issues facing the next generation of writers. (Wells, 2003, p. 168)

Tew provides a reading of postmodernism that is akin to Chow's critique of post-colonialism. In *The Contemporary British Novel* (2004) Tew realigns contemporary works in categories other than the post-modern. Tew uses issues such as class, post-coloniality and ethnicity and the mythopoeic to situate contemporary narrative practice, sceptical as he is of the claims for the simply formal and ludic, the inter-textual and ironic. Tew provides an extensive range of examples from contemporary literature to demonstrate his belief that the tag of post-modernism represents a reductive label that removes the subtleties from many novels and reduces the novel to the level of textual analysis at the expense of taking into account the cultural and socio-political symbols and thematics represented in many contemporary novels. In the epilogue Tew expresses his intention to allow for a more complete understanding of the novels than the current overreliance on the sole use of the interpretive schema of post-modernism has made fashionable, and indeed to assert that there are fashions in criticism and theory, and that these fashions should not be allowed to dictate the way that novels are read and received amongst academics to the extent that other valid interpretations are all but drowned out. Essentially, in a manner akin to Chow, Tew argues that theoreticians and students of literature should take a more open approach to the contemporary novel in order to fully appreciate the complexities and subtleties of the form's interaction with the world that has produced it. My consideration of the marginal text outside of the contexts of the post-modern and the post-colonial therefore responds to the challenges set down by Tew and Chow.

It should be recognized that the novelists under investigation in this book are themselves often concerned with what could reductively be labelled a post-modern-style of experimentation but I suggest that they evoke such experimentation as a means of revalidating the authority of narrative.

This is evident in the confident quasi-realist and yet innovative forms created by writers such as Crace, Self and Winterson whose mimetic qualities are synthesized variously with the grotesque, feminist fantasy, satire, a mythopoeic history and periodically within the texts an intermittent realism in detailed descriptions of place, motivation and authorial concepts. Arguably this is a 'post-postmodern' synthesis of a particular phase of a British-based aesthetic, a new kind of formalism (Tew, 2004). Authors such as Jim Crace, Will Self, Toby Litt and Adam Thorpe deliberately create a distancing effect in novels such as *Being Dead* (1999), *How the Dead Live* (2000), *Deadkidsong* (2001) and *Ulverton* (1992) in order to highlight the perspectival prejudices and biases of contemporary thought, in a manner that draws upon Swiftian satire but ultimately seeks also to produce innovations within the form itself, and should not be regarded solely in terms of a return to traditional forms.

Part II

Marginal Texts and Contexts

Chapter 3

The Misfit Protagonist

This chapter considers the presentation of the marginalized individual or misfit in selected contemporary British novels, and examines the changing roles and status of the misfit protagonist in the contemporary era. I examine the didactic element of the misfit protagonist in the works of authors such as Jeanette Winterson, Hanif Kureishi and Kazuo Ishiguro, and suggest that the misfit figure functions as a necessary vehicle through which a greater sense of social cohesion can be attained. I also engage with Rey Chow who suggests in *Ethics after Idealism: Theory-Culture-Ethnicity-Reading* (1998) that protagonists are now routinely depicted in terms of how they differ from dominant cultural modes.

The misfit has remained a constant in the novel form throughout its history but there has been a substantial change in the way that such a figure is perceived and defined in the contemporary period. The misfit grows in significance on the British literary landscape as the sense of alienation and distance from the real world, in the Baudrillardian sense, becomes *de rigueur*. In its contemporary setting the misfit protagonist takes several different forms:

- The child misfit (Marcus in Nick Hornby's *About a Boy* (1998)) whose central role is to remind the adults of the 'other' perspective that highlights the flaws in their own perception of the world.
- The outsider, (Mary in Martin Amis' *Other People: A Mystery Story* (1981)) who doesn't fit in because of his/her personal traits and who is thus more privileged in his ability to watch, but whose testament may be doubtful. The fact that the misfit so often provides either doubtful or in some way compromised narratives mean that the misfit is also a device that draws attention to the very process of telling.
- The newcomer (characters such as Shahid from Hanif Kureishi's *The Black Album* (1995) who move from the suburbs to the centre of London) observing the customs of another, but themselves often observed all the time.

It must be recognized that misfit characters are evident in even the earliest examples of the novel form, such as the protagonist Becky Sharpe in William Thackeray's *Vanity Fair* (1847–48), the eponymous heroine of Daniel Defoe's *Moll Flanders* (1722) and Charles Dickens' *Oliver Twist* (1837). Within the work of Dickens there is also a tradition of depicting significant misfit characters in a supporting role, such as Rosa Dartle in *David Copperfield* (1850) Miss Wade in *Little Dorrit* (1857) and Hortense in *Bleak House* (1853). These characters challenge the moral schemes and values and the linguistic norms and conventions of the traditional novel simply via their existence as alternatives to that model.

Contemporary engagements with the misfit character often dispense with Dickens's use of such characters as marginal influences and instead shift the focus of the novel onto the misfit, by casting such characters as the protagonist. Kazuo Ishiguro's Mr Stevens in *The Remains of the Day* (1989) is a well-known example of this shift in focus onto the marginal and the misfit. James Kelman's Robert Hines and Nick Hornby's Will Freeman and the many and varied misfits and outsiders that have populated children's fiction from Roald Dahl's *Charlie and the Chocolate Factory* (1964) to J. K. Rowling's *Harry Potter* series (1997–2007) stand as testimony to the fact that British fiction and the characterization of the misfit share a long tradition.

The role and status of the 'misfit' in the contemporary novel has come to prominence with texts such as Hanif Kureishi's *The Black Album* (1995) and Zadie Smith's *White Teeth* (2000) consistently reaching a widespread audience while simultaneously portraying the liminal outsider figure as heroic, and openly instigating a pluralist, rather than universalist search for the moral. Indeed in doing so such texts reinstate the search for the real or meta-real as a set of literary coordinates, considering simultaneously issues such as sexism, racism and the emergence of a new hybridized culture. In this respect, with their evocation of the marginal, their lack of homogeneity, and through an emphasis on the peripheries of society, the texts under examination here share a desire to promote a decidedly pluralistic morality, which is closer to the work of Emmanuel Levinas than to the type of nineteenth-century didacticism that is familiarly associated with the notion of morality within the novel.

A key way, in which authors who evoke the misfit protagonist have gained an ability to make ethical or moralistic statements about the state of the nation, whilst avoiding claims that it is simply a naive form of moralizing, is through the application of a seemingly innocent perspective. Nick Hornby's *About a Boy* (1998) and Hanif Kureishi's *Gabriel's Gift* (2001) utilize the child's perspective to fulfil this function of the innocent perspective upon the adult world. Hornby's popular novel *About a Boy* revisits the traditional ground of the misfit. Its central adult character Will offers a devastating portrait of the selfish, isolated, infantilized modern Man in the form of Will Freeman, who is a 36-year-old singleton, and is introduced to the reader thus:

> How cool was Will Freeman? This cool: he had slept with a woman he didn't know very well in the last three months (five points). He hadn't spent more than three hundred pounds on a jacket (five points). He had spent more than twenty pounds on a haircut (five points) (How was it possible to spend less than twenty pounds on a haircut in 1993?). He owned more than five hip-hop albums (five points). He had taken Ecstasy (five points), but in a club and not merely at home as a sociological exercise (five bonus points). He intended to vote Labour at the next general election (five points). He earned more than forty thousand pounds a year (five points), and he didn't have to work very hard for it (five points, and he awarded himself an extra five points for not having to work *at all* for it). He had eaten in a restaurant that served polenta and shaved parmesan (five points). He had never used a flavoured condom (five points), he had sold his Bruce Springsteen albums (five points), and he had both grown a goatee (five points) *and* shaved it off again (five points). (Hornby, 2000, pp. 5–6)

Will is living a life devoid of purpose: 'The thing was, Will had spent his whole life avoiding real stuff' (Hornby, 2000, p. 104), but consistently purpose is reinstated in this novel, though the existence of Marcus, a lonely child whose mother is suffering from depression and who becomes a staple part of Will's life despite Will's best efforts to remain detached from responsibility. Central to Marcus' ideology is an optimistic sense of determinism, concerning his mother's and his own fate. He deliberately attempts to procure a bigger community of friends to rely upon as a safety net for future suicide bids by his mother: 'If she had a plan, then he had a choice' (Hornby, 2000, p. 119). For this determination to come to fruition however, Hornby suggests that there has to be a return to depth and an acknowledgment of feeling over surface within the adult members of contemporary British society.

The 12-year-old Marcus is already endowed with this depth of character: 'he couldn't spot the difference between inside and outside, because there didn't seem to be a difference' (Hornby, 2000, p. 14), but Marcus' 'purity of soul' is often set against those adults around him, who should know better, but whose attitude is making Marcus, the misfit, the voice of moral reason.

> Ms Maguire was young and nervous and she was struggling he reckoned. This class could go either way.
>
> 'OK, let's put it another way. How can we tell if people are mad?'
>
> Here it comes, he thought. Here it comes. This is it.
>
> 'If they sing for no reason in class, miss.'
>
> Laughter. But then it all got worse than he'd expected. Everyone turned round and looked at him; he looked at Ms Maguire, but she had this big forced grin on and she wouldn't catch his eye.
>
> 'OK, that's one way of telling, yes. You'd think that someone who does that would be a little potty. But leaving Marcus aside for a moment . . .'
>
> More laughter. He knew what she was doing and why, and he hated her. (Hornby, 2000, p. 16)

Marcus has to set about re-educating the adults around him into acknowledging their responsibility for the next generation, and this begins with Marcus' conviction that an outsider's life simply won't do. He expresses a simple, naive belief in the power of, and the need for, community and attempts to create one for himself: 'you had to hand it to Marcus, he thought: the boy was awkward and weird and the rest of it, but he had this knack of creating bridges wherever he went, and very few adults could do that' (Hornby, 2000, p. 259). Within the confines of the novel a child misfit protagonist allows the author to achieve what would normally be regarded as a naive statement whilst managing to avoid such accusations. The reviews on the back cover of the novel testify to this. *The Literary Review* acknowledges that: 'it takes a writer with real talent to make this work.' Hornby does not simplify the misfit into being a character that can be moulded into 'fitting-in'; however, on the Penguin website for the book, Hornby sums up the role of Marcus in terms that acknowledge rather than simplify the problems that he faces:

> Marcus, who was very very loosely based on someone I used to teach, was as far removed from potential GQ-ishness as I could imagine – he's nerdy, badly-dressed, uncool, and came with all this messy emotional baggage.

I fitted in at school – I liked football and the right sort of music and so on – but Marcus doesn't and can't. He learns to, but he's lost something of himself in doing so. (Hornby, *Nick Hornby on 'About a Boy'*, 2004)

Hornby's acknowledgement that in 'fitting in' we each 'lose something of ourselves' is perhaps analogous with Michel Foucault's notion that the misfit is the only one to contain the potential to be free of the discursive practices of the dominant ideology (Foucault, 1981, p. 10) since the misfit has to some extent escaped being 'grouped' or controlled in the way that (according to Foucault) the rest of society has. For Foucault however, this self-determination involves the necessary freedom to move into a state of 'unreason'.

There are links between Bataille's notion of unreason (as discussed in Chapter 1) and Foucault's perception of the term. Foucault discusses unreason in *Madness and Civilization* (1961), which explores the changing relationship between madness and unreason. The true nature of both terms is rarely expressed or allowed to speak, and frequently one forms part of the other. Unreason is defined as 'reason dazzled' or confused in the period of confinement. In the modern period, however, unreason is pushed further beneath the surface of society, and is understandable only through certain artists; madness on the other hand, becomes mental illness, and is treated and controlled by medical and psychiatric practices. Foucault believes that 'unreason' is somehow lost after the eighteenth century, a situation that he laments.

In *Madness and Civilization*, he sees insanity as a limit of reason, and investigates the discursive origins of the practice of exclusion of insanity. What is at stake here is ultimately a rewriting of the history of science as a history of reason, attempting to come to grips with the exclusion of the insane from 'civilized' society. Like Bataille, Foucault is here interested in madness as an absolute limit, which makes the entire enterprise of reason tremble because it cannot account for it. The medical practice of psychiatric commitment is seen as a means of excluding that which cannot be accounted for. A key assumption behind Foucault's understanding of the importance of 'unreason', in an age in which he believes that linguistic structures perpetuate a given reality and then obscure the fact that that reality has arisen mostly through choices made by human agents, is made clear in the introduction to *Birth of the Clinic: An Archaeology of Medical Perception* (1963).

In our time – and Nietzsche the philologist testifies to it – [the possibility and necessity of critique] are linked to the fact that language exists and that, in the innumerable words spoken by men – whether they are reasonable or senseless, demonstrative or poetic – a meaning has taken shape that hangs over us, leading us forward in our blindness, but awaiting in the darkness for us to attain awareness before emerging into the light of day and speaking. We are doomed historically to history, to the patient construction of discourses, and to the task of hearing what has already been said. (Foucault, 1973, p. xvi)

This assumption is both structuralist and determinist, Foucault's words here express a Romantic impulse; he believes that he can uncover 'truth' through analysing and deconstructing the processes of discourses.

Colin Wilson in *The Outsider* (1956) similarly explores the 'Romantic' idea that the misfit (or the outsider) could be in some ways 'freer' from the constraints of civilization and can therefore reveal 'truth'. Wilson suggests that the outsider occupies a more 'natural' state of being that allows him to stand for the savagery that is at the heart of all humans:

The outsider's case against society is very clear. All men and women have these dangerous, unnameable impulses, yet they keep up a pretence, to themselves, to others; their respectability, their philosophy, their religion, are all attempts to gloss over, to make look civilised and rational something that is savage, unorganized, irrational. He is an outsider because he stands for Truth. (Wilson, 2001, p. 13)

For Wilson, (as for Foucault) the outsider (like 'unreason') stands for 'truth' because he lacks the 'pretence' of civilization.

Wilson implies that the middle classes are most prone to failing to see beyond the 'pretence' of civilization, and suggests that the bourgeoisie have a 'need' to see the world as a fundamentally orderly place and that this has led to the exclusion of those individuals that do not wish to see the world as an ordered place. He notes:

For the bourgeois, the world is fundamentally an orderly place, with a disturbing element of the irrational, the terrifying, which his preoccupation with the present usually permits him to ignore. For the outsider, the world is not rational, not orderly. When he asserts his sense of anarchy in the face of the bourgeois' complacent acceptance, it is not simply the need to cock a snook [sic] at respectability that provokes him; it is a distressing sense that *truth must be told at all costs'*. (Wilson, 2001, p. 15)

Peter Stallybrass and Allon White implicitly concur with Wilson on this point when they note the appeal of a character that has to see the world in a different, less ordered way. In *The Politics and Poetics of Transgression* (1986) Stallybrass and White propose that while the lower echelons of a society may be 'despised and denied at the level of political organization and social being' (Stallybrass and White, 1986, pp. 5–6) there remains a sense in which those who are otherwise derided and excluded are still 'instrumentally constitutive of the shared imaginary repertoires of the dominant culture' (Stallybrass and White, 1986, pp. 5–6). Stallybrass and White's assertion that a marginalized figure may represent a crucial position in art seems consistent with George Bataille's insistence that

> [I]n order to perceive the meaning of a novel, it is necessary to go to the window and watch *strangers* go by. Letting go of our profound indifference for everyone we don't know is the most complete protest against the face adopted by humanity as a species of anonymous passers-by. The stranger is negligible and, in a character from a novel, the opposing affirmation is implied, that this stranger has the world to himself. That he is sacred, as soon as I lift the profane mask that conceals him. (Bataille, 2001, p. 199)

Bataille's implication that the unfamiliarity of the stranger is profane until the individual gains knowledge of an underlying common humanity between himself and the stranger; and that this process is ever present in the act of reading a novel, suggests that the misfit figure functions as a necessary vehicle through which a greater sense of social cohesion can be attained.

Kureishi's *Gabriel's Gift* concerns a young teenager, Gabriel, and his struggle to deal with his parents' mid-life, 'mid-marriage' crisis. The text alludes to the notion that the stability that the grown-ups insist exists in the world may be an illusion and Gabriel is constantly made aware of the presence of the irrational, the strange and the inexplicable. Gabriel has a talent for art that his father cultivates by taking his son to see Lester Jones (a David Bowie style musical legend), who gives Gabriel a piece of his artwork and encourages the teenager to pursue his artistic talent. Significantly exactly what constitutes Gabriel's 'gift' is never fully explained in the novel. Gabriel has a talent for drawing, and for a large part of the novel his artistic creations magically come into concrete being when no one else is around, but Gabriel also feels that he can communicate with his dead brother. The 'gift' of the title might also refer to Gabriel's talent for uniting people and getting them to do what he wants; any or all of these could in fact be his 'gift'. The novel shares *About a Boy's* sense of determinism, and constantly disrupts the boundaries between what is a gift and what is a curse, suggesting that it is only when Gabriel takes control over his own fate that the 'earth can be put back onto its axis'.

> The more he considered what he had done, the more disturbing he found it. Winking daffodils tried to communicate with him. Dead brothers spoke within him. The earth, surely, had tilted and was trembling on its axis. Who would put it back before it tipped into eternity? (Kureishi, 2001, p. 22)

This assertion that the earth is in danger of tipping off its axis is by no means the first that Gabriel makes, as for the angst-ridden teenager the world is always in jeopardy. Gabriel's continued affirmations that the planet is fragile form a motif that haunts the novel, almost becoming a refrain. The notion is repeated twice in the first three pages.

> Gabriel looked around before gripping Hannah's hairy hand, something he had always been reluctant to do, particularly if a friend might see him. But today was different: the world was losing its mind. (Kureishi, 2001, p. 1)

There is only a gap of two pages before the next assertion, also from Gabriel's perspective that 'If the world hadn't quite turned upside down, it was at an unusual angle, and certainly not still' (Kureishi, 2001, p. 3). In terms of *Gabriel's Gift* the fear that humankind is forever on the verge of a violent and destructive chaotic force may at first appear to be the juvenile concerns of a particularly troubled boy, as Gabriel seems to equate the loss of stability in his own life (the death of his twin and the subsequent breakdown of his parents' marriage) with that of the entire earth. But we are told from the outset not to negate the concerns of the child, since

> [C]hildren always noticed the underneath of things; for a long time, like foot soldiers and servants, they only saw the world from below, a good position for noticing how things worked. (Kureishi, 2001, p. 80)

Indeed the notion that something is either hidden or unsaid also haunts *Gabriel's Gift*, not least because we are never entirely sure which aspect of Gabriel's unusual life and personality constitutes his 'gift' (as stated above Gabriel can speak to his dead brother, his drawings come to life and he has a particular ability to forge relationships with almost anyone he meets). This is compounded when it becomes clear that the adults are certainly not immune from the need to exorcize their demons rather than confront their problems, or from the ability to extend their own pain into their surroundings.

> [. . .] 'his teenage mother', as he called her, didn't seem well. She looked as though she wept a lot; she was losing weight and had begun to accumulate even more self-help books; her bed was full of chocolate wrappers and she drank Tia Maria in the morning. She wasn't yet old but he was beginning to see what sort of old woman she would be, and it wasn't the picture she had presented to him in Kew Gardens. It was sadder and more desperate than that. (Kureishi, 2001, p. 136)

The turmoil of Gabriel's home life is projected onto the city of London itself. The fact that it holds itself together at all is ultimately affirmed, but nevertheless the proviso 'just about' reminds us of the ever-present threat of dissolution and chaos.

> The bar was an indication of either futile hope or a new direction. The city was no longer home to immigrants only from former colonies, plus a few others; every race was present, living side by side without, most of the time, killing one another. It held together, this new international city called London – just about – without being unnecessarily anarchic or corrupt. (Kureishi, 2001, p. 8)

The use of the phrase 'unnecessarily anarchic or corrupt' here is worth examining since it implies that there is a necessary amount of corruption and anarchy that can and must occur. The novel examines and critiques the boundaries of this 'necessary' corruption and anarchy. Gabriel's parents have to make moral decisions about the extent to which they want to rid their lives of anarchy and corruption. They employ an au pair, Hannah, in order to attempt to provide order in their son's life. Hannah is a refugee and so in fact seems to embody a reminder of the troubles going on in the rest of the world: 'Hannah, a refugee from a former Communist country, was that restless eye, which slept, encased in the rest of her, on a futon in the living room' (Kureishi, 2001, p. 9). The exploitation of Hannah by Gabriel's middle-class parents and the threat of bullying posed to Gabriel by the 'rougher', more working class pupils at his school raise questions such as how much corruption and anarchy are or should be allowed.

Gabriel's older friend Speedy warns Gabriel about hero-worshipping seemingly anarchic punk musicians and artists:

> 'I know these guys, the creative artists. They're selfish and self-obsessed; the desire for success isn't pretty. It's a hunger that never goes away or can be satisfied. That's what makes people into stars.' (Kureishi, 2001, p. 124).

Gabriel's growing recognition of the difficult decisions involved in adult life cause him to feel estranged from both sanity and reality. Gabriel feels that there is much that is hidden and not talked about: 'There was a secret. The world was a façade. It was the beyond, behind and under- neath – a nether factory making dreams and stories that writhed with strange life.' (Kureishi, 2001, p. 17)

It is fitting that Gabriel does not know the correct name of the place that Hannah comes from and merely refers to it as:

> a town called phlegm, near a river called bronchitis. (Kureishi, 2001, p. 14)

It is only when Gabriel and his mother and father learn to be less selfish that the world is put back safely into orbit:

> this was the only kind of magic Gabriel wanted, a shared dream. (Kureishi, 2001, p. 178)

The misfit novel often takes the moral high ground because representing the mainstream from the margins allows for a representation that shows what is usually 'the mainstream' as 'other' and so can critique it. In many texts that contain a misfit protagonist that which purports to be 'normal' is often in fact itself a marginalized perspective (such as the religious commu- nities that Winterson and Kureishi depict in *Oranges are not the only Fruit* (1985) and *The Black Album* (1995) respectively). It is perhaps fair to say that it is common currency in the contemporary misfit novel to posit the misfit in a world that seems itself to have 'gone mad' in order to highlight the 'normative' rather than the 'marginalised' aspects of the central protago- nist for the mainstream reader.

In *Ethics after Idealism: Theory-Culture-Ethnicity-Reading* Rey Chow suggests that there is in fact a growing interest in the stranger and the 'passers-by' within contemporary fiction. Chow suggests that a shift in ideology has occurred, which means that the marginalized character now dominates the modern novel, even though this may not translate to the creation of a more democratic world. Chow notes the appeal of the 'other' and suggests that

> [I]nstead of imagining themselves to be a Pamela or Clarissa being held captive, resisting rape, and writing volumes in order to preserve the

purity of their souls (and thus their 'origins') first world intellectuals are now overtaken by a new kind of desire: 'Make me other!' (Chow, 1998, p. 31)

The shift in focus, from the Pamelas and Clarissas of eighteenth-century fiction to the marginal characters of late-twentieth-century fiction is significant. While characters such as Pamela and Clarissa may have been ostracized in the course of their respective novels such a break with the mainstream was always temporal and their re-assimilation back into society a welcome return. This pattern of separation, experience and return is transformed in the work of novelists such as Will Self and Jim Crace where the character arc is changed to one in which the individual does not return, or more importantly, wish to return to the mainstream. Such is the contemporary desire for the marginal that Chow suggests writers are now less interested in preserving the wholesomeness and ethnic 'purity' of their characters and more concerned with an often superficial representation of difference.

Although Chow's statement might suggest that the misfit is a particular result of twentieth-century conditions, there is a history of such characters in the novel form. Regardless of whether the figure is isolated through possessing superior nobility or greater savagery than the norm, on a functional level the fictional character must be made a misfit in order to act as a bridge between the make believe world on the page and that of the reader. By not entirely fitting into the world of the novel the misfit is able to comment on the complexities of their fictive world.

One major reason for the post-1975 growth in the appropriation of the misfit is the growing sense that a dislocation has occurred between the individual and the 'real world'; one that has created feelings of isolation, alienation and disorientation that have permeated into the 'mainstream' bourgeois population. Martin Amis explores the extent of this penetration in *Einstein's Monsters* (1987), commenting that:

Our time is different. All times are different, but our time is *different.* A new fall, an intimate fall, underlies the usual – indeed traditional presentiments of decline. To take only one example, this would help explain why something has gone wrong with time – with modern time: the past and the future, equally threatened, equally cheapened, now huddle in the present. The present feels narrower, the present feels straitened, discrepant, as the planet lives from day to day. It has been said – Bellow again – that the modern situation is one of *suspense*: no one, no one at all, has any idea how things will turn out. (Amis, 1987, p. 32)

Amis was to explore further the nihilistic nature of the modern condition in his novel *Other People: A Mystery Story* (1981). In the novel Amis uses a technique (made popular by Craig Raine in his poem 'A Martian Sends a Postcard Home' (1979)) in which familiar objects and activities are described in unfamiliar ways (as if from an alien perspective). The protagonist of *Other People: A Mystery Story*, Mary, awakens one morning in an institution suffering from some kind of psychosis; she is unable to recognize the world around her and remembers nothing about her former life. She describes walking down the corridors with 'heavy curved extensions' (Amis, 1981, p. 14) that the reader can infer are nothing more unusual than her shoes. Mary also uses equally outlandish descriptions for motor vehicles, describing them as 'trolleys charging noisily along the street' (Amis, 1981, p. 16). Clouds are described as 'extravagantly lovely white creatures – fat sleepy things' (Amis, 1981, p. 17), while aeroplanes become: 'slow moving crucifixes' (Amis, 1981, p. 17).

Mary's changed mental state causes her to feel and become an outsider, a misfit with literally no place that she can recall as 'home'. As the novel opens Mary begins a journey of self-education, which involves starting with an investigation of the bottom rungs of humanity; entering a world of violence and malevolence that is aimed, it seems, at disorientating many of the readers in the same way that Mary herself is disorientated. For Mary (and conversely the reader) the world has become the mystery story alluded to in the title.

Other People: A Mystery Story can be read as a stinging critique of the capitalist values of mainstream Western society during the 1980s. Like Amis' other attack on the decade, *Money* (1984), which is discussed below, *Other People: A Mystery Story*, presents the reader with a mirror image of their own society in order to highlight its social and moral failings. In an interview with James Diedrick, Amis positions himself far to his father's (Kingsley Amis) left:

> The thing about him and his contemporaries – these former Angry Young Men, all of whom tend to be right-wing now – is that while they weren't born into poverty, they didn't have much money. Then they made some money, and they wanted to hang on to it. And they lived through a time when the left was very aggressive and when union power made life unpleasant. There are many aspects of the left that I find unappealing, but what I am never going to be is right-wing in my heart. Before I was even the slightest bit politicized, it was always the poor I looked at. That seemed to be the basic fact about society – that there are poor people,

the plagued, the unadvantaged. And that is somewhere near the root of what I write about. (Amis, 'A biographical sketch: An interview with James Diedrick', 1995, p. 35)

In *Other People* Amis makes the novel, in part, an examination of the lives of the most dispossessed, as because of her memory loss Mary is forced to start her life again from scratch. Living in a women's refuge and working as a dishwasher in a local café Mary begins her search from the bottom of the social ladder. Amis uses this Dickensian plot device in order to alert the comfortable bourgeois reader to the realities of living on the poverty line. Many of Mary's dealings with other characters in the novel involve violence, broken faces (Mary beats her lover with a brick), and various other broken bones, such as a broken back (Mr Botham's in defending Mary). Amis' text depicts a difficult and harsh world, in which the 'other people' referred to in the title often operate as a reminder of how Amis depicts British society as being violent and unsympathetic to the misfit.

In *England, England* (1998) author Julian Barnes explores the relationship between the lack of a clear and defined personal identity and the perception that in the contemporary period a loss of reliable 'national' memory has occurred that essentially makes misfits out of all of us. Barnes depicts an England that is selling off its history, with the protagonists engaged upon setting up a kind of heritage theme park on the Isle of Wight that gathers, replicates and displays the landmarks of England, whilst offering the chance to experience the traditions of England's past. Like Amis, Barnes equates the problematic nature of asserting a complete national identity with the equally problematic nature of asserting a coherent personal identity: 'it was like a country remembering its history: the past was never just the past, it was what made the present able to live with itself. The same went for individuals, though the process obviously wasn't straightforward' (Barnes, 1998, p. 6).

The protagonist Martha Cochrane personifies the lack of a fit between an individual and their perception of their place in the world. Martha's understanding of herself and of her national identity is directly influenced by her earliest memory. Martha can remember herself as a child trying to complete a jigsaw depicting the English only to find that, symbolically, one piece of the jigsaw is missing (Barnes, 1998, p. 5). The sense of incompleteness and betrayal that the recollection of this missing piece evokes in Martha accompanies her throughout the novel; as she tries to find her 'true self' in order to become a: 'mature, ripened person' (Barnes, 1998, p. 205). Martha begins to doubt more and more that such a pure and natural self exists: 'for all a lifetime's internal struggling, you were finally no more than what others saw you as' (Barnes, 1998, p. 259). Critic Sarah Henstra notes in 'The McReal Thing: Personal/national identity in Julian Barnes' *England, England*' that this depiction of England and English identity as being constructed is a state more usually associated with thinking about 'Third World' countries and their national, cultural identity (Henstra, 2005, p. 98). Indeed, Barnes implies that through losing a sense of the 'real' past and insisting instead upon a sanitized and literally 'theme park' version of the past which prizes antique objects above 'real' memory, the characters in the novel have become spiritually impoverished by losing the contact and community that an emphasis on shared memories would allow. The novel promotes a version of the past that prioritizes communal experiences and 'myth making' rather than precious artefacts.

Ultimately Martha has to discover the only way to achieve a semblance of authenticity is through contact with other people, and the opportunity for sharing in the common myths of identity and nationhood that this allows for. The 'Heavens to Betsy' myth[1] being one such example of a myth whose questionable truth value once blinded Martha to the value of the story, but by the end of the novel Martha is converted to the belief that the value of the story lies in its ability to forge an idea of shared magic and myth around which an identity (national and personal) could be forged.

Figures such as Barnes and Amis utilize the misfit protagonist as a means of suggesting that a breakdown in community has occurred in the contemporary era (particularly in the 1980s) or as means of explaining and analysing behavioural patterns within society at large. In *The English Novel in History 1950–1995* Steven Connor notes that

> [M]any of the most striking and significant explorations of the conditions of national identity in the post-war British novel have been the product not of inside-out excursion but of an outside-in recursion, as outsiders who were previously held spatially and culturally at a distance have returned or have doubled back to the distant imperial centres to which they had previously been connected, as it were, only by their separation. (Connor, 1996, p. 85)

Indeed the post-colonial and post-feminist context that Connor highlights is a major contributory factor to the return to a socio-politically aware misfit in the contemporary novels of writers such as Winterson and Kureishi. In novels such as *Oranges are not the only Fruit* and *The Black Album*, the misfit works along much the same lines as Dickens' *Oliver Twist*, being a misfit only by virtue of the machinations of a corrupt and/or prejudiced world. Such novels perhaps inform the contemporary period's engagement with the figure.

Critic Sukhdev Sandhu notes that the fiction of those who have been 'socially side-lined', has all too often been driven out of the mainstream by being classified as 'single issue' writing. In his text *London Calling: How Black and Asian Writers Imagined a City* (2003) Sandhu describes how this side-lining process presented, and left, the marginal author with only

> [T]hat turgid stage so familiar to students of minority literatures in which ethnic writers spend years churning out angry, joyless polemics which counter-productively enjoin 'society' to respect and reimburse the communities they oppress. (Sandhu, 2003, p. 230)

For Sandhu, Kureishi deliberately stands against this categorizing into the bracket of serious, polemical 'minority', or 'ethnic' text. Instead Sandhu notes how 'Ribaldry and bawdiness were more to Kureishi's liking. . . . His work featured drug-pushers, tyrannical ex-foreign Ministers, bogus mystics, brutalizing landlords, togged-up likely lads and sex-hungry cripples' (Sandhu, 2003, pp. 230–1).

In the light of Sandhu's comments it is interesting to note the similarities between Kureishi's *The Black Album* and picaresque novels such as *Don Quixote* (1605) and more recently James Joyce's novel *A Portrait of the Artist as a Young Man* (1916). This is particularly evident in Kureishi's depiction of the internal triumvirate struggle in the protagonist between a fundamentalist version of the Islamic faith, a transgressive, hedonistic even dangerous love, and a secular academic thirst for knowledge. In such a reading the central character of *The Black Album*, Shahid, becomes a modern incarnation of the adoptable picaro; literally everyone wants to adopt Shahid in order it seems to convert him to their own ideology. Significantly Kureishi presents any character that is doggedly bound to a constricting or one-sided ideology as unable to laugh fully. Chad is a case in point, and consequently Shahid finds it difficult to comprehend Chad's position.

> Shahid was in a turmoil, concerned that he had disturbed his new companions so much that they wouldn't want his friendship. He liked Chad. Laughter took place all over his body – his shoulders, stomach, chest – and his hands quivered like fans, as if someone had activated a motor

in his stomach. Yet he had also chosen the arduous task of policing this excess laughter: Chad seemed ashamed of finding so much mirthful. (Kureishi, 1995, p. 12)

In *The Black Album* laughter serves to liberate characters from the problems of the world around them; they are externalized in the act of laughing and thus liberated from what Bataille calls their own science [this term can perhaps be better understood in terms of ideology]: 'someone who laughs, in principle, does not abandon his science, but he refuses to accept it for a while . . . laughter has the ability to suspend a very closed logic' (Bataille, 2001, p. 144). In the novel laughter seems to be both the most natural and human of reactions but also one that has to be constrained and policed. Shahid cannot agree with the group's notion that comedy and laughter are not appropriate, mature responses to the human condition.

Shahid views both worlds from the margins, finding a home in neither and experimenting with various different guises before finding the confidence to select those aspects of both worlds which he desires and reject those that he finds suffocating. Love is the saving grace that allows Shahid to be himself. But this is not a simple and wholesale rejection of one way of life in favour of another more perfect one.

The growing influence of writers such as Hanif Kureishi has meant that not only did the margins come to be thought of as comprising also of those areas such as race, sexual, cultural and gender politics, but that the margins are not in a fixed place. *The Buddha of Suburbia* exemplifies this point; in it there are characters that are just as marginalized by the pettiness of their suburban existences as they are by the wider issue of race. The suburban misfit Karim dreams of a world in which the colour and vibrancy that he perceives is everywhere in the metropolis is accessible even on the margins of the urban landscape, but finds that the suburbs offer only 'security and safety' as 'the reward of dullness' (Kureishi, *The Buddha of Suburbia* , 1990, p. 8). As Sandhu notes 'Kureishi's white suburbanites shudder at the idea of sharing the same environment with people of different races' (Sandhu, 2003, p. 235). For Karim the margins of suburbia represent something from which he must flee if he is to find freedom. Like Shahid in *The Black Album*, Karim feels that he must run towards the centre; London offers freedom within both *The Black Album* and *The Buddha of Suburbia*, as Anthony Ilona notes of the later: 'London is celebrated as a location of cultural diversity without the stifling tensions seen in the suburbs' (Ilona, 2003, p. 101).

For Karim the margins are not a place to linger for the young Asian male. Upon visiting his white girlfriend Helen, Karim is faced with her father's

'Alf Garnett style' declaration that the family are in fact aligned with the 'Rivers of Blood' mentality that has already cast him as an outsider in white suburbia: 'We're with Enoch' (Kureishi, 1990, p. 40). This rejection of the idea that suburbia is a safe place goes further than simply the rejection of the insidious racism that Kureishi portrays as existing in such areas. Instead Karim embodies a greater rejection of the domesticity and ordinariness of life at the suburbs (margins) of the city. As figures such as Kerouac had done for a generation earlier in America, writers such as Kureishi tap into a new fascination with the Bohemian city.

Kureishi suggests that something of an embryonic and long overdue cross-fertilization could be discerned, as the metropolitan outlook of the city space could no longer be ignored. As witnessed by the disillusionment felt by the other children in Charlie's class in *The Buddha of Suburbia*, when Charlie's manager collects him from school in a pink Vauxhall viva:

> 'Wanker,' the other boys said despondently, devastated by the beauty of the event. 'Fucking wanker.' We were going home to our mothers, to our rissoles and chips and tomato sauce, to learn French words, to pack our football gear for tomorrow. But Charlie would be with musicians. He'd go to clubs at one in the morning. He'd meet Andrew Loog Oldham. (Kureishi, 1990, p. 70)

For Kureishi the problem with suburbia seems to lie in the fact that he feels that real and meaningful human interaction of the kind that form society and that generate what can be termed 'culture' have all but disappeared. Kureishi made this explicit in a 1988 essay 'Finishing the Job'.

> Walking past the homes of my childhood I noticed how, in an orgy of alteration they had been 'done up' [. . .] it was DIY they loved in Thatcherland, not self-improvement or culture or food, but prosperity. Display was the game. (Sandhu, 2003, p. 241)

Indeed for Kureishi unsympathetic characters such as Eva in *The Buddha of Suburbia* can be found engrossed in the pettiness of decorating and DIY whereas the sympathetic characters can often be found living in ramshackle, disorganized homes (Sandhu, 2003, pp. 241–3). But there is also another link, the ramshackle homes with soul are nearly always in the centre; the done up to the nines, soulless houses are the staple of suburbia. Eva takes her compulsion to decorate to the extremes becoming an interior designer; Shari's parents and sister-in-law both take pride in the appearance of their houses while they ignore the degeneration of nearly every other aspect of their lives. Deedee and Shahid, however, both live in untidy homes, complete with the smells, sights and sounds of the other inhabitants. For Shahid particularly the communal aspect of his accommodation seems striking: 'the different odours of Indian, Chinese, Italian and Greek food wafting from open doorways gladdened Shahid, as they had done the first time he passed them, full of anticipation and expectation' (Kureishi, 1995, p. 3).

Both Karim and Shahid believe there to be soul in the communal living of the inner city, the centre of town is what they crave:

> Before crossing the river we passed over the slums of Herne Hill and Brixton, places so compelling and unlike anything I was used to seeing that I jumped up, jammed down the window and gazed out at the rows of disintegrating Victorian houses. The gardens were full of rusting junk and sodden overcoats; lines of washing criss-crossed the debris. (Kureishi, 1995, p. 43)

Kureishi's work suggests that it is not enough for immigrant communities to retreat to 'a quiet life' in the suburbs; he suggests that the centre must not be given up by those that would otherwise be so easily marginalized, and it is not simply that within Kureishi's novels the margins hold as much racism as the centre. Rather as Sandhu notes of the property developer in *Sammy and Rosie Get Laid* (1987) who enjoys bulldozing the makeshift homes of the beggars and the junkies, 'I'm proud to say – [we're] making London a cleaner and safer place'. Sandhu notes the implications of the developer's words for characters such as Shahid and Karim.

> What the developer is saying, of course, is 'a cleaner and safer place *for people like us*'. This is the totalitarian language of social hygiene. Glossy, streamlined, showpiece – all yuppie adjectives. Kureishi believes in urban messthetics – the idea that dirt, confusion, and contamination define urban life. (Sandhu, 2003, pp. 245–6)

Much of the misfit fiction in this chapter is ingrained with a sense of urbanity and a desire for the urban is expressed by many of the characters, from Shahid and Karim in *The Black Album* and *The Buddha of Suburbia* to Jeanette in *Oranges are not the only Fruit* and Lily in Timothy Mo's *Sour Sweet* (1982). One reason for the prominence of the urban in the misfit novel is that the city is often depicted as the place in which the past and the future can collide. The city can to some extent be moulded into a form that will accept the misfit, even if their hometown will not.

The title of Mo's novel is integral; *Sour Sweet* expresses the perfect integration of two seemingly opposed elements. The novel's depiction of the Chinese community in London presents the reader with a version of the margins and the centre coexisting. Yet this relationship is not as simple as it first appears. Instead, like the carefully balanced food that Lily gives to her husband to keep his Yin and Yang in perfect harmony, the correct balance may not be immediately obvious or even desired by its recipients, but nevertheless *Sour Sweet* suggests that it is adaptation and adjustment that is necessary in order for balance to be achieved: 'there had been parturition, the single cell had contracted, swelled, and through the wall had escaped matter from its very nucleus. Now there were two cells, sharing the same territory, happily co-existing but quite autonomous' (Mo, *Sour Sweet*, 1999, p. 285).

The misfit appeals to the human psyche as it forms a means of 'attacking the system' but in an optimistic way with a view to the possibility for change and renewal: 'He is an outsider because he stands for Truth' (Wilson, 2001, p. 13). Wilson writes further about the rebellious aspects of the misfit in *The Outsider*. He expounds his theory of the outsider as a 'type', and further as a title worthy of nearly all the greats across nearly all the arts, from Nietzsche to Van Gogh and from Kafka to Hesse. For Wilson a sense of truthfulness occupies the very essence of the outsider: 'the outsider is not sure who he is. He has found an "I", but it is not his true "I". His main business is to find his way back to himself' (Wilson, 2001, p. 147).

The Outsider provoked a great deal of academic discussion upon its publication in 1954. Kingsley Amis complained that Wilson concerned himself with 'those characters you thought were discredited, or had never read, or (if you were like me) had never heard of' (Phelps, 1979, p. 44). Despite Amis' review *The Outsider* quickly gained an audience. Its sense of alienation, existential angst, even downright nihilism, that so typified the mode of thought of Wilson's outsiders seemed to reflect a mood that appealed to the contemporary sensibility. In the introduction to the updated edition of the text Wilson notes:

> Osborne and I were supposed to prove that England was full of brilliantly talented young men who couldn't make any headway in the System, and were being forced to go it alone. We were supposed to be the representative voices of a vast army of outsiders and angry young men who were rising up to overthrow the establishment. (Wilson, 2001, p. 7)

For Wilson the misfit is always imbued with a noble sensibility 'He is an outsider because he stands for Truth' (Wilson, 2001, p. 13). At a cultural level the misfit is more likely than any other figure to remind the reader of a savage truth that the world needs to be reminded of.

> The outsider's case against society is very clear. All men and women have these dangerous, unamiable impulses, yet they keep up a pretence to themselves, to others; their respectability, their philosophy, their religion, are all attempts to gloss over, to make look more civilised and rational something that is savage, unorganised and irrational. (Wilson, 2001, p. 13)

By depicting figures such as Nietzsche, Van Gogh, Kafka and Hesse as outsiders, Wilson denies them any position of intellectual centrality within the British literary hierarchy. An essential aspect of the misfit is that no group within the margins can object to the misfit on the grounds that their interests are excluded, the misfit automatically speaks to no group, and thus effectively sidesteps issues of representation, allowing the figure instead the potential to speak to everyone at once. With the general perception of the breakdown of community, and the concurrent increase in the production of a media-induced metropolitan outlook, the figure of the misfit becomes ever more relevant in the modern literary landscape.

Echoes of Antonio Gramsci's realization, in *Avanti!* (1929) (quoted in Ian Haywood) that 'The proletariat must face the problem of winning intellectual power' (Haywood, 1997, p. Npag) can be found in Wilson's text, as through *The Outsider* Wilson seems to have heralded something of this claiming of figures such as Nietzsche and Dostoevsky for those not at the centre. If figures like Nietzsche and Dostoevsky can be seen as outsiders or misfits then this in turn leads to the outsider being associated with a position that *entails* the ability to comment upon the human condition.

The misfit's distance from the mainstream of society undoubtedly enables the figure to be used as a vehicle through which a value system can be conveyed that may stand in opposition to that of 'the status quo', and further that this voice may form a radicalizing presence, but may not necessarily be overtly confrontational.[2] It has become something of a staple of the novel to produce a hero that is only a misfit within the realms of the novel and is intentionally appealing to the reader. This provides a voice of solemnity at a moment when the world has seemingly gone mad. The characters of Shahid in Kureishi's *The Black Album*, and Jeanette in Winterson's *Oranges Are Not The Only Fruit* (1985), and Will and Marcus in *About a Boy* (1994), exemplify this role, in that they all find themselves the sane ones, in a world that is no longer willing or able to contain them.

Jeanette Winterson expresses the internal conflict of those misfits who find themselves in a world that no longer fits their experiences, and suggests that for the misfit 'home' is not necessarily a place of safety and acceptance. In novels such as *Oranges are not the only Fruit* the central protagonist cannot find a place in the world. The misfit is removed, even from the intimate world of their parents, hometown and birth community. The misfits find greater acceptance in the Bohemian areas of London, and this is where characters such as Shahid, Karim and Jeanette end up. Significantly the crossover is permanent, and transference between the two worlds of province and Bohemian city space is only one way. Jeanette, the narrator of Winterson's *Oranges are not the only Fruit* notes that 'People do go back, but they don't survive, because two realities are claiming them at the same time. Such things are too much' (Winterson, 1991, p. 156).

Jeanette exists as a voice of sympathetic reason, calling for massive change in a world that turns the usual symbolic hierarchy on its head. Winterson suggests that: 'Oranges is a threatening novel. It exposes the sanctity of family life as something of a sham; it illustrates by example that what the church calls love is actually psychosis (Winterson, 1991, p. xiii) whilst also acknowledging that 'Oranges is a comforting novel. Its heroine is someone on the outside of life. She's poor, she's working class but she has to deal with the big questions that cut across class, culture and colour' (Winterson, 1991, p. xiv). Indeed, Jeanette's loneliness is spiritual and perhaps represents a common feeling that does cross the barriers listed above: 'I miss God. I miss the company of someone utterly loyal. I still don't think of God as my betrayer. The servants of God, yes, but servants by their very nature betray. I miss God who was my friend. I don't even know if God exists, but I do know that if God is your emotional role model, very few relationships will match up to it' (Winterson, 1991, p. 165).

The loss experienced by Jeanette as she is made an outcast of her religious community upon the discovery that she is gay, finds an echo in the loss experienced by Mr Stevens in Kazuo Ishiguro's *The Remains of the Day* as the decline of the British aristocracy leaves him without a role. The novel narrates the delusional memories of Stevens, a butler who reminisces of his experiences working in the 1930s, specifically the years directly preceding the Second World War, when the rise of Fascism across Europe was gaining support amongst certain quarters of the upper classes in Britain. The novel's narrative style means that the reader is allowed to 'read between the lines' of Stevens' testament and reveals that Stevens is regarded by those around him as a misfit who is caught between two worlds – the new world of openly expressed feeling and emotion, which he fears – and – the old world of outmoded servitude, that is dying.

There is a bifurcation of effect between Stevens' narration, which seems lyrically proximate in certain of its qualities to poetry and the banality of his actions, which come close to seeming those of an emotional cripple. It is in this divide, the separation of lyrical effect and a cold-hearted quality, that the audience glimpses the fragility and fragmentary nature of Stevens' humanity, and this forms a vital tool for understanding the nature of the misfit.

Georges Bataille's attempts to theorize a form of absolute negativity also largely revolve around the central notion that the universal could be perceived as the parochial, the misfit can in such a situation stand for the universal. However this took the form for Bataille of an analysis of what he termed the formless, Bataille defined the word formless in the 'critical dictionary' published in *Documents* (1929) thus:

> FORMLESS – a dictionary would start from the moments in which it no longer provides the meaning of their words but their job. *Formless* is thus not merely an adjective with such and such a meaning but a term for lowering status with its implied requirement that everything have a form. Whatever it (formless) designates lacks entitlement in every sense and is crushed on the spot, like a spider or an earthworm. For academics to be content, the universe would have to assume a form. All of philosophy has no other goal: it is a matter of fitting what is there into a formal coat, a mathematical overcoat. On the other hand, to assert that the universe resemble nothing else and is formless comes down to stating that the universe is something like a spider, or spit. (Bataille, 2001, p. 31)

Thus Bataille's definition of 'formless' forms a conceptual framework that can be applied to *The Remains of the Day*, since the primary events in the novel that have led to Stevens' marginalization, as relayed through his reminiscences, seem also to hinge upon notions of negation in the form of sacrifice and loss, the loss of a father, the loss of a possible lover, the loss of youth. Even the experience of these events appears to have been sacrificed, or lost, as they are reduced to the narration of a memory, rather than a true enactment within the novel.

Stevens' narration as a misfit, forms a moving, simultaneous exteriority and a kind of intimacy, as Stevens relates these experiences for his future self, he describes his father's death mostly in terms of his schedule, which he says doesn't permit the time to see his father in his dying hours. Stevens' dialogue is often moving, but it is questionable as to how far he is redeemed in the same way that misfits such as Jeanette or Shahid are, both of whom reach some kind of resolution, even reunification with the system that once excluded them; they have the power to change their surrounding, even though only on an individual basis. Stevens has no such power.

John Self, the protagonist of Martin Amis' *Money*, represents a different sort of misfit altogether. Initially the character of Self appears to consist of nothing that would not fit into the picture of the twentieth century that Amis creates; he has a lot of money, is relatively successful in his career and wants the kind of sexual thrills and short-term fulfilments that Amis hints have come to typify the twentieth century. But it soon becomes obvious that Self represents the extremes of these positions, becoming through the course of the novel, a man who is violent towards men and women alike, an attempted rapist, an alcoholic and a pornography addict amongst other things. Through Self, and with a narrative which aims to compel and alienate the reader in equal measure, Amis chronicles what he sees as the cheapening of humanity. Amis attributes this phenomenon to the unique situation of the twentieth century, in which he believes that the age of the television has created a false sense of collective life experience that actually creates isolated individuals, because it is only the semblance of a collective existence and not the real thing. Isolated as they are, these individuals become as morally bankrupt as they are socially inept.

The moral bankruptcy that typifies the fictive world of Amis' *Money* means that the world is full of danger and pitfalls for Self despite his status as someone who has superficially 'made it' it in the capitalist lottery. Self cannot contain the world that has offered him so much, and is thus in the process of being consumed by the very pastimes that he indulges in. According to Amis, Self is:

> [. . .] consumed by consumerism . . . . I also mean him to be stupefied by having watched too much television – his life is without sustenance of any kind – and that is why he is so fooled by everyone; he never knows what is going on. He has this lazy, non-effort response, which is wished on you by television – and by reading a shitty newspaper. Those are his two sources of information about the planet. (Haffenden, 1985, p. 5)

Despite the fact that Self's only two sources of information are tabloids and television, the novel is littered with references to literature, from the pub that Self was born in that is known as 'The Shakespeare' to the surname of Martina Twain and the fact that an author named Martin Amis appears in the novel. Despite Self's professed illiteracy 'the big thing about reading is that you have to be in condition for it. Physical condition too. This body of mine is a constant distraction' (Amis, 2000, p. 203). *Money* provides plenty of hints for the reader that it is literature that could have a transformative effect on its protagonist. Self's only glimmer of enlightenment comes in the form of the novels that he is introduced to by Martina Twain.

Amis implies that John Self would profit intellectually and morally from reading fiction, not least because it provides an antidote to the isolation that the excesses of pornography and alcohol have induced in Self. Within the novel Martina introduces Self to the novels of George Orwell, he begins by reading *Animal Farm* and his time with Martina is typified by a sense of calmness: 'she looked at me with her long eyes and nothing happened. Why should something always be happening?' (Amis, 2000, p. 229).

This sense of calm that Martina's brief introduction to literature offers Self is not too distant from Amis' own experience of fiction. In conversation with Ian McEwan, Amis said that he became a writer because '[Life] is all too random. [I have] the desire to give shape to things and make sense of things,' and he adds 'I have a god-like relationship with the words I've created. It is exactly analogous. There is creation and resolution, and it's all up to [me]' (Alexander V. N., 2005).

Amis provides a very clear definition of what an author's relationship with his text should be when Victoria N. Alexander asks him whether he thinks an artist should 'discover' meaning or 'give' meaning. According to Alexander

> [H]e answered my question automatically, as if he had been asked the time of day. 'The artist rearranges things to give point and meaning . . . The difference between *In Cold Blood* and *The Executioner's Song*, say, and *Crime and Punishment* is that Capote and Mailer are just given the facts and cannot arrange them to point up a moral – or just arrange them to point up various ironies. What they're left with is *life*, which I say is kind of random. (Alexander V. N., 2005)

Amis points to a position that he returns to in a later paper included in Zachary Leader's *On Modern British Fiction*. This position affiliates Amis with Iris Murdoch, who suggests that fiction has the capacity to contain and translate the moral weight for the reader. Murdoch insists that

> [A]rt transcends selfish and obsessive limitations of personality and can enlarge the sensibility of its consumer. It is a kind of goodness by proxy. Most of all it exhibits to us the connection, in human beings, of clear realistic vision with compassion. The realism of a great artist is not

a photographic realism, it is essentially both pity and justice. . . . if there is any consolation it is the austere consolation of a beauty which teaches that nothing in life is of any value except the attempt to be virtuous. (Murdoch, 1967, pp. 14–15)

Murdoch believes that good art contains a transformative power that transcends both the need for absolute verisimilitude and the everyday limitations of the human condition, its transformative power originating in its ability to prioritize the value of virtue. Amis shares this conviction to the extent that he declares that he does not consider Mailer and Capote as 'artists' because he discerns in their work the lack of an ability to exert a 'god-like' control over their material (Alexander V. N., 2005).

Amis does include Saul Bellow in his list of 'moral artists' and cites Bellow's 'Jefferson Lectures' as forming some of the inspiration behind Self, specifically, Bellows insistence that 'this person is our brother, our semblance, our very self. He is certainly in many respects narrow and poor, blind in heart, weak, mean, intoxicated, confused in spirit – stupid. We see how damaged he is, how badly mutilated. But the leap towards the marvellous is a possibility he still considers' (Alexander V. N., 2005). Amis adheres to this model with Self, who dreams of an escape in the form of a whole body transplant that will rid him of the toxins that keep him addicted to the excesses of the twentieth century.

Zadie Smith's *White Teeth* (2000) ensured that Penguin began the twenty-first century with the publication of the kind of expansive novel that had become the staple of the greats in British writing; in this, Smith echoes predecessors such as Salman Rushdie and Angela Carter, who each incorporate within single novels what seems like an entire world of influences from around the globe, and in one novel often cover enormous time periods. Also like these novelists Smith is at pains to incorporate a sense of the misfit in the most sympathetic of her characters. Irie is perhaps the most promising and accessible of the characters. She is both likable and intelligent but perhaps even more importantly she is also almost utterly at odds with the world around her; the most obvious manifestation of this is Irie's figure. Irie's story is set in the 1990s, in a world of heroine chic and the super waif, super model; against this backdrop Smith introduces Irie thus: 'There was England, a gigantic mirror, and there was Irie, without reflection. A stranger in a stranger land' (Smith, 2000, pp. 265–6).

Irie is not the only character to feel externalized; every character in the novel fails to 'fit in'. Archie and Samad feel that their experience of the Second World War is shameful because it is not filled with dangerous exploits but with waiting and inaction; the Chalfens are isolated to the extent that the children have to be introduced to new people artificially (in the form of Irie and Millat) in order to aid their development. Clara is isolated from her mother's religious conviction and Magid and Millat both fail to conform to their father's hopes for them thus isolating them from the family unit that should provide a place for them to be themselves.

Despite the many misfit characters that populate *White Teeth* (the suicidal mid-life crisis of Archie, the unrequited love of the quietly disaffected school girl in the form of Irie, the militant vocally disaffected youthfulness of Millat, and the stranger abroad of Samad, to name but four of the ways in which Smith creates characters that pertain to the misfit and marginal categories). Smith does something greater than simply provide an identifiable character for almost every 'type' of misfit residing in Britain at the turn of the twenty-first century. Instead the novel shifts the ground upon which the characters, classes and races in this novel interact with one another; the activism of the Chalfens is one of the things that make them seem so out of step with the society that the young Irie and Millat have come to understand. Rather for Smith the action through which the characters influence each other's lives is no longer the great political gesture, we learn that 'In Glenard Oak Comprehensive, black, Pakistani, Greek, Irish – these were races. But those with sex appeal lapped the other runners. They were a species all of their own' (Smith, 2000, p. 269). Smith depicts a Britain in which the ground has shifted to the personal, the next generation are not interested in racial prejudice as much as a kind of consumer-driven competitiveness over who can wield the most power through their own sexual attraction.

Indeed the action of this novel takes place in the houses of its characters rather than in the streets of London and the clubs and universities and schools that proliferate in Kureishi's work, or the boarding houses and parks of Sparks, or the pubs and cars and busses of *Lucky Jim*. But again more than this, think about how many times the action takes place in the inner sanctum of the home; *White Teeth* is a novel in which at least 50 per cent of the action takes place in the kitchen; it is here that the Chalfens choose to educate their new found foundlings, it is here that Alsana and Clara discuss what should be done about the loss of their children to the English middle classes and it is here that Hortense takes in and feeds Irie after her escape from both Chalfens and parents. This is a novel in which the intimacies, subtleties and everyday meetings of the novel's characters are prioritized. And in this the relations between the races that the novel contains are also shifted to the personal – the friend/enemy, the lover/ spouse, and the neighbour.

The politics that concern the figures in *White Teeth* who are politically active is the politics of the minority activist group and the pressure group, be it religious, scientific, egalitarian, or vegetarian. Smith presents a picture of Britain at the turn of the century in which organizations, groups and societies are the primary ways in which people make political or moral gestures, and it is as much about navigating your way through these as choosing a path of tradition or hybridized modernity that the younger characters of the novel have to come to terms with. The novel presents a picture of the unspoken and subtle ways in which people of different classes, religions, races and genders, influence, infect and enhance each other's lives. Smith suggests that this process both dilutes and enriches what was there before but in ways that are perhaps more subtle and complex than might have previously been imagined.

The novel shifts the ground upon which Britain's future will be shaped into the realm of the personal, and thus implies that it may be possible that the powerful hold that mainstream (white) culture initially has over Irie, and that immigrant nostalgia has over Samad, and that the fundamentalist activist group has over Millat might start to lose its grip in the new millennium. Smith uses this move into the personal to complicate where the blame for such a restricted idea of beauty lies. Irie is unsure about how her body might fit into a Western ideal that is different from her Caribbean genes but Smith provides us with the words of the shopkeeper from whom Irie purchases the straight hair that she thinks will make her fit in. The shopkeeper complains that she should not be blamed for providing the customer with what they want, even if what they want seems to be to deny an entire aspect of their cultural make-up.

But this is not to suggest that Smith does not address issues such as what might be the cause of fundamentalism. This is perhaps felt most keenly in the depiction of the Islamic fundamentalist group KEVIN. The depiction of this group is not short on satire, not least in the unfortunate acronym of the group's name. Smith is also at pains to point out that racism and the isolation that it can produce for a marginalized character can be a contributing factor to the formation and the recruitment of such groups. Millat decides to travel to Bradford with members of KEVIN to participate in a demonstration against the publication of Salman Rushdie's *The Satanic Verses* (1988). During this incident the narrator alludes to the fact that the demonstrators have not read the book that they are about to burn, but rather than suggesting that Millat's actions are solely born of ignorance, Smith is at pains to point out that fundamentalism can be the result of prejudice and discrimination. Millat may not have read the novel but he feels the rage that is directed at it, primarily because of his understanding of the same feelings in his own life. Smith tells us that Millat 'recognised the anger, thought it recognised him and so grabbed it with both hands' (Smith, 2000, p. 202).

The novel reaches its crescendo as Millat produces a gun at the public presentation of a genetically modified mouse.[3] Archie places himself between the bullet and the scientists on the stage (Marcus Chalfen and his mentor, the aging Nazi, Dr Perret Sick. Archie, of course has saved the Nazi collaborator before and it is revealed that it is the same scientist that we now discover he failed to shoot on the infamous night in France in 1945, when he and Samad decided to 'do their bit' in stopping the Nazis. It is now revealed that Archie decided to free the doctor, rather than execute him (in the process Archie ended up getting shot in the leg).

Archie is shot once more at the FutureMouse presentation, and thus saves the scientist for a second time. This act is not simply an act of either weakness or kindness on Archie's part; rather it can be read as a demonstration of the lack of power of Perret's Nazism, since Archie has led a life that promotes hybridity, multi-ethnic mixture and conglomeration. Samad may save a Nazi twice in the novel, but his life, and everything he stands for is in fact a powerful statement against Nazism. Archie stands as an example of how despite the continuation of notions of a restricted version of 'purity', the persistence of monomania and cultural bigotry (in any and all of its many forms in the novel), hybridity and change are not fragile elements in need of protection and artificial life support (such as that attempted by Mrs Chalfen). In *White Teeth* hybridity is a powerful and even an unstoppable force that has survived every attempt made in the last century to end the process. The search to control or to stop processes of heterogeneity is in fact pointless.

The importance of Archie is hinted early in the novel, as he is thwarted in his attempted suicide.

> Archie dragged his head off the steering wheel. And in the moment between focusing on the sweaty-bulk of a brown-skinned Elvis and realizing that life was still his, he had a kind of epiphany. It occurred to him that, for the first time since his birth, Life had said Yes to Archie Jones. Not simply an 'OK' or 'You-might-as-well-carry-on-since-you've-started', but a resounding affirmative. Life wanted Archie and Archie, much to his surprise, wanted Life. (Smith, 2000, p. 7)

After the shooting at the FutureMouse presentation, both Magid and Millat receive reduced punishments since they are almost totally indistinguishable from one another; the result is that both extreme responses to the colonial situation, the assimilator and the dissenter are essentially treated in the same way by the host state. Both are symbolically channelled into a communal project; they are both required to become gardeners in a millennial garden as a form of community service. The title of the garden and the nature of the project are similarly suggestive of a new, more organic future, and in itself perhaps an extension of Rushdie's imagery in *The Satanic Verses* of immigrants and their descendants as the new gardeners of Britain.

Samad initially feels betrayed at Archie's failure to kill Perret in 1945. He feels that his relationship with Archie has been built upon a lie. A moment of reconciliation occurs however when Samad realizes, that this story will now provide entertainment for the next 50 years. It is this notion of shared personal histories, shared narratives that binds communities that are otherwise genetically disparate. As such, although mindful of the abuses that man has committed against man,[4] the novel becomes a celebration of the chaotic and the haphazard ways in which we share our heritage, regardless of the theories, politics and sciences that surround us.

> [A]nd it is young professional women aged eighteen to thirty-two who would like a snapshot seven years hence of Irie, Joshua and Hortense sitting by a Caribbean sea (for Irie and Joshua become lovers in the end; you can only avoid your fate for so long), while Irie's fatherless little girl writes affectionate postcards to *bad uncle Millat and good uncle Magid* and feels free as a Pinocchio, a puppet clipped of paternal strings? And could it be that it is largely the criminal class and the elderly who find themselves wanting to make bets on the winner of a blackjack game, the one played by Alsana and Samad, Archie and Clara, in O'Connell's, 31 December 1999, that historic night when Abdul-Mickey finally opened his doors to women?
>
> But surely to tell these tall tales and others like them would be to speed up the myth, the wicked lie, that the past is always tense and the future, perfect. And as Archie knows, it's not like that. It's never been like that. (Smith, 2000, p. 541)

Significantly it is the misfit that is prioritized in such a setting, as it is Archie, the novel's biggest misfit, who provides the most opportunity for 'accidental' newness to be born.

The novel thus relegates the divisive aspects of the politics of race to a secondary position in relation to the everyday interactions that bind people together; Archie finds a home within his friendship with Samad, and this the novel suggests is all that really matters. In Smith's novel, a newness that seems akin to Rushdie's desire in *Imaginary Homelands* seems to be both inevitable and only ever accidental in its true form, those (be they the Chalfens, FATE, KEVIN or the Nazis) who attempt to force such change are always thwarted by happy accidents, such as the inevitable escape of the aptly named FutureMouse.

> Archie [. . .] watched the mouse. He watched it stand very still for a second, with a smug look as if it expected nothing less. He watched it scurry away, over his hand, and through the hands of those who wished to pin it down. He watched it leap off the end and disappear through an air vent. *Go on my son!* thought Archie. (Smith, 2000, p. 542)

In this the novel is certainly one of the most optimistic to come out of the new era, *White Teeth* suggests and provides a celebration of the fact that the processes of Britain's multicultural future are both underway and irreversible, and relegates the debates surrounding the subject to the level of secondary narrative with little relation to the real relationships, both good and bad, that exist between the many different peoples in Britain. For the characters of *White Teeth* the future, represented by the allusions to the advent of the next millennium, is a thing to be relished and anticipated, but more than this, the future is happening, regardless of the debates taking place at the meetings of KEVIN, FATE or indeed any of the other organizations in the novel.

To conclude, the role that the marginalized character or misfit plays in the post-1975 novel is an interesting if complex one. Primarily writers seem to utilize the marginalized figure in a social role to humanize a particular political stance, the thinking being that if the reader is able to sympathize with a character then they are also likely to consider the potentialities of any idealist view that is espoused through them. In this manner the misfit functions as an answer to John Brannigan's call for the novel to become 'available as a voice for the silenced, and as an imaginative space for dissidence, critique and reinvention' (Brannigan, 2003, p. 204). Writers depict characters excluded from the structures and value systems of the mainstream, either because of age (Gabriel and Marcus), ethnicity (Irie, Lily), social background (Mr Stevens), in order to damn the ideology of the mainstream and to suggest the need for a greater degree of the plurality and individual liberty which Wilson proposes is required for the well-being of society.

While this chapter has explored the marginal as it is incarnated in character, in dealing with the marginal, many post-1975 British novels simultaneously express either an explicit or an implicit desire for a return to a narrative that often utilizes the stylistic and formal experimentation of post-modernism but ultimately is not led by such technical flourishes. Chapter 4 details this return to narrative by authors such as Barker, Evaristo and Crace whose revisionist novels centre on those previously marginalized in history books.

Chapter 4

Revised Histories and Renewed Myths

This chapter examines selected contemporary texts that engage with the historicizing process. Authors such as Pat Barker, John Fowles, Peter Ackroyd and Jeanette Winterson interact with the exclusionary nature of 'history' in order to suggest the need for a multiplicity of narratives. In novels such as *Regeneration* (1991), *The Magus* (1977) and *Hawksmoor* (1985), Barker, Fowles and Ackroyd attempt to re-evaluate the importance of the historical narrative to account for the marginal experience, in the process attempting a democratization of narrative. Several of the writers in this chapter fuse the historical with the mythic in order to critique the claims to absolute 'truth' made implicitly by 'history books'.

The novel *Hawksmoor* fuses historical narrative with fictional narrative as the fictional life of Nicholas Dyer apes the life of the real person, Nicholas Hawksmoor, who rose through the ranks from apprentice mason to principle deputy of Christopher Wren. In the novel, it is the fictional seventeenth-century Dyer whose life follows this pattern, with Hawksmoor making an appearance as a twentieth-century detective. The novel interacts with the specifics of each period in a way that one might expect; seventeenth-century Dyer experiences all of the defining events of the seventeenth-century, the plague has killed his parents, the Great Fire has provided the means for his new designs to be built and Dyer feels an affinity with the roving societies of beggars who frequent the newly forming, newly modern London city. He reflects on the indifference and hypocrisy of the urban middle classes in the same way that one might expect a Jacobean city comedy to do. In contrast, and perhaps in keeping with the novel's engagement with popular constructions of historical periods, including the contemporary, in the twentieth-century chapters Nicholas Hawksmoor seems deprived of such awareness, but as Edward J. Ahearn notes in his essay, 'The modern English visionary: Peter Ackroyd's *Hawksmoor* and Angela Carter's *The Passion of New Eve*', 'a sense of vast alienation, loneliness, family fragmentation, homelessness, and sordid crime is nonetheless conveyed' (Edward J. Ahearn, 2000).

This blending of the mythic, or the invented with the verifiably historic is not without literary precedent for as Eleazar M. Meletinsky notes in *The Poetics of Myth* (1998), the relationship between the two has long been considered as symbiotic: 'The Romantics did not see myth and history as opposed but instead continually tried to reconcile differences between the two' (Meletinsky, 2000, p. 273). While Meletinsky suggests that there is an older tradition, deriving from the Romantics, of approaching myth and history as interchangeable narratives, Philip Tew notes the manner in which the links between these two forms have continued into the present era.

> Cultural changes after the 1960s have created the conditions for a huge expansion of history and history-making in the novel that engages more broadly than simply working through imperial loss. Nostalgia and myth-making have synthesised with and transmuted the historical. (Tew, 2004, p. 124)

This chapter engages with a still emerging group of novelists that includes those already mentioned, in addition to other examples that embody a self-reflective attitude to narrative (be it historical or mythic), but whose prime engagement seems to be with a definite (at times perhaps, seemingly naive) assertion of the importance of a multiplicity of narratives both complimentary and oppositional that together will incorporate marginal as well as mainstream historical narratives.

Critical material on the subject of revisionist historical narrative often highlights how the process of rewriting historical narratives to account for the experiences and perspectives of the marginal often entails an 'updating' of these histories, in effect imbuing well-documented episodes from history with a more 'politically correct' viewpoint. Lane, Mengham and Tew dedicate a section of their book *Contemporary British Fiction* to the subject of myth and history, and suggest a political impetus for the contemporary interest in the historiographic and the historical.

> After 1979 Britain seemed tentatively aware that a new phase of history might well have begun, which if acknowledged, separated it from the earlier post-war period. A new generation of writers, responding to their literary antecedents, developed a newly focussed literary consciousness. This was not simply a matter of reflecting historical events or trends. In politics, the reality and myth of Margaret Thatcher and an attendant concept of history were dominant. The themes of myth and history long considered by literature acquired a currency in the public sphere.

Novelists responded to both the contemporaneous political domain and their literary predecessors. The place of history in our everyday lives, its literary recovery and the question of its status recur in a variety of contemporary British fictional texts. (Lane et al., 2003, p. 11)

Therefore, this chapter will examine the process, common amongst contemporary British writers, of rewriting history from the perspective of the marginal. More specifically I will explore the various ways in which these writers produce revisionist novels that both critique traditional historical narratives and simultaneously assert the relevance and need of narrative per se in the contemporary era. Writers such as Barker, Evaristo, Fowles and Winterson infuse historical narratives with different perspectives to the ones that are conventionally documented, in effect asserting the existence of the marginal in history, be it through the assertion of the histories of alternative sexualities, oppressed races or genders. Steven Connor, in his essay, 'Rewriting wrong: on the ethics of literary reversion' (2000) suggests that much contemporary literature has arisen out of and is itself haunted by narratives of the past be they historical or literary what Connor terms the 'imperative of the eternal return' (Connor, 2000, p. 123). He lists some of the likely candidates for such a reading:

Barth's literature of 'exhaustion', Genette's 'literature to the second degree', Kristeva's 'intertextuality', or Baudrillard's 'regime of the simulacrum', or instanced by Beckett's obsessive auto-iterations, Barth's sequels to the *Odyssey* and *Don Quixote* in *Tidewater Tales*, Robert Coover's skilful parodies of movie genres in *A Night at the Movies* and his extrapolation of the Pinocchio story in *Pinocchio in Venice* . . .. [Connor's list continues for half a page]. (Connor, 2000, p. 123)

Indeed, much has been written concerning the tendency amongst contemporary British writers to engage with the past through what can adequately be described as a revisionist approach. Marguerite Alexander notes that, '[. . .] some of the more exciting developments in later twentieth century fiction have emerged through writers exploring the connections between history and fiction, personal and national myth' (Alexander M., 1990, p. 126). Philip Tew notes that the 'reworking of long established modes of narration [. . .] marks out one major strand of contemporary novels that transform history, parable and myth into something contemporaneous' (Tew, 2004, p. 118). While this process serves to highlight the fictiveness of all historical narratives it can lead to the undermining of the notion of narrative itself, suggesting when taken to its conclusion that nothing in narrative can be trusted. This, in turn, can lead to an implicit devaluing of the form's worth.

Mikhail M. Bakhtin, and particularly his essay 'Forms of time and of the Chronotope in the novel: notes towards a historical poetics', is important to this chapter as Bakhtin insists upon an underlying historicizing force that operates within literature. Bakhtin chooses to construe this relationship in an interesting way as he claims an historical essence for all novels, rather than stating the fictional or imagined qualities that often appear in historical texts. Bakhtin places an emphasis on creating a philosophical understanding of the nature of the spatial and temporal embodiment of the historic (the Chronotope), noting that

> [W]e might put it as follows: before us are two events – the event that is narrated in the work and the event of narration itself (we ourselves participate in the latter, as listeners or readers); these events take place in different times (which are marked by different durations as well) and in different places, but at the same time these two events are indissolubly united in a single but complex event that we might call the work the totality of all its events [. . .]; thus we perceive the fullness of the work in all its wholeness and indivisibility, but at the same time we understand the diversity of the elements which constitute it. (Bakhtin, 1981, p. 255)

Much contemporary writing is concerned with the task of presenting and understanding the diversity of the elements which constitute the narrative of history (including the place of the mythopoeic within the historical). As such the place and 'worth' of history and myth in the novel has occupied a central position in the fiction of the contemporary period, and has long been discussed, disputed and examined both within the form itself and by the critics and philosophers who comment upon it. Authors such as Pat Barker, A. S. Byatt, Peter Ackroyd and John Fowles have all turned their attention to the historical subject.

Critic Marguerite Alexander suggests that the historic can be viewed as an impulse that has driven the creative world since ancient times; she notes that the 'use of historical material in imaginative writing is part of the development of literary genres before the novel' (Alexander M., 1990, p. 124). Alexander implies that the representation of the historic and the mythic within the novel should be viewed in the context of the established notion that 'The need to understand, celebrate or assess a national past is a central impulse in all epic' (Alexander M., 1990, p. 124). The Marxist critic and philosopher, Georg Lukács identifies a similar pattern but is however more concerned with the political essence of the literary recording of history; in *The Historical Novel* (1962) Lukács saw the development of the form as separate to the mainstream novel, and deplored what he perceived as 'the appearance of reality in an external, decorative, picturesque manner by means of the conscientious application of archaeology' (Lukács, *The Historical Novel,* 1962, p. 224).

The contemporary engagement with the processes of revision and re-alignment has not stopped at the level of creating texts that contain nostalgia for an imagined aesthetic of a particular period. Rather there has been an explicit move towards creating novels that fulfil a particular social function with regards to how we view the historic novel itself, and in some senses can be seen as a treatment that is fully mindful of the faults that Lukács highlights within the genre. John McLeod suggests that the contemporary novelist has moved beyond the 'archaeology' that Lukács so disapproves of. He states the aim of the next generation of historical novelists in directly political, post-colonial terms:

> The social and political future of the British Isles rests upon the ability of its conflicted population to reconceive of Britain's past and present in transcultural terms, recognising and prizing the unruly rhythms of arrival, settlement and departure which London particularly, but not exclusively, exemplifies. (McLeod, 2004, p. 178)

The sense of 'unruliness' that McLeod notes is not limited to the post-colonial historical novel, but is also evident across many of the other genres in post-1975 British fiction. Indeed many of the authors discussed in this chapter (in particular Fowles and Barker) do not stop at the act of depicting a different history. Rather their interrogation of the particular versions of history that have governed our understanding of 'where we are now', also inevitably incorporates an interrogation of the processes of narrative. This impetus towards revision and renewal as an integral and ongoing part of narrative, rather than a process that leads to a finished and perfect article and then ceases, traces its origins to the very beginning of the contemporary period.

In 1977 John Fowles revised and re-published his already successful novel *The Magus,* (1966) the unusual aspect of this revision being the very popularity of the previous version of the novel. In both versions the novel concerns itself with two 'marginal' histories. The first of these 'marginal' histories is the personal history of the character Nicholas, an anti-heroic newcomer to the Greek island of Phraxos who escapes in order to get away from a deteriorating relationship with his girlfriend and his sense that his adult life has been a failure. Through the character of Nicholas, Fowles shifts the focus of the novel on to an outsider, presenting us with a protagonist who is failing to live up to the bourgeois ideal. The second marginal history is that of Conchis, a suspected Nazi collaborator, who tells and retells the island's history under occupation and in so doing shifts the focus away from the heroic individuals who fought the Nazis and onto the lesser-told stories of those who surrendered.

Although in the introduction to the revised edition Fowles stresses some imperfections in *The Magus* that he felt needed dealing with, it is fair to suggest that this was not a revision of an otherwise unworkable text. Instead, the revisions seem to hint at a more general concept that revision and counter-narrative can and should be ongoing processes of narrative discourse. Bakhtin's dialogic word has a bearing here, since the process of revision that Fowles undertakes has the effect not so much of replacing the original in the minds of the fans but rather of coexisting alongside and containing within it the 1960s version, commenting on the earlier edition, and itself representing part of the ongoing (and twin) processes of fiction and history. Marguerite Alexander explains:

> [. . .], part of the interest of the novel now is in its curious effect of historical layering. On the one level it is a distillation of the 1960s attitudes overlaid by sober afterthoughts; on another (the first version, still perceptible in the second) it is a critique on England in the early 1950s from the perspective of the mid-1960s. (Alexander M., 1990, p. 170)

Connor expresses the central role that such a revisionist approach to narrative gained in the later half of the twentieth century, in his essay, 'Rewriting wrong: on the ethics of literary reversion', he notes that '[. . .] it is plain that, in contemporary fiction, telling has become compulsorily belated, inextricably bound up with retelling, in all its idioms: reworking, translation, adaptation, displacement, imitation, forgery, plagiarism, parody, pastiche' (Connor, 2000, p. 123).

In *The Magus* Fowles seems close to producing a novel that fulfils Meletinsky's belief that the novel stands at the fore of contemporary engagement with the narratives and processes of myth and history. During the course of the long and complex non-realist plot of the novel Fowles depicts a set of symbolic and fantastic episodes through which the text deconstructs any assured or stable view of a historical narrative. In its conflation of myth and 'fact' *The Magus* echoes Meletinsky's notion that

> [M]ythification is a trait of twentieth century literature. It implies a particular worldview and an artistic strategy. It goes well beyond merely using mythical motifs for artistic purposes. Although mythification is a feature of drama and poetry, its most recent incarnation is especially visible in the contemporary novel. (Meletinsky, 2000, p. 275)

Set in the 1950s the plot of *The Magus* follows the life and thoughts of its first person narrator, Nicholas Urfe, who professes to despise the petty privileges that his middle-class, minor public school education has granted him. Nicholas removes himself from situations where he may be happy, such as with his lover Alison, in order to search for a Utopian perfection that he only comes close to achieving with Conchis, a Nazi collaborator and millionaire on the Greek island of Phraxos.

The notion that fashion as much as ethics might dictate taste and values underpins the philosophy of the novel (and thus by logical extension specifically the fashion of the particular period in which a character finds themselves). And true to form it is Nicholas's sense of the Romantic that purveys much of his narration. The character's Romantic pretensions are the means by which he justifies and accounts for his libidinous disposition. Nicholas' belief that he is in possession of a Romantic vision is somewhat mocked through the exaggerated language that Nicholas employs, he describes the possibility of a sexual encounter with one of the twins in terms of justification, 'my selfishness, caddishness . . . could now be justified. It was always to be this, and something in me had always known it' (Fowles, 1977, p. 210). The novel challenges the assumptions upon which a character such as Nicholas could read himself as a Romantic hero, and begins to engage in a somewhat dialogic relationship with its own material, in which Nicholas himself starts to feel that history will remember him incorrectly; he laments that 'They had been wrong, at the trial. It was not that I preyed on girls; but the fact that my only access to normal humanity, to social decency, to any openness of heart, lay through girls, preyed on me' (Fowles, 1977, p. 608).

The Magus incorporates an implicit interrogation of the relationship between narrative and truth, particularly regarding historical narratives. Early in their relationship, the eccentric Conchis (Nicholas' somewhat mystifying mentor) tells Nicholas that he has burnt all of the novels that he ever owned, asking, 'why should I struggle through hundreds of pages of fabrication to reach half a dozen very little truths?' (Fowles, 1977, p. 96). Furthermore, we learn that Conchis himself has been guilty of fabrication, not least in his dealings with Nicholas (he lies to him in letters, in person and with the appointment of actresses, Julie and June, who act out roles that Conchis has written for them during Nicholas' stays at the villa). Conchis tells Nicholas 'stories' of his experiences in Nazi occupied Phraxos, some of which are verified, others which are later revealed to be false and the rest remain left to the readers' own judgement. This mixing of aspects of the text that we are asked to believe in and those that we are told are false, serves in part to ensure critical reactions such as David Lodge's. Lodge notes in *The Modes of Modern Writing* that the plot of *The Magus* belongs to a group of contemporary novels which 'we shall never be able to unravel [. . .] for they are labyrinths without exits' (Lodge, 1979, p. 226).

While *The Magus* suggests an uneasy relationship between the discourses of fiction and the search for historical truth (or indeed any other kind of truth), then it does appear to believe in the validity of narrative rather than seeking to undermine it completely. Significantly Nicholas 'feels' this as he searches for (and believes that he has found) 'meaning' in Conchis' tales, but (perhaps symbolically) Nicholas can't fully articulate what he is feeling. After hearing one of Conchis' stories about the war, in which Conchis reports that he once refused to murder a member of the Greek Resistance even though he understood that this refusal would lead to his own death and the deaths of 80 other members of the village at the hands of Nazi soldiers. Conchis tells Nicholas that he escaped the Nazis by chance rather than design. Upon hearing the story Nicholas' reaction is significant. He feels that he must philosophize on what appears to be an example of some uniquely human strength; he feels that the Utopian perfect freedom that he sought at the start of his journey might be defined in terms other than the nineteenth- and twentieth-century philosophies of existentialism and nihilism that the book engages with. Nicholas talks about a feeling, induced by his interpretation of the story, that he can only explain in oblique terms, he suggests that the story conveys '[. . .] something much older than the existentialist freedom . . . a moral imperative, an almost Christian concept, certainly not a political or democratic one' (Fowles, 1977, p. 440). As such the novel offers an oblique and implicit reassertion of the very narratives that it has brought into question, but perhaps significantly the worth of the tale is measured in the almost exclusively Bakhtinian terms of its ability to produce a response. Bakhtin prioritizes the 'continual mutual interaction' of the 'real world (which obviously is in constant flux, and the world represented in the text, which although initially the product of only one particular moment in time, Bakhtin suggests that

> [T]he work and the world represented in it enter the real world and enrich it, and the real world enters the work and its world as part of the process of its creation, as well as part of its subsequent life, in a continual renewing of the work through the creative perception of listeners and readers. Of course this process of exchange is itself chronotopic: it occurs first and foremost in the historically developing social world, but without ever losing contact with changing historical space. We might even speak of a special *creative* chronotope inside which this exchange between work and life occurs, and which constitutes the distinctive life of the work. (Bakhtin, 1981, p. 254)

Essentially *The Magus* offers very little in terms of closure on the issues that it raises concerning the philosophical and historical stability of narrative, rather as Marguerite Alexander notes, 'In *The Magus* it is the journey itself, what is irreducible in the text that matters' (Alexander M. , 1990, p. 175).

Fowles' revision of his own novel and the subsequent prioritizing of the 'the journey' that Alexander notes seems to have heralded something of a culture of revision that does not necessarily seek to replace an older version of history but rather attempts to add and to embellish (in the fashion of Bakhtin's dialogic word). Writers such as Evaristo, Barker and Graham Swift all incorporate a sense of widening rather than of correcting the historical perspective, so that stories sit alongside one another rather than battling for supremacy or attempting to become *the* definitive historical narrative. Evaristo provides an account of black history in London in Roman times to sit alongside both the 'Windrush-centric history' of black experience in Britain, and also to sit alongside the predominantly white-centric account of British history. Barker provides a narrative on the Great War that incorporates both stories from the home front and a working class and female perspective on the war, not to replace the trench narratives of Owen and Sasoon, but to sit alongside and to suggest possible other views that did not get recorded or have not survived.

Jeanette Winterson's *Oranges are not the only Fruit* (1985) embarks on a different journey of revision to *The Magus*. The novel consists of eight chapters, each taking the title of one of the first eight books of the Old Testament, but the constant interruptions of other narratives over this framework constantly draw the readers' attention to the fragmentation within the biblical framework that has shaped the life of the young character, Jeanette.

These intrusions, 'which become increasingly unmotivated in realist terms, serve to fragment the text and give it something like the heterogeneity of collage' (Suleiman, 1990, p. 137). Images of the 'un-Christian' literature of myth and legend sit alongside the evocations of the books of the Bible referred to in the titles of each of the segments that constitute the novel. Kim Middleton Meyer notes in her essay, 'Jeanette Winterson's evolving subject' that the 'biblical thematics give way to vignettes that parallel Jeanette's disenchantment with the church' (Middleton Meyer, 2003, p. 212). One of the stories concerns a heroine called Winnet, the easy rhyming with Jeanette conveying the allegorical quality of the story for the protagonist of the frame narrative.

The tale of Winnet concerns a young girl who has spent her formative years under the tutelage of a sorcerer. The sorcerer proceeds to cast the young girl out of his kingdom when she crosses the physical boundaries that he has set for her. Winterson's story is a subversion of the biblical tale of Adam and Eve, which casts Winnet as the Eve character and suggests that she gains from being cast out of the sorcerer's kingdom, in that it allows her to grow spiritually rather than suffering for it. The novel suggests that this very process of subverting traditional narratives represents the very essence of human interaction with narrative.

> That is the way with stories; we make them what we will. It's a way of explaining the universe while leaving the universe unexplained . . . Everyone who tells a story tells it differently, just to remind us that everybody sees it differently. Some people say there are true things to be found, some people say all kinds of things can be proved. I don't believe them. The only thing for certain is how complicated it all is, like string full of knots. It's all there but hard to find the beginning and impossible to fathom the end. The best you can do is admire the cat's cradle, and maybe knot it up a bit more. (Winterson, 1991, p. 91)

Winterson's narrative philosophy 'insists upon a poetics of uncertainty' (Middleton Meyer, 2003, p. 212) and warns that taking only a single 'story' for 'gospel' and simply ignoring the wealth of other interpretations on offer will lead only to the fossilization of peoples and cultures. The imagined character of the orange demon warns the young Jeanette that trying to remain whole and singular at the expense of those forces that bring hybridity and multiplicity will not make those forces go away.

The orange demon's warning can be read as an implicit suggestion of the positive aspects of the marginal. The explicit linking of narrative with the marginal that occurs at this point represents a trend that spans many of the contemporary novels under discussion in this chapter; one that suggests that a more democratic attitude towards narrative is preferable to an exclusionary approach. Winterson's text moves beyond a statement of a belief in the beneficial effects of a more egalitarian multiplicity of narratives to suggest that this diversity is the only way in which we can even hope to effectively understand the world around us.

In *Oranges* it is through the evocation and the persistence of the unproven and the mythic (set against the sacred and the pragmatic) that this 'truth' is conveyed. The orange dragon tells Jeanette that ignoring the multiplicity of narrative is dangerous because a simplification of the plenitude of narratives and histories inevitably involves a simplification of the self, 'If you ignore us, you're likely to end up in two pieces, or lots of pieces, it's all part of the paradox' (Winterson, 1991, p. 106). Meletinsky suggests that the evocation of such a narrative technique in the contemporary novel functions a means of providing narrative coherence.

> Mythification characterizes many novels of the post-World war II period, not as a global model but as an instrument that uses mythical parallels to accentuate particular situations and conflicts. (Meletinsky, 2000, p. 330)

Meletinsky highlights the use of the mythic as a tool that through its tendency towards exaggeration can be used to create a literature which spans the distance between realism and the imagined world. For Meletinsky the mythic often employs an almost surrealist style that suggests that the moral world, and indeed the world of the novel may not be finally easily rationalized. The move into the mythic however does not necessarily lead to the complete debunking of ontological belief, and revels instead in a kind of aporia that leaves things finally unresolved. The mythic and the historic are not entirely satisfactory for the young Jeanette of *Oranges*, something else is required something altogether more mundane and immediately 'real'.

> I starred into the fire waiting for her to come home. Families, real ones, are chairs and tables and the right number of cups, but I had no means of joining one, and no means of dismissing my own; she had tied a thread around my button, to tug when she pleased. (Winterson, 1991, p. 171)

While *Oranges* seems to discuss the positive effects (and inevitability) of a multiplicity of narratives the novel also complicates matters by stating that the act of looking back, revisiting and re-evaluating the past can create a nihilistic effect for the individual when the novel warns that the process of undermining supposedly factual, historical narratives (of the past) may leave the individual feeling adrift, disconnected from the world around them.

> I'm always thinking of going back. When Lot's wife looked over her shoulder, she turned into a pillar of salt. Pillars hold things up, and salt keeps things clean, but it's a poor exchange for losing yourself. People do go back, but they don't survive, because two realities are claiming them at the same time. (Winterson, 1991, pp. 155–6)

Peter Ackroyd's *Hawksmoor* (1985) is an example of a contemporary novel that discusses the ability that an exploration of the past has to dislocate and demoralize the individual. The novel provides a perspective on the past that is inevitably bound up with a dialogue on the boundaries of 'reality'. The novel fuses the eighteenth-century murders committed by architect Nicholas Dyer with the murders that twentieth-century detective Nicholas Hawksmoor has to investigate. The narrative hints that it is portraying a marginalized or silenced history by suggesting that there is a 'demonic' or 'satanic' element to the construction of several London churches.

Interestingly *Hawksmoor* contains allusions to the shared imagery between the demonic and the saintly: 'on the day of St Paul's conversion it was the custom in London to bring in procession to church a wooden staff in which was cunningly wrought a snake or a serpent' (Ackroyd, 1993, p. 56). *Hawksmoor* fuses history with the present as the consciousness of the seventeenth-century character; Dyer seems to leak into the present during the course of the twentieth-century detective Hawksmoor's investigation. Connor notes that *Hawksmoor* regards history as 'occurring all at once' (Connor, 1996, p. 144) and that it is 'rooted in the visionary tradition as the novel unfolds into a spatial rather than a developmental view of history' (Connor, 1996, p. 144). Ackroyd uses the historical setting of the novel to merge the present 'reality' of Nicholas Hawksmoor with the past 'reality' of Nicholas Dyer, such that the novel begins by alternating the two stories until the narrative becomes almost confused, the reader is not always immediately sure whether they are reading about the seventeenth or the twentieth century.

The prologue begins this process of 'stretching' the past 'over' the present; the depth of the shadows cast by the fire in the extract below implies that the past has penetrated the present more absolutely than first appearances might suggest.

> This is the vision we still see and yet now, for a moment, there is only his
> heavy breathing as he bends over his papers and the noise of the fire
> which suddenly flares up and throws deep shadows across the room.
> (Ackroyd, 1993, p. 1)

Shadows become the leitmotif of the novel, as the past constantly casts its
own metaphorical shadows over the contemporary setting of the novel; the
first-person narrative of Nicholas Dyer becomes interspersed with a seemingly omniscient recounting concerning murders at the sites of seven
London churches. In the second part of the novel, the detective Nicholas
Hawksmoor tries unsuccessfully to solve murder cases in twentieth-century
London, and as he does so the past and the contemporary period seem
to intersect with one another. Ackroyd achieves the effect of interweaving
both the seventeenth- and the twentieth-century narratives by describing
the same historical buildings, so that the reader often doesn't know at first
which century the novel has taken them to, as Hawksmoor finds himself
in buildings that Dyer is building. Dyer even likens the architectural designs
that cover the walls of his room to a narrative or a story itself.

> I have finished six Designes of my last church, fastned with Pinns on the
> walls of my closet so that the Images surround me and I am once more at
> Peece. In the first I have the Detail of the Ground Plot, which is much like
> a Prologue in a Story; in the second there is all the Plan in a small form,
> like the disposition of Figures in a Narrative; the third Draught shews the
> Elevation, which is like the Symbol or Theme of a Narrative, and the
> fourth displays the Upright of the Front, which is like to the main part of
> the Story; in the fifth there are designed the many and irregular Doors,
> Stairways and Passages like so many ambiguous Expressions, Tropes, Dia-
> logues and Metaphoricall speeches; in the sixth there is the Upright of
> the Portico and the Tower which will strike the Mind with Magnificence,
> as in the Conclusion of a Book. (Ackroyd, 1993, p. 205)

The fusion of narrative and architectural forms is such that Ackroyd presents a city which is constructed as much out of the subconscious of its
inhabitants as it is by town planners and architects, 'could it be that the
world sprang up around him only as he invented it second by second and
that, like a dream, it faded into the darkness from which it had come?'
(Ackroyd, 1993, p. 158). Such a reading seems to encompass and accept
both the ephemeral nature of narrative alongside an evocation of its
power.

In *Hawksmoor* Ackroyd seems to be creating a novel that to some extent embodies Lukács' suggestion that there should be a complex but direct link between the individual character and history in the historical novel, in order to present an accurate portrayal of the relationship between individuals and their own historical moments.

> This indirect contact between individual lives and historical events is the most decisive thing of all. For the people experience history directly. History is their own upsurge and decline, the chain of their joys and sorrows. If the historical novelist can succeed in creating characters and destinies in which the important social-human contents, problems, movements, etc., of an epoch appear directly, then he can present history 'from below', from the standpoint of popular life. (Lukács, *The Historical Novel*, 1962, p. 285)

Dyer is involved with a murderous demonic sect, and delineates his own place in history accordingly, as such his conception of religious architecture, and of the city of London, is infused with a sense of the sacrificial and an ancient evocation of the demonic.

Dyer's predicament does not solely depict the struggle of one man with the forces of the satanic; however, rather it also represents the coming together of marginalized and mainstream narratives. Dyer sees this other narrative, the satanic, everywhere he looks, contained within the very architecture of the holy, indeed the novel depicts the fragmenting of the Christian world view within Dyer, but significantly depicts a multitude of openings for other narratives to seep through, rather than encompassing only a single alternative.

Hawksmoor feels that in order to adequately explain the past events of a murder it might be necessary to 'invent a past from the evidence available' (Ackroyd, 1993, p. 157). The obvious problem of such a stance with regards to solving crime and to writing historical fiction lies in the dubious reliability of some of the available evidence, such that the novel lacks the clear distinction between the past and the present that would allow for a detachment from the historical subject matter. Instead an 'eternal dialogue' seems to be established between the past and the present in *Hawksmoor*.

The appeal of an 'eternal dialogue' is evident in Salman Rushdie's novel, *The Satanic Verses* (1987). Rushdie's book was published ten years after the revised edition of *The Magus*, and Rushdie presents the reading public with a novel that is perhaps even denser with historic, mythic, sacred, literary and cultural references than Fowles' work. Rushdie juxtaposes and combines apparently conflicting literary modes, providing the reader with a style that sets political satire alongside religious fable and stark realism. Such an overlaying of narratives prompted critic Dominic Head to suggest, in *The Cambridge Introduction to Modern British Fiction*, that, 'the complexity can seem contrived . . . making it difficult to forget the grand design whilst reading the book' (Head, 2002, p. 179).

The novel has a range of temporal and geographical settings, from the seventh to the twentieth century, and from mythical Jahilia, to Bombay and London in the 1980s. The two central protagonists, Saladin and Gibreel are 'reincarnated' in the various settings in which they find themselves, as each time they move country they become altered by the experience almost to the extent that they become born again as different people.

In some respects Rushdie's text is 'heavy handed', nevertheless it still marks a significant staging post in the development of a new type of revisionist historical novel, and this is particularly evident if seen in terms of Lukács' notion that the historical novel needs to be reclaimed by 'the people', so that it is no longer solely presided over by the bourgeoisie. Rushdie embarks upon a process of dramatically altering the composition and the scope and the subject of the traditional historical novel. In doing so, he seems to adhere to Lukács' insistence that

> [. . .] where it is a question of changing every principle of composition so that the voice of popular life should be heard for itself and not just the writer's attitude to popular life, such a resolve can only be realised gradually and unevenly, only after searching questions have been asked in the domains of history, ideology and art. (Lukács, *The Historical Novel*, 1962, pp. 282–3)

Whether we as readers consider Rushdie's text to espouse an authentic version of the popular life that Lukács talks about or not, it cannot be denied that *The Satanic Verses* contains a critique of a series of narratives, be they mythical, religious or artistic, and attempts at least to re-align and to ask questions of the historical novel. Rushdie incorporates mythic and invented events alongside actual documented events; he combines mythic places with real places and documents eras that he cannot have experienced alongside the present that he is still living in.

In one interesting example Rushdie provides his own version of John O'Gaunt's 'This other Eden' speech from William Shakespeare's *Richard II*. The speech depicts England as a lost Eden that has fallen into corrupt hands and is in danger of being sullied beyond recognition. Rushdie re-creates the speech, but he subverts the culturally conservative, nostalgic imagery that is often associated with it and forges a means for the Edenic garden metaphor to become a call for change.

> We are here to change things. I concede at once that we shall ourselves be changed; African, Caribbean, Indian, Pakistani, Bangladeshi, Cypriot, Chinese, we are other than what we would have been if our mothers had not crossed the oceans . . . We have been made again, but I say that we shall also be the ones to remake this society, to shape it from the bottom to the top. We shall be the hewers and the gardeners of the new. It is our turn now. (Rushdie, 1988, p. 414)

By subverting the Eden myth Rushdie explicitly exposes the propagandist nature of nostalgia. He sets the ideal of newness against his depiction of a national obsession with looking backwards, and thereby, embarks upon an interaction with the nostalgia that contributes towards shaping a national consciousness.

In *The Mirror in the Text* (1977) Lucien Dällenbach notes that the mythic form itself is suited to producing reflection, rather than universal truth, the mythic contains 'an inexhaustible supply of meanings' and therefore lends itself to the cause of democratizing narrative through focusing on the marginal experience.

> The tale is suited to the propagation of universal truths, since it can be universally appreciated. As for myths, even if they are being brought into an allegorical context, they never quite lose all of their original character: 'symbols extended into narrative form', they 'make me think', and in moving the narrative into an unreal register, none the less produce an inexhaustible supply of meanings. (Dällenbach, 1977, p. 59)

Dällenbach insists upon the ability of the mythic tale to facilitate thought in the reader precisely through their ability to remove the ideological constraints that may be silently limiting our ability to see alternatives to the current way of doing things. Dällenbach suggests therefore that the mythic or invented text can be politically useful in an attempt to democratize or overcome an inherent bias. A politically driven motivation for destabilizing and rewriting 'mainstream history' is seen by many as a result of the Second World War; as Marguerite Alexander explains:

> It seems likely that the second world war, which was even more of a 'mass experience' than the French Revolution and the Napoleonic wars, has helped to foster a new sense of history; and among writers since the war,

realist and non-realist alike, there has been increasing unwillingness to concentrate on private emotional and psychological experiences as though they existed in a social and historic vacuum. (Alexander M., 1990, p. 126)

Alexander may be correct to a point but the personal and the psychological still exist in some popular and well-known texts. Ian McEwan's *The Child in Time* (1987) is perhaps the most obvious example of an intimate, psychologically oriented text that deals with the very private loss of a child, and the subsequent marital breakdown of the parents. In contrast to Alexander's suggestion *The Child in Time* approaches the problem of representing reality precisely from the perspective of personal history and the emotionally driven concepts of time and memory. McEwan's novel focuses on the emotional life of its protagonist, Stephen, who experiences the action of the majority of the novel in what seems like a pause in time. Due to the trauma of losing his daughter, Stephen has lost perspective on time itself.

The novel opens with a traffic jam, itself a suspension of time, but Stephen avoids this 'dead time' by walking past the jam, to the government committee meeting on child rearing he is meant to attend. However, this external escape is not mirrored in Stephen's emotional life, indeed his inner life consists of the dead time of the past. Since the abduction of his child, and finding it impossible therefore to move forward, the narrative of the novel, echoing Stephen's emotional life, becomes ever more concerned with the very intimate and personal experience of 'time'.

The first chapter is both framed by the non-moving 'bureaucratic time' of the committee and filled with Stephen's memories of his childhood, and his haunting recollections of the days surrounding and the day of his daughter's disappearance. McEwan eschews chronological time in favour of a non-linear narrative, as Stephen seems intent upon pursuing the moment of 'uninterrupted time' (McEwan, 1997, p. 10) that he believed was attainable through his own and his wife's proposed lovemaking before Kate's abduction; however, through the course of the novel McEwan seems intent upon deconstructing this notion of 'uninterrupted time'. The presence of memory and emotion ensures that such a proposition is untenable in the realms of human experience, since 'time . . . monomaniacally forbids second chances' (McEwan, 1997, p. 10). All that is left is memory; as such history in McEwan's novel becomes a very personal, intimate space, in which we learn of little that is going on outside of Stephen's own psyche. Stephen's memories become more fantastic as he 'remembers' events before his birth.

It is solely Stephan's responses to events and to time that are being recorded in this novel. Thus, whilst the novel does contain clear criticisms of Thatcherite policies, McEwan shifts the ground of the novel into the personal and defies Alexander's belief that the contemporary novel avoids such personal and psychological investigations.

Pat Barker's *Regeneration* represents another example of a revisionist approach that chooses to emphasize the importance of personal histories while consciously placing the epic and grandiloquent into the background. Barker's novel both incorporates the suggestion that a socially democratizing polyvocality is needed when considering historical narratives, and starts to re-evaluate the traditional weighting between public and private spheres.

The action of Barker's novel concerns the experiences of a number of officers from the Great War, who are in various states of recovery and degeneration at the Craiglockhart hospital in Edinburgh, under the care of leading neurologist and anthropologist Dr Rivers. Several of the characters are based on real people,[1] and much of the action also concerns itself with several of the 'real events' of the First World War.[2]

Barker uses Sassoon's letter to *The Times* newspaper of 1917 stating his objection to the continuance of the war, and the time that he subsequently spent at Edinburgh's Craiglockhart hospital, as a device to shift the focus of the Great War epic onto those who are not (for the moment) fighting the war. Through the hospital ward at Craiglockhart, Edinburgh, Barker portrays the experiences of many marginalized groups during the war, specifically the working classes, women, homosexual members of the military, and those with neurasthenic conditions. Barker presents a novel that deals with the imagined histories of those that have not had the privilege of being recorded; the girls at the munitions factory, Sarah, Lizzie and Betty, represent a newly working, working class woman. Craiglockhart inverts the usual power relationship between the sexes and the classes. The men at the hospital can be detained and reprimanded by the female nurses and V. A. Ds, as evidenced when Prior is denied access to the outside world after returning late from his first night with Sarah.

The *Regeneration* trilogy – *Regeneration, The Eye in the Door* (1993) and *The Ghost Road* (1995) provides a commentary of otherwise excluded narratives, homosexual experience, female experience, working class experience, the experience of the hurt and the injured both mentally and physically; Barker invents a part of their stories, in a novel that embodies Connor's notion that '[. . .] the perspective that takes novels as a resource for history – as a certain kind of historical evidence, for example – must at some stage acknowledge the uneasy overlap between novels and history as forms of narrative' (Connor, 1996, p. 128).

Lynn Wells suggests a greater sense of verisimilitude and fidelity to the 'facts' that works against the kind of post-modern relationship with history and the past made popular by the metafiction of prominent contemporary authors like Salman Rushdie in texts such as *Midnight's Children* and *The Satanic Verses*. Wells notes that *Regeneration* constantly undercuts its own mimetic processes. Well's notes that the novel suggests:

> How the oppositional impulses of realism and modernism are both in play even in novels that appear to have aligned themselves clearly with one pole or the other. What those verisimilar listings reveal is that the majority of the main characters are based on actual literary figures of some renown (such as Siegfried Sassoon and Wilfred Owen), and that they and the other characters derived from real people (like Dr Rivers) have been constructed on the basis of texts written by and about them. (Wells, 2003, p. 121)

Through this merging of the historical with the fictional Barker draws attention to the fact that she is writing about a period that has been recorded as much by the work of poets, essayists and letter writers (both professional and personal), as it has by historians and statisticians. Barker essentially fuses the twin narrative forms of fiction and reported history, finally prioritizing neither of the two narratives. Mengham, Lane and Tew note:

> History in contemporary fiction reaches for an extended sense of its interpretive possibilities (in myth, and in the placing of signification or meaning), drawing themes from the present, such as sexual orientation and gender that Pat Barker, for example, makes central to the social reading of war and its effects in the *Regeneration* trilogy. (Lane et al., 2003, p. 12)

Barker's trilogy of novels was published at a time in which as Marguerite Alexander notes:

> There have been changes in the concept of history – in the way that historians themselves approach their subject, in the teaching of history in schools and in universities – which match those changes in the theory of fiction underpinning postmodernist writing. (Alexander M., 1990, p. 127)

Barker's trilogy conforms to Alexander's statement to some extent, but departs from Alexander's following suggestion that

> [I]n both [history and Postmodern fiction] there is a greater awareness of the unreliability of all narratives, whether purporting to be fact or fiction, and a corresponding impulse to expose the processes by which narratives are made. They share an unwillingness to attribute too much to individuals, but instead examine the forces which shape the terms of individual action. Both novelists and historians allow more of a place in the story to those previously unsung, in history and fiction. (Alexander M., 1990, p. 127)

Departing from Alexander, *The Regeneration Trilogy* suggests that rather than simply debunking the notion of the 'Great individual' in history in order to portray a fuller picture that includes previously marginalized perspectives, it is in fact more prudent to supply as many individual experiences as possible. The trilogy concerns itself with including previously marginalized or silenced perspectives alongside those that are already well documented. The author's note at the end of *The Ghost Road* (1995) serves as a final reminder that the trilogy is including non-documented histories deliberately alongside, and in the same manner as, the previously exalted:

> The reader may wish to know more about some of the historical characters encountered in this novel.
> Colonel Marshall-of-the-Ten-Wounds was killed attempting to cross the Sambre-Oise canal, having led his men 'without regard for his personal safety'. He was awarded a posthumous VC.
> Wilfred Owen's MC for gallantry in capturing an enemy machine-gun and inflicting 'considerable losses' on the enemy at the battle of Jancourt was awarded after his death.
> Rivers drew on his Eddystone data in several published papers, but the major work he and Hocart planned was never written. His notebooks are in the Rare Manuscripts Department of Cambridge University Library.
> Njiru, Kundaite, Namboko Taru, Namboko Emile, Lembu and the captive child are also historical, but of them nothing more is known. (Barker, 1996, p. 591)

The trilogy consistently reminds the reader of the potential to ghettoize the narratives of the marginal if they are to be presented in completely different terms to their historic predecessors. Barker does not simply transfer the attention from traditional 'great' historical figures onto the many and varied 'ordinary' characters of her novel. Instead she takes great pains to forge together the verifiable and the fanciful, the central and the marginal, but in such a way that neither narrative is lost or undermined. The emphasis is on the coexistence of multiple and dialogic versions of the Great War.

The historical subject matter is infused with class-consciousness, as *Regeneration* becomes a commentary also on the processes of recording and commenting on the moments of our past that make it into the annals of history. In this respect Barker seems close to Lukács' representation of the relationship between character (whether fictional or not) and historical moment in what he terms 'the classic' historical novel.

> In this mass experience of history the national element is linked on the one hand with problems of social transformation; and on the other, more and more people become aware of the connection between national and world history. This increasing consciousness of the historical character of development begins to influence judgements on economic conditions and class struggle. (Lukács, *The Historical Novel*, 1962, p. 25)

But if Barker is presenting history 'from below' as Lukács requires then she is keen to point out that it is only fiction that can facilitate this process of aligning history to account for the experience of previously under-represented groups. Barker's novel reflects a wider trend that Lane and Tew note operates 'Throughout contemporary fiction [in which] the adjacency of past and present becomes an aesthetic dynamic, a motive force for narrative, self-identifications and cultural models in a changing society. History is both interrogated and becomes interrogative' (Lane et al., 2003, p. 12).

Mythic and historical narratives, viewed critically, have now come to form part of the means by which authors comment on contemporary reality as they see it. The parabolic and the didactic elements of mythic and historic narrative have been resurrected in its recent incarnations in the contemporary British novel. Part of this practice involves a deconstruction of traditional history that is achieved by bringing into question the 'truth' of historical narratives through the introduction of the mythic.

Kazuo Ishiguro's *The Remains of the Day* (1989) has parallels with Barker's *Regeneration* trilogy in its attempts to shift the focus of a well-documented period (the lead up to the Second World War) onto a narrative that is largely ignored in Britain, that of the Fascist sympathizers in the British aristocracy. Ishiguro depicts the events at Darlington Hall in the lead up to 1939, through the reminiscences of an aging butler.

The novel depicts two time periods; first, the 1930s lead up to the Second World War which is recounted through the reminiscences of the butler, Mr Stevens, and second, the present of the novel, the 1950s in which seemingly little remains of the stately home's heyday. Lord Darlington is dead, the house has a new owner and only the butler, Mr Stevens (the narrator) remains of the once extensive staff, but the house's untold history seeps into Mr Stevens' narrative despite his efforts to deny this aspect of Darlington Hall's history.

Mr Stevens' narrative portrays at first the privileged, isolated world of Darlington Hall which hints at an isolated society, seemingly detached from national and international affairs. Yet it gradually becomes clear that the late Lord Darlington was a Nazi sympathizer, a fact that Stevens struggles throughout the text to reconcile with his own view of his employer as a great man. Darlington Hall's new master, an American businessman, encourages Stevens to take some time off. As he travels in his borrowed car, to the West Country to visit former housekeeper, Miss Kenton, Stevens' memories unfold in the form of a travelogue/journal. Stevens' flashbacks help us to make sense of his past and simultaneously reveal to the reader that his conscious recollection of that past is provisional, partial and unreliable: 'I recall thanking him for his kindness but quite probably I said nothing' (Ishiguro, 1990a, pp. 3–4). As the novel progresses, we learn that Stevens helped his master entertain Fascist leaders like Mosley and that he has played a part in the dismissal of two Jewish maids. Stevens attempts to remove blame from himself by simply refusing to admit any liability for his own actions: 'It is hardly my fault if his lordship's life and work have turned out today to look, at best, a sad waste – and it is quite illogical that I should feel any regret or shame on my own account' (Ishiguro, 1990, pp. 3–4).

The Remains of the Day sees Ishiguro making explicit the status of memory as both an individual and a cultural object that is constantly formed from half-truths and from cultural re-shaping that inevitably excludes some perspectives. This is true in both the lives of individuals (Stevens' insistence that there is dignity in his sacrifices such that they were somehow noble) and the collective ability of England to forget the role of some of its number in the rise of Fascism within Europe. In this reminder Ishiguro essentially extends the questioning of history to account for the marginalized experiences and suggests that individual memory can be just as partial. Ishiguro constructs the text in such a way that the reader can infer far more than Stevens ever openly offers. In an interview with CNN Ishiguro himself suggests:

I'm interested in memory because it's a filter through which we see our lives, and because it's foggy and obscure, the opportunities for self-deception are there. In the end, as a writer, I'm more interested in what people tell themselves happened rather than what actually happened. (Ishiguro, CNN Book News, 2000)

It can be argued that the very lack of reliable memory in Ishiguro's novel serves to highlight what critic Alec McHoul regards as the essential 'misappropriation' of any concept through which we can define or finally close the debate about the nature of our existence or our memory. McHoul proposes that the definition of culture can become its tendency to undermine absolutes, and to contaminate 'pure' identities; these identities can then be remembered or lived. In the case of *The Remains of the Day*, the dissolution of the absolute of memory into the fragments of a narrative can be seen as the contamination of the purity of memory itself through the cultural phenomena and the convenient lies that we use to construct each of our individual pasts. Stevens' conscious memory denies his own implicit (and his boss' explicit) involvement in British support for fascism. Undermining the completeness of memory lays it open to the same interrogation that Barker suggests we should impose on the processes of national histories. Barker and Ishiguro combine to suggest that the processes of remembering can be complicit in denying marginal narratives from the stories of history.

Adam Thorpe's novel *Ulverton* (1992) incorporates an analysis of the recording process of history, and akin to Barker and Ishiguro, shifts the focus of historical narrative onto the 'ordinary', previously untold histories of peasant villagers. The novel is concerned with a historical period that spans nearly half a millennium, 1650–1988 and begins by recounting the tale of William, a shepherd who resides in a newly puritan area of rural England. William's life is briefly touched by the tumultuous events of war when mercenary soldier, Gabby, returns from the war in Ireland claiming to have shaken hands with Oliver Cromwell at Drogheda. William affirms the partial nature of memory (in a manner akin to Ishiguro's treatment of Stevens) when he tells us, that although it seems unlikely, 'I had no cause not to believe him. Whether a man has done a thing or no, I know when he believes he has, and that is all the same in the end' (Thorpe, 1994, p. 3).

Gabby enters the novel in a manner akin to a mythical resurrection; we are told that after many years of absence, and having been presumed dead, Gabby 'appears' on the top of a misty, medieval earthworks, watched by our narrator William, a lowly shepherd, tending his sheep.

> [. . .] he appeared on the hill at first light. The scarp was dark against a greening sky and there was the bump of the barrow and then the figure,

and it shocked. I thought perhaps the warrior buried there had stood up again to haunt us. (Thorpe, 1994, p. 3)

William muses on the new puritan age, and laments the loss of mysticism that the defeat of Catholicism has entailed, Cromwell's army are in the process of attempting to make history change 'overnight' and to deny the catholic heritage of villagers such as William. Whitewashing the church represents a change in religious orientation, but in opposition to this 'silencing' of their past, the villagers' lives continue in a steady stream, changing slowly and in difficult and complex ways, William wishes that his mind could accurately reflect the simplicity of the change that occurs at the level of his concrete surroundings.

I asked God if he could whitewash all my thoughts like the soldiers had covered over the old paintings that I had known as a boy and a man. But thoughts were not on walls but ran like deer and the smell of whitewash mocked me. (Thorpe, 1994, p. 16)

Similarly the story in which the character of Anne is revealed to be a witch affirms the novel's interaction with the persistence of the mythic as a means of interpreting the world. Anne is 'enchanting' in the proper sense of the word, she retains the sexual voraciousness associated with witches and fulfils the narrator's sexual desires as well as his desire for magic and intrigue.

[. . .] we lay on bluebells and it were sticky, and in the autumn the bed-wine dropped his old man's beard into her black hair and I said it was her crown of silver, but she said nothing. In the winter I brought a fleece with me and wrapped her in it so she wouldn't shiver. For it snowed some of the times.

And this went on, oh, for years, until I couldn't see the bedwine plumes in her hair no longer before I blew them off. Then she sickened and died one winter. Sometimes she would whisper the name of Gabby in my ear. And I am an old man!

She was the last witch I ever knew. I was a little mad, probably. That's the story. (Thorpe, 1994, p. 18)

The lives of otherwise ordinary villagers form the central concern of the novel; this has two effects. First, it lends a sense of human proportion to these otherwise distant and ancient characters; second, it suggests that the everyday lives of ordinary people are only briefly touched by history before finding their way back to a pragmatic struggle for survival. Ideals are given little credence when set alongside the very real struggles that the everyday presents. The big historical events of the period are in some senses being removed from an otherwise historical novel. Characters such as William and Gabby continue the tradition of Walter Scott in that as characters who reside at the margins rather the centres of power they are only touched briefly by history and do not see themselves as active participants in the processes of change.

Indeed the cyclical structure of the book – the novel begins with the shepherd's story and ends with the mention of the shepherd's pipe music – works to undermine the teleological history of the type found in textbooks. Hence the reference to 'shepherd's pipe music' (Thorpe, 1994, p. 382) that concludes the novel indicates this shift from the epic to the individual and through its echoes of the initial story of the shepherd adds to the sense of narrative continuity between the ancient and the contemporary settings.

Writers such as Thorpe, Barker and Ishiguro suggest that the marginal and the previously untold histories of Britain do still impact upon the present. For Stevens the suppression of his sense of responsibility for the past has led also to the suppression of his deeper feelings for Miss Kenton. In *Regeneration*, Rivers' suppressed feelings of guilt at sending men back to the front line of battle eventually lead to his breakdown. While in Thorpe's novel the shepherd's music that concludes the text suggests that the 'mystical' and superstitious beliefs that Cromwell's army attempt to suppress at the very start of the novel can still be felt six centuries later.

For writers such as Bernadine Evaristo however, the process by which marginalized or untold histories can assert themselves will not happen organically, untold histories will not assert themselves without the help of contemporary writers and readers. Evaristo sets herself the task of asserting the previously untold history of black people in Britain prior to the arrival of the *Empire Windrush*. For writers like Evaristo narrative is needed as a tool that can redress the suppression of particular historical stories, only if authors deliberately draw attention to the previously untold narratives of their forefathers.

Evaristo's working ethics is based upon the belief that narrative can portray historical truth without being a historical novel in the traditional sense (i.e. based upon documented history). Evaristo describes her aim in writing thus: 'I am committed to exploding the myth of Britain as monocultural and "racially" pure until 1948. There are so many layers of British history to be peeled back' (Evaristo, 2004, p. 291). Evaristo's novel *The Emperor's Babe* (2001) traces the little known history of a black woman living in London in the third century A.D. The novel challenges the British colonial perspective on history that prioritizes solely the experience of post-Windrush immigrant communities.

In an interview with Alastair Niven, Evaristo explains some of the popular assumptions about the history of black people in Britain. She notes:

> What's interesting is that when people read about the book they always presume she is a slave, which I find fascinating because she isn't a slave and there are no references to her being a slave. But at certain moments of history, black people are seen as victims, as downtrodden and enslaved. (Evaristo, 2004, p. 282)

Evaristo's novel re-aligns black history in Britain, incorporating historical research with myth and imagination to tell the story of Roman London through the eyes of Zuleika, a young Londoner of Sudanese parentage growing up eight centuries ago. The novel is also written in verse with the effect that the imaginative, artistic impulse behind the historical research that has gone into the novel is not hidden, but rather prioritized.

The novel is prefaced by Oscar Wilde's aphorism: 'The one duty we owe to history is to rewrite it' (Evaristo, 2001, p. i). It is with this aim in mind that Evaristo's novel embarks upon a knowing rewriting of the history of Roman Britain. The novel is not simply a rewriting, 'this isn't a Greek tragoedia, though it could be mistaken for one' (Evaristo, 2001, p. 245). *The Emperor's Babe* purveys a sense that it does not represent the inclusion of a marginal character in an already established form, but is a new and different form. The novel seems to stand outside of its own preface. It is not simply about rewriting a single narrative, called history, but rather about the creation and the coexistence of alternative histories and alternative myths of our genesis as human beings; as John McLeod notes, Evaristo '[. . .] has striven to show that the fortunes of black people in history are not marginal or of interest only to black readers, but play a central part in the wider historical narrative of the British Isles and make a mockery of notions of cultural and racial purity' (McLeod, 2004, p. 177). Significantly, the novel ends with an evocation of the intimacy that narrative can provide, even after the death of the protagonist.

> Zuleika moritura est.
> Now is the time. I glide to where you lie,
>
> Look upon your pink robes, ruched,
> Décolleté, a mild stir with each tired breath,

> Pronounced mould o your face, odsidian
> With light and sweat, so tranquilla
>
> In your moment of leaving. I slip
> Into your skin, our chest stills, drains
> To charcoal. You have expired Zuleika,
> And I will know you, from the inside. (Evaristo, 2001,
> p. 253)

Evaristo's novel suggests that acquiring real truth entails the ability to remain unfulfilled by what appears to be an explanation, and to continue the search for alternative narratives.

Evaristo's belief that a multitude of narratives is the only way to truly democratize history finds an ally in Winterson's novel *Lighthousekeeping* (2004). *Lighthousekeeping* contains a multiplicity of narratives without prioritizing any one point of view. The novel constructs an analogy between lighthouse keeping and storytelling; the art of storytelling protects the narratives of the marginalized in the same way that the lighthouse protects the lives of those at sea. In *Lighthousekeeping* the art of the storyteller is itself shown to be in danger of becoming a marginalized art. Winterson employs characters such as Darwin and Robert Louis Stevenson in order to suggest that there was a time when the art of storytelling was not opposed to the development of science.

The novel forms what can be best described as a quasi-historical narrative. In a manner similar to Barker's *Regeneration*, Winterson's text depicts real historical people, such as Charles Darwin and the Stevenson family, but interweaves their narratives with the fictionalized people of the seaside town of Salts. Each of these characters is engaged in storytelling of one sort or another. The creation of a story that can adequately explain the origin and purpose of man's existence on earth is the preoccupation of most of the stories whether they are religious, mythical or scientific accounts. Winterson suggests that although during the course of the novel one interpretation often seems to attempt to exclude the other narratives and to marginalize those who insist on the feasibility of what are now outdated accounts. It is only through the art of keeping otherwise marginalized myths and stories alive that humans can fully interact with each other on a spiritual level.

> These stories went from man to man, generation to generation, hooped the sea-bound world and sailed back again, different decked maybe, but the same story. And when the lighthouse keeper had told his story, the sailors would tell their own, from other lights. (Winterson, 2004, p. 39)

The stories that are exchanged form a means for the marginalized histories of those who don't fit in (such as Babel Dark, Silver herself and Pew) to be heard. The lighthouses provide 'a known point in the darkness' (Winterson, 2004, p. 39), the novel suggests, stories also provide 'lit-up moments' (Winterson, 2004, p. 134), in the dark and disjointed narrative of human existence.

Lighthousekeeping suggests that if documented histories fail to account for the experiences of many of the figures within the novel, then the new fantastic tales that Pew and Silver advocate may provide a more democratized narrative of our many different versions of the past. Pew and Silver both indulge in non-realist and magical realist stories that contain a mythopoeic element in that the stories that Pew and the lighthousekeepers, (eventually including Silver herself) tell are ultimately distinct from what is understandable as rational fact but they concern themselves with providing an explanation of how we came to be where we are.

Lighthousekeeping proposes that the greatest and most important myth of all being the myth of one's provenance, Silver tells us that 'My mother called me Silver. I was born part precious metal part pirate' (Winterson, 2004, p. 3). This tale ultimately prioritizes the romantic over the realist, but nevertheless something is still identifiable as 'truth' in the suggestion that a child may be both strong and precious. The reader can understand Silver's point about the 'preciousness of children' even though it is made in an abstract way. The statement about her origins works on another level even though the metaphor is extended beyond realist expression.

The story therefore has a value of its own, and a value as a story, a myth that needs no grounding in the rules of rationality, but nevertheless reveals something vital about the nature of human existence; as Silver comments: 'the story tells you everything you need to know' (Winterson, 2004, p. 135). Narrative in *Lighthousekeeping* has priority as a means of providing balance and comfort in a world that is shown through the experiences of the orphaned Silver and Babel Dark to be both cruel and chaotic, and in which the old order that would have provided stability has been shaken. As Winterson reminds us:

> Darwin overturned a stable-system of creation and completion. His new world was flux, change, trial and error, maverick shifts, fateful experiments, and lottery odds against success. (Winterson, 2004, p. 170)

In moments when transience and change are felt keenly, it is narrative that is left to provide comfort and a means of interacting with the world, for those who have otherwise been excluded from it. *Lighthousekeeping* does not prioritize one narrative over any other, but simply elevates the importance of interrogating and making new narratives and myths as a means of providing 'a known point in the darkness'. The analogy with the lighthouse seems apt, as like stories lighthouses are often regarded as much for their aesthetic value as they are for their pragmatic purpose. *Lighthousekeeping* suggests that stories should be prized just as much for their ability to construct myths, as a means of asserting a common humanity even in the most uncertain of worlds.

> It is true that words drop away, and that the important things are often left unsaid. The important things are learned in faces, in gestures, not in our locked tongues. The true things are too big or too small, or in any case always the wrong size to sit in the template called language.
>
> I know that. But I know something else too, because I was brought up to Lighthousekeeping. Turn down the daily noise and at first there is the relief of silence. And then, very quietly, as quiet as light, meaning returns. Words are the part of silence that can be spoken. (Winterson, 2004, p. 135)

Philosopher Ernst Cassirer suggests that mythic comprehension differs from the purely rational perspective: 'For where we see a mere analogy, i.e. a mere relation, myth sees immediate existence and presence' (Cassirer, 1955, p. 68). It is the lack of narrative that ultimately destroys Babel Dark, as he cannot allow the different narratives that exist within him equal existence and instead attempts to force one narrative to predominate at the exclusion of all others; Darwin warns him of the consequences of this, suggesting that in order 'to avoid either extreme [of Jekyll or Hyde], it is necessary to find all the lives in between' (Winterson, 2004, p. 161). It is precisely his inability to reconcile the different sides of his character that eventually destroys Babel (Winterson, 2004, p. 120). Conversely the Pews have a sense of timelessness and permanence:

> The Pews have been lighthouse keepers at Cape Wrath since the day of the birth. The job was passed down generation to generation, though the present Mr Pew has the look of being there forever. He is as old as a unicorn, and people are frightened of him because he isn't like them. Like and like go together. Likeness is liking, whatever they say about opposites.
>
> But some people are different, that's all. (Winterson, 2004, p. 15)

The apparently ageless quality of Pew adds to the notion that the novel is primarily concerned with an examination of the importance of narrative to afford the marginalized a place in human societies; as Cassirer notes: 'death by no means signifies a sharp division, a parting, of the soul from the body. [. . .] such a distinction, such a definite contrast of the conditions governing life and death, is contrary to the mythical mode of thought' (Cassirer, 1955, pp. 159–60). In Winterson's novel timelessness itself becomes a quality that is afforded to the Pews since those who choose not to ignore myth can revel in the advantages that it offers. Pew has the ability to allow the different stories and competing narratives room to exist without needing to promote one single narrative, Pew understands that, '[. . .] nothing is gone, that everything can be recovered, not as it was, but in its changing form' (Winterson, 2004, p. 150). Pew also exists in this realm, being recovered in a slightly different form in all of the generations in which 'there has been a Pew' (Winterson, 2004, p. 150) at the lighthouse.

The novel intimates that although the loss of past narratives may initially seem nihilistic: 'If one thing is taken away, another will be found' (Winterson, 2004, p. 48). The novel takes an approach to the understanding of the limits and uses of rational knowledge that corresponds to Cassirer's account of the patterns of human culture; as Cassirer suggests:

> [. . .] knowledge can never reproduce the true nature of things as they are, but must frame their essence in "concepts." But what are concepts save formulations and creations of thought, which, instead of giving us the true forms of objects, show us rather the forms of thought itself? (Cassirer, 1955, p. 7)

Lighthousekeeping assumes a specific tone, and a set of political, and historical concerns that the author hints will not be resolved through linear and binary rational practices but which will instead require the exploitation of the ambiguous space that opens up when such practices are broken down. The narrator suggests that a reassertion of what increasingly comes to seem like faith in the magic of narrative is needed. She asserts that

> [N]ames are still magic; even Sharon, Karen, Darren and Warren are magic to somebody, somewhere. In the fairy stories, naming is knowledge. When I know your name, I can call your name, and when I call your name, you'll come to me. (Winterson, 2004, pp. 155–6)

The novel also hints at the transitional, marginal quality of such a space, similar to Cassirer's understanding of what he terms mythical consciousness.

. . . [which] is not, like the theoretical consciousness, concerned with gaining fundamental constants by which to explain variation and change. This differentiation is replaced by another, which is determined by the characteristic perspective of myth. The mythical consciousness arrives at an articulation of space and time not by standardizing the fluctuation of sensuous phenomena but by introducing its specific opposition – the opposition of the sacred and the profane – into spatial and temporal reality. (Cassirer, 1955, p. 81)

In *Lighthousekeeping* mythical consciousness in its oppositional role to that of the theoretical consciousness, permits the realm of emotions and ideals to exert a tangible power upon the action of the novel, and thus it is love that finally provides the 'anchor' to the rest of the world that the marginalized Silver requires: 'I had lost the few things I knew, and what was here belonged to somebody else. Perhaps that would have been alright if what was inside me was my own, but there was no place to anchor' (Winterson, 2004, p. 21). The novel suggests that love will provide a form of sustenance but this sustenance will not be straightforward, in the traditional sense of the 'happy ending' in which the reader knows that the hero and the heroine will find eternal happiness in their love for one another. Rather Winterson suggests that in this novel love must be understood in its own terms:

I used to be a hopeless romantic. I still am a hopeless romantic. I used to believe that love was the highest value. I still believe that love is the highest value. I don't expect it to be happy. I don't imagine that I will find love, whatever that means, or that if I do find it, it will make me happy. I don't think of love as the answer or the solution. I think of love as a force of nature – as strong as the sun, as necessary, as impersonal, as gigantic, as impossible, as scorching as it is warming, as drought-making as it is life-giving. And when it burns out, the planet dies. (Winterson, 2004, p. 199)

Significantly this is not intended as a complete move away from the romantic, since we are informed that Silver still is 'a hopeless romantic'; instead new versions of eternal human qualities are being sought, away from the universal, Pew warns Silver that she needs to remember that, although a knowledge of stories is vital to human existence it is not the ability to command knowledge over such narratives that is treasured since the novel applies Cassirer's notion that 'knowledge . . . (is frequently) reduced to a kind of fiction' (Cassirer, 1955, p. 7) but rather the narratives themselves, with a full understanding of the limitations of 'stories':

> You don't need to know everything. There is no everything. The stories themselves make the meaning.
>
> The continuous narrative of existence is a lie. There is no continuous narrative, there are lit-up moments, and the rest is dark. (Winterson, 2004, p. 134)

To conclude, the mythic and the historic elements of the novel thus become in the contemporary British setting a set of image-borne strategies aimed at destabilizing the official worldview and promoting a marginalized perspective. These texts imply that a line can be drawn and should not be overstepped in which newness should be created whilst preserving some of traditions of narrative. Ingrained in this always is the notion of return, Lukács famously called for such a return in terms of the historical novel: 'The perspective for the development of the historical novel depends then on the resumption of classical traditions, on a fruitful assimilation of the classical inheritance.' (Lukács, *The Historical Novel*, 1962, p. 344). A part of this return will also include a reassessment of the post-modern perception of the relationship between man and narrative. That this return would also incorporate a re-establishing of the primacy of narrative amongst the work of many contemporary authors would seem to hint at a future direction for the form. It may be necessary to concede critic Seyla Benhabib's affirmation of the power of narrative and the need for multiple stances, since these novels suggest that 'to deny that the play of language games may not turn into a matter of life and death, and that the intellectual cannot remain the priest of many gods but must take a stance is cynical' (Benhabib, 1984, p. 124).

Lukács provides a socio-political context for the changing form of the historical novel when he notes that

> [T]he difference of principles between the historical novel of the classics and of decadence etc. has its historical causes [. . .] the historical novel in its origin, development, rise and decline follows inevitably upon the great social transformations of modern times [. . .] its different problems of form are but artistic reflections of these social-historical transformations. (Lukács, *The Historical Novel*, 1962, p. 17)

Lukács' observation concerning the importance of the influence of what he terms 'social-historical transformations' on the form seems to apply to the contemporary situation in a very specific way. The contemporary historical novel has indeed become a product of its era, created out of a period that exists in a literary world that is (self) consciously aware of the destabilized position that history must now occupy within the novel. Indeed many novelists interested in the historic form have eschewed both the quasi-realist methods of the traditional historical novel and the 'external, decorative, picturesque manner' that Lukács disapproves of. The renewed critical attention that contemporary historical novels have brought to texts that deal with history or practices of historical narrative have formed a large part of the contemporary scene. From Fowles and Rushdie to Winterson and Evaristo, such novelists seek to interrogate the processes of history as much as they attempt to evoke them, producing meta-historical narratives, which place the documented and imagined, previously marginalized histories side-by-side in their deliberate attempts to erase the boundaries between the two.

Chapter 5

Satire and the Grotesque

This chapter examines the grotesque in contemporary British fiction. The grotesque is important as it represents a fusion of the marginality of the misfit figure explored in Chapter 3 and the contemporary desire for a reassertion of the importance of narrative that was discussed in chapter four.[1] My definition of the grotesque follows Wolfgang Kayser's model set out in his seminal work *The Grotesque in Art and Literature* (translated into English in 1957). Kayser's text represents a lengthy interaction with the theme of the grotesque and thus a large part of this chapter is dedicated to interacting with Kayser in particular, but it should also be noted here that, although on a smaller scale, critical notions of the grotesque feature in a wide range of theoretical work dedicated to providing an understanding of literature which refuses to uphold the classical ideal, and that instead promote a more marginalized perspective.[2]

It is now commonplace to see an appropriation of the grotesque as an affirmation of vitality against a moribund and bureaucratic system; akin to Rushdie's call for 'newness' within literature. The grotesque provides this opportunity for a 'new' perspective. Carol Shields evokes this sense that the grotesque can offer a sense of vitality when she notes in the *Guardian* that *The Girls of Slender Means* (1964) contains a refreshing and darkly comic 'grotesque dénouement in which naked girls smear their bodies with margarine and, amid great confusion, crawl through a bathroom window to safety' (Shields, 2003). In the introduction to his text about American author *Saul Bellow* (1965) Tony Tanner comments more generally on what he classifies as 'art associated with negation' (Tanner, 1965, p. 115), a category in which he places the grotesque. Tanner notes that

[A]rt associated with negation, art that shocks its readership or that gives us a regulated glimpse of Avernus or of chaos is not 'negative art' at all. I think it can be argued that there is in fact a literature of negative energy which is yet affirmative of life. (Tanner, 1965, p. 115)

The primary way in which the grotesque can contain this element that is 'affirmative of life' is through its ability to shift the focus of the novel onto new ground, and it is this aspect of the theme that has interested those wishing to portray a newer or a previously marginalized perspective within literature.

Kayser's text is seminal because it marks a turning point in the manner in which the grotesque should be perceived. This turning point is largely due to Kayser's insistence that the grotesque must be regarded as a comprehensive structural principle (Kayser, 1963, pp. 29–47). Kayser suggests that there must be a certain pattern that is peculiar to the grotesque and 'a fundamental structure that is perceivable in any grotesque work and its effect' (Thomson, 1972, pp. 18–19). Philip Thomson helpfully summarizes this pattern as three overlapping properties that the grotesque work must contain:

(1) The grotesque is the expression of the estranged or alienated world, i.e. the familiar world must be seen from a perspective that suddenly renders it strange (this strangeness may be either comic or terrifying, or both).

(2) The grotesque is a game with the absurd, in the sense that the grotesque artist plays, half laughingly, half horrified, with the deep absurdities of existence.

(3) The grotesque is an attempt to control and exorcise the demonic elements in the world. (Thomson, 1972, pp. 18–19)

The category of the grotesque as outlined by Kayser offers the possibility to portray a marginalized perspective because of its insistence upon the possibility for an alien or demonized perception within art.

Contemporary critics have detailed the growing evocation of an ever-present threat of alienation and violence, which creates an aesthetic that is remarkably close to Kayser's three elements of the grotesque. Gilbert Phelps in *Modern Britain: The Cambridge Cultural History* (1972) notes that: 'all post-war English literature has been overshadowed by a sense of social and cultural disintegration and of the ever-present threat of violence and chaos' (Phelps, *Cambridge Cultural History of Britain*, 1992, p. 198). Philip Tew notes in *The Contemporary British Novel* (2004): 'an evolving British aesthetic is concerned variously with a familiarity of location, a disrupted conventionality, and a sense of otherworldliness' (Tew, 2004, p. 29).[3]

Rey Chow, whose work implicitly informs much of my own in this book seems particularly relevant here. Chow implies that we need to understand the processes of marginalization noting that '[. . .] a monstrous aesthetics is also an aesthetics of *making* monstrous, of demonstrative magnification and amplification' (Chow, 1998, p. 16). In Chow's terms the grotesque could be seen to offer a means for the subject that has been 'made monstrous' to speak back to the mainstream audience that has been implicit in this process of 'making monstrous'. Therefore the grotesque can be seen as containing a radical, democratizing element.

It is interesting to compare Kayser's notion of the grotesque with some contemporary novels that engage with the theme. Will Self's novel *Great Apes* (1997) exemplifies the contemporary engagement with the notion of perspective. The novel details an alternate universe with both comic and terrifying elements, in which apes are the evolutionary successful species, having created a civilization remarkably recognizable for the human reader.

The artist Simon Dykes becomes our psychotic guide into this world. Simon begins the novel as a successful artist who indulges almost fully in a narcotic-enhanced world of excess, but waking up one morning to find his partner has mysteriously turned into a chimpanzee over night, Simon slowly reaches the realization that even when the effects of the drugs wear off he is still having to accept that the rest of his ape world consider him nothing more than an ape suffering the delusion that he is human.[4] Simon becomes entirely marginalized, locked in an institution, and with no fellow believers in the possibility that he was once human.

Self prioritizes perspective within the novel; it is *the* means by which the humans that open the novel interact with their environment, influencing concepts of time, and of reality itself.

> [. . .] It's perspective that provides the necessary third continuum for vision and maybe consciousness as well. Without it an individual might no longer be able to apprehend time, might . . . have to relearn time in some way, or be left in a sliver of reality, imprisoned like a microbe in a microscope slide. (Self, 1998a, p. 3)

Adhering to the pattern of Kayser's formula concerning the grotesque shift in perspective *Great Apes* proceeds to drastically alter Simon's perception of the world around him, through questioning his assumption that he is human. However, in Simon's world of cosmopolitan London, perspective is always already flawed.[5]

It is not at the point at which Simon is convinced that the rest of society are chimps that the shift in perspective occurs. Rather Simon occupied a marginal or externalized position from the very beginning of the novel; he actually begins to provide an altered, drug-induced perspective on humanity whilst still believing that he and the rest of society are human. Simon persists in reducing that humanity to a grotesque series of parts and functions: 'Male, female, whole, crippled, it hardly mattered. What he desired was a flesh pit full of writhing naked bodies, smeared with glycerine; or better still a conga-line of copulation, where a cock-thrust here would produce a cunt-throb way over there' (Self, 1998a, p. 10).

In its human state Simon's body continually causes him to feel misaligned, and it is here that the novel seems most to espouse a peculiar kind of didactic teaching, hinting that if humans think that they can escape the confines of their animal bodies they may find that they have overreached themselves. The recreational drugs that were supposed to lift him out of the confines of his physicality and transcend the constrictive perspective of the human body conspire in their after-effects to imprison him in his fleshy frame, despite his feeling that he doesn't fit any longer: 'for now his bodily awareness was one solely of constraint, of resistance, of a missing fit between every ligament and bone, every cell and its neighbour' (Self, 1998a, p. 12). Simon's body is depicted as an evil twin to his psyche, continually conspiring to hold him back.[6]

The success of *Great Apes* as a grotesque novel is in large part due to the completeness with which Self achieves the shift in perspective into 'chimpunity'.[7] The depiction of Ape civilization is posited between those aspects that can be effortlessly transposed into the human world; there are chimp versions of famous figures such as Sigmund Freud, O. J. Simpson and Jane Goodall (an ape who studies wild humans), and the depiction of differences between the two worlds that alienate the human reader. Self employs a narrative that evokes the grotesque through a series of rapid and disorientating transformations from stark realism to horrific farce. Self renders the most poignant subjects at once real and grotesque, such as Simon's sense of separation from his children following the breakdown of his marriage.

> No matter how much he saw them now, how many times he picked them up from school, how many times he made them oven chips and fish fingers, how many times he petted them, kissed them, told them he loved them, nothing could assuage this sense of wrenching separation, their disjunction from his life. He may not have snacked on the placenta, but somehow the umbilici still trailed from his mouth, ectoplasmic cords, strung across summertime London, snagging on rooftops, car aerials, advertising hoardings, and tied him to their little bellies. (Self, 1998a, p. 13)

With a narrative that seems at times reminiscent of Jonathan Swift, Self turns his novel into a high-powered satirical weapon aimed at a wide range of political and cultural figures.[8] But Self is not simply creating a transient sardonic comedy. In scope too *Great Apes* is reminiscent of Jonathan Swift's *Gulliver's Travels*, which made similar use of anthropomorphized beasts to satirize the general corruption and foolhardiness of the human race. In a moment of reflexivity (on Self's part) Busner remarks to Simon at the conclusion of the novel:

'It crossed my mind – and I hope you'll forgive me for this speculation in advance if you cannot concur – that your conviction that you were human and that the evolutionarily successful primate was the human was more in the manner of a satirical trope.' (Self, 1998a, p. 404).

Self constantly reminds the reader of the humanity of the figures residing at the heart of his grotesque tale, and *Great Apes* can be unexpectedly moving, as in the passage where Simon's human mind/chimp body problem takes the form of a drug-induced feverish dream:

He identified the lost infant as himself – or to be more precise his lost body. He saw his infant's body, standing, shivering, naked of its protective coat. Little Simon, as gracile as a young bonobo; head fur blond and cropped at the back, features refined and serious. . . . Simon turned towards the lost infant, wafted across the grassy floor to get him. But as he drew nearer the infant's blue eyes widened, and his red red lips parted, and the sapling body bent in an afflatus of anguish. Then Simon heard the awful, meaningful vocalizations; so guttural – but so just. 'Get away! Get away, Beelzebub! Foul beast! Ape man!' (Self, 1998a, p. 283)

In such moments the radical alienation that Simon feels in terms of [or from] his environment, his family, and even his own nature becomes more than just an appealing comic device. Instead these moments prioritize the notion that it is something about the contemporary Western world that has produced a sense of lost perspective for the individual.

The human body had – Simon felt – been pushed out over a purely local void, an overhanging of time; it dangled there, a Navaho on a steel girder, pitting its head for heads against the sheer cliff of just-constructed, concretised techno. The wind had changed and left Simon's human subjects distorted in the attitudes required to live in this world of terminal distressing. (Self, 1998a, p. 25)

Simon, the human-minded ape, could at times be speaking for all those who feel that they have lost their sense of perspective. Self employs animal imagery in order to reproduce the effect for the reader, as the narrative leaps from the urban and the urbane to the fantastic and the animalistic, but by avoiding the appropriation of the exotic through evoking the image of domesticated sheep, rather than any more glamorous creature, Self makes the image grotesque by denying the classical and 'bringing back down to earth' the otherwise classical image of the kiss.

The outer eddies from the opening reached the two men, a skirl of chamber music nouveau, a waft of Marlboro smoke, a couple of youngsters, who leant against a nearby pillar, the girl's sateen-hosed thigh gently rubbing her companions corduroy crotch, while sheep-like they cropped on one another's faces. (Self, 1998a, p. 2)

The fact that Self so obviously seems to have a political or social 'point' to his work and that he uses a process of alienation to achieve the desired effect links his work to an older (often neglected) set of coordinates set out by Marxist critic Georg Lukács. In his discussion of 'reification' Lukács was among the first to reintroduce the idea of alienation as central to Marxist thought. According to Lukács, the formal fragmentation of modernist texts participates in the process of reification. Realism is the only literary mode capable of representing the totality of society. Bourgeois thought is repeated in naturalism and subjectivism. Naturalism is for Lukács a degraded form of realism and limits itself to description instead of narration. Subjectivist art elevates art as the product of the superior subjective consciousness of the creative artist.

The goal of art is to provide a picture of reality in which the contradiction between appearance and reality, the particular and the general, the immediate and the conceptual, etc., is so resolved that the two converge into a spontaneous integrity . . . The Universal appears as a quality of the individual and the particular, reality becomes manifest and can be experienced within appearance. (Lukács, 'Writer and Critic 1970', 1980, p. 76)

Within *Great Apes* Self combines the idea that reality can be regarded as manifest with an evocation of the more established theme of corporeality.

The sound of the ringing reverberated in the confined space, creating a split-second echo, a distortion in sonic registration that Simon connected with his own sense of dislocation from his body, of the mismatch between psychic and physical. (Self, 1998a, p. 157)

John R. Clarke writing about the development of the grotesque form in literature and theatre in *The Modern Satiric Grotesque And Its Traditions* (1991) opens his text with a reminder of how the grotesque would have been interpreted in the past: 'the literature of the modern era immerses us again and again in disillusionment, anomie, alienation and wretchedness' (Clarke, 1991, p. 1). Clarke's statement can be traced back further than the modern era with similar sentiments being expressed by prominent critics from the last three centuries. From as early as 1853 Mathew Arnold notes that 'the dialogue of the mind with itself has commenced; modern problems have presented themselves; we hear already the doubts, we witness the discouragement of Hamlet and of Faust' (Arnold, 1965, p. 591), similarly in *Human All Too Human: A Book For Free Spirits* (1878) Friedrich Nietzsche notes the importance of what he calls 'an art of the ugly soul':

One imposes far too narrow limitations on art when one demands that only well-ordered, morally balanced souls may express themselves in it. As in the plastic arts, so in music and poetry too there is an art of the ugly soul beside the art of the beautiful soul; and the mightiest effects of arts, that which tames souls, moves stones and humanises the beast, have perhaps been mostly achieved by precisely that art. (Nietzsche, 1986, p. 82)

Though discussion on the 'art of the ugly soul' can be found in the nineteenth century, twentieth-century critics are concerned with the self-conscious analysis of what they discern to be the proliferation of the grotesque within the twentieth century. As early as the 1920s Thomas Mann was predicting that no manner or mode in literature would be as typical or pervasive in the twentieth century as that of the grotesque. Mann notes that

[. . .] broadly and essentially, the striking feature of modern art is that it has ceased to recognize the categories of tragic and comic, or the dramatic qualifications tragedy and comedy. It sees life as tragicomedy, with the result that the grotesque is its most genuine style. (Mann, 1968, pp. 240–1)

This notion that the grotesque can offer the genuine is largely the result of two fundamental attributes of the form. First, through the inherent opportunity that the genre provides for a disruption of the perceived 'rationalised', predictable outcome of any given situation, and second because of the dominant, slightly exterior position to which the reader is often privileged as the grotesque provides a similar distancing effect to what Bakhtin terms the 'laughing context'.[9] It is through these qualities that the grotesque can be seen as in some way enabling the contemporary search for a fiction that can adequately represent the marginal as a more 'genuine', or 'realistic' depiction of the human condition.

John R. Clarke elucidates the growing sense of alienation in contemporary literature:

> Modern interest in the psyche, in Man's troubled inner life, renders the gloomy strategies of Gothicism and grotesquerie more pertinent and apt. The tactics and themes of the grotesque are well suited to exaggerate the dark side of human nature, to shock the audience with scenes of the startling, the disturbing, the unnatural, and the absurd. [. . .] Such darkling artistry cannot help but alienate its audience and upset the bourgeoisie; indeed, it is thus that the traditional satiric artist, treating serious subjects, gains serious attention. Surely he wants it that way. (Clarke, 1991, p. 7)

It is interesting to note that in *Great Apes* Self initially imbues his application of the grotesque with a sense of it being the only means through which Simon can interact with the newspaper headlines that serve to both disturb and distance him from the world around him.

> Simon struck the set and looked to his right where a freestanding rack of newspapers stood. He scanned the headlines: 'More Massacres in Rwanda', 'President Clinton Urges Ceasefire in Bosnia', 'Accusations of Racism in O. J. Simpson Trial'. It wasn't, he reflected, political news; it was news about bodies, corporeportage. Bodies dragged by thin shanks through thick mud, bodies' smashed and pulverised, throats slashed red, given free tracheotomies so that the afflicted could breathe their last. There was some fit here, Simon realised, between the penumbra around his life, the darkness at the edge of the sun, and these bulletins of disembodiment, discorporation updates. His imagination, always too visual, could enter into these headlines readily enough, but only by casting Henry, his eldest, as Hutu; Magnus, the baby, as Tutsi; then watch them rip each other to shreds. (Self, 1998a, pp. 13–14)

The image of babies re-enacting some of the most violent incidents of the latter half of the twentieth century serves as a device to both highlight the inhumanity of the reduction of people into parts and numbers that form what Simon terms the 'corporeportage' of the headlines, and to highlight the potential in all humanity to enact violence. Simon's reaction to the stories of the genocide in Rwanda reflect what seems to be a human propensity towards imagining the grotesque as a first reaction to real events that seem so brutal as to be beyond understanding or reason. The grotesque then fulfils the political and social function of exploring 'man's inhumanity to man' in the post-Second World War era.

James Wood emphasizes the political nature of the grotesque when he argues in his essay 'V. S. Naipaul and English comedy' (Wood, 2002, p. 9) that of all of our literary predecessors it is Charles Dickens who has been the decisive influence on postwar English comedy. Dickens' influence has been primarily to create the kind of comic genre that revels in grotesque portraiture and satiric caricature usually with a political target in mind. In addition Dickens' work often engages in an implicit questioning of all 'representations of reality' in order to foreground the otherwise marginalized working classes. Wood argues that the presence of Dickens's influence can be felt in the work of almost any contemporary author; he details the extent to which Dickens can be felt in contemporary British fiction thus:

> [. . .] in Muriel Spark, in early Naipaul, overwhelmingly and detrimentally in Angus Wilson, also in Salman Rushdie (again detrimentally), in Angela Carter and Martin Amis, one finds Dickens' impress, in particular the interest in the self as a public performer, an interest in grotesque portraiture and loud names, and in character as caricature, a vivid blot of essence. (Wood, 2002, p. 9)

Novels such as Angela Carter's *The Passion of New Eve* (1977) and *Nights at the Circus* (1984), Irvine Welsh's *Trainspotting* (1993), Jim Crace's *Being Dead* (1999) and *Arcadia* (1992), Will Self's *Cock and Bull* (1994) and *Dorian* (2004) (amongst other examples too numerous to mention here)[10] provide evidence that the appropriation of the grotesque can often be both politically motivated and mordantly sardonic, designed to shock the reader via an exhibition of excess and exaggeration. If the grotesque marks the boundaries of what is and is not acceptable then it will always form the ground upon which the struggle for definition and for acceptance and rejection will be played out.

Wood's evocative description of the characters created by authors such as Carter and Rushdie as 'a vivid blot of essence' can be appealing; it would, however, be unfair to assume that these authors limit themselves to creating characters that are nothing more than 'caricature'. The authors Wood lists often go further than simply creating 'a vivid blot of essence' and in a Bakhtinian sense each incorporates 'the corrective of reality' (Bakhtin, 'The Prehistory of Novelistic Discourse', 1982, p. 58) creating not merely vibrant and sardonic recreations of fundamental human characteristics but also creating what Bakhtin terms 'intentional dialogised hybrids' in which the primary perspective is knocked out of kilter in order for another, newer voice to spring forth, enriching rather than mocking the subject. (Bakhtin, 'The Prehistory of Novelistic Discourse', 1982, p. 58)

Georges Bataille frames the process by which a subject could be enriched by satire philosophically when he notes that 'knowledge enslaves us, [. . .] At the base of all knowledge there is a servility, the acceptation of a way of life wherein each moment has meaning only in relation to another or others that will follow it' (Bataille, 2001, p. 129). Akin to this notion that at the base of human knowledge there is a discernable partiality which conspires to restrict true knowledge in order to confine the human in servitude is the twin notion, acknowledged by critics such as Bataille, Bakhtin, Arthur Clayborough, Wolfgang Kayser and J. R. Clarke that the restrictive nature of knowledge may be at least partially overcome in forms such as the comedic, the parodic and the grotesque. These forms contain the potential for establishing a new way of sensing the world, incorporating forms as multiple and varied as parody, satire, invective, caricature, burlesque, black comedy, the macabre and the pathological, which by incorporating the previously silenced or marginalized aspects of humanity will open out meaning, and thus will act partially as a counter to the reductive nature of accepted knowledge. Such a reading necessarily incorporates an evocation of the carnivalesque-grotesque, in which laughter accompanies a sense of survival: 'The world has always moved on, and in the fracturing between character and world, there is much laughter: huge stomach-churning bursts of laughter, countered by a redemptive/narrative force that may, or may not be a result of that laughter' (Lane, 2003, p. 28).

For the contemporary British novelist the carnivalesque and grotesque form seems to offer an escape route, if only a partial one, in which the grotesque fantasy is not the deformer but the vessel of a kind of 'truth', as Iris Murdoch notes: 'we are not isolated free choosers, monarchs of all we survey, but benighted creatures sunk in a reality whose nature we are constantly tempted to deform by fantasy' (Murdoch, 1977 [1961], p. 20). The prevalence of this desire to deform connects the contemporary British novel with a distinctly modernist agenda in the manner of Joyce's concept that the ideal text will fulfil the author's desire to rebel.

> [I will] not serve that in which I no longer believe whether it call itself my home, my fatherland or my church, and I will try to express myself in some other mode or life or art as freely as I can and as wholly as I can, using for my defence the only arms I allow myself to use: silence, exile and cunning. (Joyce, 1993, p. 200)

The grotesque represents an ancient artistic urge to create a text that will challenge the traditional progressive mode of understanding, and prioritize instead a newer or a previously unheard narrative. This has been achieved within the realm of the parodic grotesque by relegating the classic or the sublime to the level of the base and the human, forging an analogy between the grotesque world on the page and the 'real' world outside, seeming therefore to work in a manner akin to Linda Hutcheon's understanding of post-modernism.

> [. . .] it seems reasonable to say that the postmodern's initial concern is to de-naturalize some of the dominant features of our way of life; to point out that those entities that we unthinkingly experience as "natural" (they might even include capitalism, patriarchy, liberal humanism) are in fact "cultural;" made by us, not given to us. (Hutcheon, 1989, pp. 1–2)

While Hutcheon helps to define the function of the grotesque in terms of the post-modern, Bakhtin provides a much older set of literary coordinates in order to locate this process culturally. Bakhtin would understand the ability of a text to destabilize normative thinking in terms of the *potential* of the carnivalesque, grotesque or parodic form to express and make powerful the otherwise marginal in society.

Bakhtin's notion of potential extends even to the most ancient of folkloric fiction. *Potential* is illustrated through the figures of the clown, the fool, and the rogue (Bakhtin, 'Forms of Time and of the Chronotope in the Novel: Notes Towards a Historical Poetics', 1981, p. 159). By its very nature *potential* is a presence that is not represented in completeness but for Bakhtin the fulfilment of *potential*, its realization in tangible or measurable form is not entirely necessary. Rather, *potential* represents the right to be more than any given role (Saul and Emerson, 1990, p. 436). As Bakhtin puts it 'the right to be *other* in this world, the right not to make common cause with any single one of the existing categories that life makes available' (Bakhtin, 'Forms of Time and of the Chronotope in the Novel: Notes Towards a Historical Poetics', 1981, p. 159).

If we follow the logic of Bakhtin's concept then characters exhibiting *potential* can be said to exploit alternative positions made available through the masks of foolery, roguishness and so on; they are constructs with limits in their understanding and incarnation in the 'real' world. Such characters are however the perfect didactic tool for showing the inconsistencies of the 'real world', not least because of the appeal to exteriority that the laughing element of the grotesque encompasses: 'In laughing I can introduce a judgement – evidently pure knowledge being what it is can enclose laughter, but laughter too can enclose knowledge' (Bataille, 2001, p. 172).

Kayser's second property of the grotesque 'the grotesque is a game with the absurd, in the sense that the grotesque artist plays, half laughingly, half horrified, with the deep absurdities of existence' (Thomson, 1972, pp. 18–19), also concerns the notion that the grotesque is a kind of game that the artist plays, half laughingly, half horrified, concerning the deep absurdities of existence. The existence of such a game is evident in Toby Litt's *Deadkidsongs* which evokes the 'grim graveyard humour' and the ever-present threat of chaos amidst civilization. The novel concerns a single summer in the lives of a group of boys who decide to kill the grandparents of their friend after he dies of meningitis, believing that it was their slow reaction to his illness that resulted in his death. The novel has two endings; a 'grotesque' ending in which most of the characters are brutally murdered and the violence that stems from the abuse of Andrew by his father extends across the entire novel, and an alternative 'realistic' ending in which the violence is mostly consigned to the realm of fantasy. By placing the chaotic violent ending first Litt ensures that the threat of the violence is felt forcibly even as we read the more 'realistic' ending.

Chaos is also firmly placed within the boys' minds and hearts themselves, as it is primarily boredom and *ennui* that will call the absurd and the anarchic into being in the very heart of supposedly civilized, middle England. Indeed boredom is a persistent theme of the grotesque; we are frequently told in *Deadkidsongs* that the boys are bored, and further that 'of all emotions the one that causes young men most suffering is boredom' (Litt, 2001, p. 94). The boredom that the boys suffer is more than simply a transient feeling that must be endured from time to time, rather their boredom is so frequently mentioned that it becomes a driving force in itself, leading to despair, and violence, such that, the text begins to fulfil Lee Byron Jennings' assertion of the ludicrous in the grotesque:

> The familiar structure of existence is undermined and chaos seems imminent. This aspect is intensified when concrete manifestations of decay appear and a feeling of hopelessness and corruption is developed. The ludicrous aspect, in turn, arises from the farcical quality inherent in such scenes of absurdity and approaching chaos. (Jennings, 1963, p. 51)

Clarke theorizes this position, noting that like the Romantics, we still desire both action and a sense of purpose surrounding that action; we still want, at least on some level (according to Clarke) revolution, imagination, extremity. However, unlike the Romantics our manner is no longer exalted, earnest, serious or holy; 'instead, we provoke the paroxysm of hopeless laughter and desperate, unnatural comedy' (Clarke, 1991, p. 13). This hopeless and desperate comedy produces its own logic and its own boundaries of taste and decency. In *Deadkidsongs* the liberal attitude of Paul's parents is unfathomable to their own son, who can only see that he is being stifled by their protective instincts. The narrator notes:

> It was a conflict in which one of the sides was fighting against the very idea of conflict itself. Paul's parents under their political delusion were trying to make the world a better, less violent place, by bringing their son up in what they saw as a better, less violent way. Paul, like all of Gang [sic], saw beyond his immediate circumstances, and out into the wider world, a world which was not improving, which, if anything, was becoming worse. Paul was readying himself for a situation he knew existed; his parents, manipulating him to be part of a situation they vaguely hoped could be brought about, if enough people like them did enough manipulating of their children. It is not difficult to see whose logic was the clearer. (Litt, 2001, pp. 85–6)

It is interesting to note that the novel is in fact far more forgiving of the parents' hopeful romantic vision than might first appear and ends in an affirmation of love in spite of the grotesque and hopeless tale that forms the main part of the novel. At the close of the novel the keeper of the manuscript that contains the main part of the action of the novel, Paul's child states that '. . . my father was a great man. Whatever he did, or didn't do, I loved him' (Litt, 2001, p. 401).[11]

Paul's father explains what seems like very rational reasons for disapproving of Paul's friendship with the abused and damaged Andrew. He tells his wife that

> 'I don't like the values he's picking up from them. They're all of them completely in thrall to Andrew's father. He's got just the kind of skewed logic that appeals to boys that age. It's all to do with physical strength. Nothing to do with compassion. Nothing to do with real friendship.'
> (Litt, 2001, p. 65)

His appeal falls on deaf ears, because essentially the grotesque is attractive to the boys; the marginal, the uncivilized and the chaotic excite them.

Litt draws this appeal of the grotesque as a particularly masculine phenomenon, presenting the idea that both the denial of feelings and the brutalizing of boys as represented by Andrew's father (perversely nominated as the 'Best Father' by the other boys) has lead to an era in which the boys feel that they have no place in the 'civilised' middle-class society of their village life. Their dislocation from the civilized world draws them to the grotesque, and towards pushing the limits of acceptability, but their choice of leader in this social experiment is of vital importance. The boys choose a leader who is at once so disturbed that his violence reaches extremes by the standards of a civilized society, but who will also immediately be seen as the sole cause for their actions, as a result of his abuse.

Andrew acts as a great 'excuse' for the others to express that side of them that is implicitly drawn to the grotesque: 'As always, his strength must derive from the fact that he is willing to do more, to do worse, than the others would ever have done' (Litt, 2001, p. 252). Andrew is a presence so disturbed that violence is something that he finds irresistible; he is compelled to violence and it is the responsibility of the others to police this compulsion in him. The character of Paul notes that 'Andrew can't just kill it for the sake of killing it. If he gets too keen on killing something, then we'll just have to let him find some ducks, like always' (Litt, 2001, p. 280).

Andrew is explicitly drawn to the grotesque because of the sense of powerlessness he feels due to his father's abuse. He articulates how it feels to be on the receiving end of his father's abuse:

> 'It's like being on top of a tiger's cage containing a tiger and a tiger's rage to be outside the cage. I know my father is about to come upstairs. I know what he s going to do but I don't know *exactly* what he is going to do. Which is why it's so awful.' (Litt, 2001, p. 341)

In the novel Andrew commits acts of violence towards animals in order to vent his frustration with his situation; after killing a dog Andrew feels: 'so full of hatred, so grotesque with it, that I have to do something, say something' (Litt, 2001, p. 358). Andrew's sense of helplessness can be interpreted as a metaphor for the helplessness felt by the individual in the face of the 'system'. This innate wish to revel in the base, the excluded and the accompanying fascination with notions of the 'other', that Bataille asserts have characterized the twentieth century provide a space for the overturning and the mocking of the dominant ideology. The grotesque text can also provide a means for artistic forms that were once marginalized to become subsumed and curiously sanitized by a newfound status in the realms of high culture. Baudrillard argues:

> A surplus of violence does not suffice to open up reality. Because reality is a principle, and that principle is what is lost. Reality and fiction are inextricable. . . . Violence in itself can be banal and inoffensive, only symbolic violence generates singularity. (Baudrillard, 2002, p. 2)

The third point that Kayser highlights as being integral to the grotesque is that it is an attempt to control and exorcize the demonic elements in the world. In this sense the grotesque is a method of making us perceive the paradoxical, the form of the unformed, the face of the world without face.

Hanif Kureishi's *Gabriel's Gift* (2001) deals with the uneasy relationship between the classes. The reader is told repeatedly that Gabriel is concerned that he is losing his 'working class' credibility at school; his parents have hired an au pair and Gabriel feels that he wants to conceal his parents 'middle class' aspirations from the other pupils at his school because of the ridicule that will ensue from the largely working class population of his school. For Gabriel the working class that surrounds him and his parents form a malevolent presence, which consumes aspiration. The men in the pub represent the working classes; the unemployed or barely employed underclass of London are depicted as narrow-minded, and old-fashioned, and are described as being variously 'musty', and 'grey-faced':

> The place was full of childish men from the post office and the local bus garage, gazing up at the big TV screen. Dad's grey-faced mates were playing pool. They all looked the same to Gabriel, with their roll-ups, pints and musty clothes. They rarely went out into the light, unless they stood outside the pub on a sunny day, and they were as likely to eat anything

green, as they were to drink anything blue or wear anything pink. (Kureishi, 2001, p. 139)

These men are depicted as zombies in the scene when Gabriel and his father have to escape a fight from their local pub over money that Gabriel's dad supposedly owes Pat, one of the other drinkers. As they run away Gabriel's dad notes of his old friends who have been consigned to rotting in the local pub after years of unemployment separated by short term dead end jobs: 'Gabriel, don't they look like corpses ready for the grave? I won't be going in there again! The whole atmosphere is rancid, hopeless, violent! I can't believe I was ever like those men' (Kureishi, 2001, p. 143).

The men in the pub have a hold over Gabriel's father, but they are themselves trapped in a situation in which because 'everyone owes everyone else' (Kureishi, 2001, p. 143), there is no way out. No one can advance because any advantage is already owed to someone else, so when Gabriel's father begins to make money and to become upwardly mobile he must disassociate himself from his old friends, lest he be dragged back into the despair that typifies their and his former existence. The easiest means of achieving this separation is to paint the 'grey men' as grotesque rather than human.

The novel does not blame Gabriel and his father for wishing to escape the drudgery of life on the 'dole', but highlights the fact that Gabriel and his father fulfil the wishes of every one of the grey men in finding an escape. Gabriel and his father's actions and the guilt associated with escape are never easily simplified in the novel. Gabriel and his parents have to make very difficult choices, and with very little guidance. Jake, the movie producer asks: 'who do we have to turn to these days for spiritual guidance? Not the priests, politicians, or scientists. There are only artists left to believe in' (Kureishi, 2001, p. 161).

Jake highlights the lack of spiritual guidance available in mainstream, secular Britain, and suggests that artists are the only ones left who can fulfil this function. There is however a difference between the priests, the politicians, the scientists and the artists and that is that whilst the first three have consistently sought to deny the grotesque, artists of both the visual and the literary world have never conspired to do the same thing, or at least never as successfully. Instead there have always been dissenters, vocal and efficacious who have employed the grotesque as a means of depicting something essential about the human world. Immanuel Kant notes the spiritual element within the grotesque when he states his belief that the grotesque is enshrined in the classical rituals of religion, and in categorizing works of art into the sublime, the noble, the grotesque and the trifling, he highlights two essential elements of the grotesque, which combine to allow the form to challenge any dominant perspective so effectively.

First, Kant suggests that the grotesque is quite literally enshrined in the very traditions of religion; it is only the perspective that allows us to worship the bones of saints whilst recoiling from the bones of men, Kant notes:

> Monasteries and such tombs, to confine the living saints are grotesque. Subduing one's passions through principles is sublime. Castigation, vows, and other such monks' virtues are grotesque. Holy bones, holy wood, and all similar rubbish, the holy stool of the High Lama of Tibet not excluded, are grotesque. Of the works of wit and fine feeling, the epic poems of Vergil and Klopstock fall into the noble, of Homer and Milton into the adventurous. The Metamorphoses of Ovid are grotesque; the fairy tales of French foolishness are the most miserable grotesqueries ever hatched. Anacreontic poems are generally very close to the trifling. (Kant, 1960, pp. 56–7)

Second, in taking his examples of what constitutes the 'grotesque' from religious icons that are typically regarded as classic or 'pure' Kant highlights the potentially transient and culturally specific nature of categories such as 'grotesque', 'sublime' and 'classic'. In doing so he highlights that the defining line between what is grotesque and what is beautiful can, in the end, be little more than a matter of ideology.

Novels such as *Trainspotting, Great Apes* and *Dorian* go further than simply evoking the term or the image of the grotesque in a general sense to convey the horror or awfulness of any given situation. All three of these novels contain knowing and carefully crafted allusions to the nature of grotesque art itself, and locate the term aesthetically, positing themselves as being at least in some part a knowing exploration of the theme. Self actually describes the workings of the grotesque form through Simon's experiences:

> Everywhere Simon directed his gaze he saw something familiar, a shop sign, a petrol station decal, a peg board menu in a café window. To be confronted with such a mundane, familiar scene only served to enhance the distortions which had been wrought upon it. (Self, 1998a, p. 223)

Self explains how the grotesque works through a sequence which alternates between the familiar and the surreal until eventually perspective is lost entirely and the human mind can no longer react 'rationally' and a baser instinct begins to dominate:

> Even the greatest of shocks can be negotiated by the mind, which is, after all, a homeostatic device, constantly labouring towards equalisation – a steady state. So it was that Simon Dykes, the artist, in a suitable pose: recumbent, covered in his own shit, slowly came round, slowly admitted the fact of where he was and what had happened, just in time for it to happen again. (Self, 1998a, p. 102)

Self punctuates *Great Apes* with references to the critical notion of the grotesque, and constantly reminds the reader that the grotesque is a tried and tested satirical tool and that the novel is aware of its status and perhaps anticipates its own critical reception.

The most infamous example of a text that seems to anticipate its own reception is Irvine Welsh's *Trainspotting* (1993). After the massive and popular success of *Trainspotting*, many of the reviews for Welsh's subsequent novels heaped praise on the author; *Sunday Times* noted that 'Welsh writes with a skill, wit and compassion that amounts to genius' and the *Guardian* named Welsh 'the most gifted of the younger writers working in Britain today'. It seems almost ironic then that given the swiftness of the establishment to attempt to contain and absorb its author, one of the primary concerns of *Trainspotting* is: 'the capacity of modern societies to contain dissidence' (Sinfield, 1997, p. xii). Renton, the novel's protagonist notes how the marginal can be easily absorbed into the mainstream without sufficiently changing the ethos of that mainstream: 'Society invents a spurious convoluted logic tae absorb and change people whae's behaviour is outside its mainstream' (Welsh, 1993, p. 187).

Trainspotting confronts its 'mainstream' reader on several levels, not least through the 'countercultural' alignment of drug use with the freeing of the human spirit:

> Suppose aw knew the pros and cons, know that ah'm gaunnae huv a short life, am ay sound mind etcetera, etcetera, but still want tae use smack? They won't let ye dae it, because its seen as a sign ay thir ain failure. The fact that ye jist simply choose tae reject whit they huv tae offer. Choose us. Choose life. Choose mortgage payments; choose washing machines; choose cars. . . . well, ah choose no tae choose life. If the cunts cannae handle that, its thair fuckin problem. (Welsh, 1993, pp. 187–8)

The working class Scots dialect of some parts of the novel purposely impedes readers from any other background, and the continual use of the most taboo vocabulary, the word 'cunt' appears frequently, alongside the frequent depiction of emotional and physical violence that is described in such a way as to potentially offend both traditional and progressive sensibilities.

At points in the novel it seems the very intention is to find a form that will offend, alienate or otherwise shock each and every sensibility equally. The purpose behind creating this shock being that a response is called for in the act of shocking since, as Pierre Macherey notes the response is the most necessary part of the process of reading such a text, 'for there to be a critical discourse which is more than a superficial and futile *reprise* of the work, the speech stored in the book must be incomplete; because it has not said everything, there remains the possibility of saying something else, *after another fashion*' (Macherey, 1978, pp. 82–93). This intention to shock is not without literary precedent, from Jonathan Swift, to James Joyce, Alan Sillitoe and James Kelman, the 'mainstream' has often been 'shocked' and yet simultaneously impressed by a 'marginal' novel.

This facet is crucial to the contemporary novel as a form of social critique. While the claim that the masses are tied down by responsibility and consumerism is far from radical by the 1990s, Renton's claim that heroine addiction can be seen as an assault on the capitalist machine, an assertion of the free human spirit, certainly stretches even the liberal imagination; not least because Renton as a drug user is not free from the endless cycle of money and need himself.

It is not just Renton's now (in)famous speech about drugs being an alternative 'lifestyle choice' that marks *Trainspotting* out on the literary landscape. There are other, perhaps more overt innovations, the first is simply the extent to which the violence and marginalization of the disaffected urban underclass pervades the novel. Whereas characters such as Arthur Seaton in Sillitoe's *Saturday Night, Sunday Morning* (1958) can be seen to have what Sinfield typifies as a 'live and let live' policy (Sinfield, 1997, p. xiii), Welsh's Begbie is pathologically violent while Sickboy is so named because of his supposedly 'sick' temperament towards violence. Perhaps the most marked difference between *Trainspotting* and its literary predecessors is the extent to which Welsh's text seemingly critiques the progressive argument of culture, as Sinfield notes, 'what is even more uncompromising in *Trainspotting* is a resentful and dismissive attitude to high culture' (Sinfield, 1997, p. xiv).

Sinfield notes that Renton's use of a bluebottle to create what he calls art on a toilet wall is provocative mainly because of his claim to have produced art that is akin to that being produced on the first day of the Edinburgh Festival, the day that the bluebottle incident occurs. Renton smears the insect into the word 'HIBS' (to denote the football team) exclaiming that 'the vile bluebottle, which caused me a great deal of distress, has been transformed intae a work of art which gives me much pleasure tae look at' (Sinfield, 1997, p. xiv). In narrating his own story, Renton has control of the narrative, he doesn't wish to be seen in a tragic light and refuses to become solely a tragic literary example of what can happen to a disaffected marginalized youth, knowing itself to be deprived both socially and culturally.

Renton, in providing a bridge for the middle-class reader (having spent a year at university, and being both literate and socially aware) also fulfils a more radical departure from the usual tragic figure. Renton reflects a breakdown in the cultural authority of the arts, and the class hierarchy enshrined therein. There is a sense in which if it can happen to Renton, a socially aware, articulate and considerate young man with all the benefits of a place at university then it could happen to anyone.

Sinfield suggests that Welsh's novel is radical because it eschews the notion that it is only the uneducated that are drawn into self-destruction (Sinfield, 1997, p. xiv). Renton has been given access to a university education in the arts, but is still drawn in a different direction. *Trainspotting* suggests that the issue for the liberal reading classes to deal with is not so much that the high-minded liberal, venturing into the depths of the working class, may encounter an illiberal attitude or two, but rather that those illiberal attitudes could conceivably break into the realm of the cultured. Setting the novel against the backdrop of the Edinburgh festival; an icon of culture, emphasizes this point: 'the noise of the two arseholes has been replaced by the appreciative chattering ay groups ay middle-class cunts as they troop oot ay the opera' (Welsh, 1993, p. 306).

In many ways Welsh's novel can be read as an epochal moment in the history of how we classify literature, as Sinfield suggests:

> Let's recap: the initial idea of literature and literary criticism was to discriminate between fine writing which generates a significant view of life, and crude or manipulative writing which exploits prurient emotions. It wasn't always specified in the theory that the latter was likely to be 'popular', but quite often it turned out that way. . . .
>
> With *Trainspotting*, as for instance with the work of Robert Mapplethorpe, Dennis Cooper and Della Grace, it becomes far more difficult to

posit a distinctive realism, let alone a superior realm, in which art and literature are created and appreciated. (Sinfield, 1997, pp. xv–xvi)·

Through the implicit removal of Renton from bourgeois society and his subsequent immersion in the grotesque underclass of drug users the novel places the reader in a distanced position. In the process the novel dares to suggest parallels between the classes and remove the 'safety barrier' between the cultured and the vulgar. In this sense *Trainspotting* is almost archetypically grotesque in that it can be found straddling the dividing line between humour and horror or even tragedy. The novel typifies Highet's notion that

> [T]he purpose of invective and lampoon is to destroy an enemy. The purpose of comedy and farce is to cause painless undestructive laughter at human weaknesses and incongruities. The purpose of satire is, through laughter and invective, to cure folly and to punish evil; but if it does not achieve this purpose, it is content to jeer at folly and to expose evil to bitter contempt. (Highet, 1962, p. 156)

In *Working Class Fiction: From Chartism to Trainspotting* (1997) Ian Haywood notes that: 'The discovery of such cultural squalor beneath the beauty and antiquity of the capital city [of Scotland] revived the old class imagery of 'two nations'. It seemed that the response of youth to the prospect of a future on the 'broo' was self-abandonment and an immersion in a hedonistic, self-destructive underclass existence cut off from all conventional moral discourse' (Haywood, 1997, p. 158).

> Drug addiction has become the demonic and demonised reflection of a commodified, fetishized and irresponsible capitalist system. Addiction ritualises the alienation of the body by inducing a relentless cycle of narcissistic pleasure and loss of self-control. (Haywood, 1997, p. 158)

The image of Rentboy rooting around in his own faeces for the opium suppositories provides a comic reworking of the Freudian notion of excrement as infantile 'gold'. Rentboy's friend, Kelly (a waitress) similarly resorts to contaminating the café's food with every bodily emission imaginable in order to rebel against her customers' superciliousness. The episodes with Kelly's waitressing allow Welsh to rework and thereby evoke Orwell's *Down and Out in Paris and London* (1933) in which an anarchist *plongeur* spits into the soup before it is served.

The characters are involved upon a search for themselves; above all else they hate dishonesty. Whether they see it in the capitalist system itself or the betrayal of all of the previous 'big ideas' these characters feel intrinsically betrayed and all instigate an ontological search for truth. The grotesque therefore is just another part of the whole self that the system has forbidden and the grotesque must be recovered for the self to be reclaimed. It should be noted here that there is an undeniably Gothic element to such a reading of the grotesque, incorporating such an appeal to the possibility of producing decay as a force that will strip the contemporary world of artifice.

An element of the Gothic is incorporated in the concept of the grotesque prevalent in the twentieth century. Since the eighteenth century the ghost of the Gothic has been a constant reminder that ruin and invasion by darker forces pose an ever-present threat to civilization. Sir William Temple and Jonathan Swift often appealed to the cyclical nature of human history, suggesting that every Roman Empire will eventually be overturned.

Continuing this tradition *Trainspotting* includes the haunting of Renton by the dead baby, Dawn. The motif of the death of the child forms the perfect metaphor for what Clarke identifies as a growing trend for the grotesque and the Gothic within literature and art. Clarke notes that:

> With the twentieth century the ideal of inevitable progress came terribly crashing to the ground, shattered by monumental world wars, revolutions, indeterminacy, atomic energy, the Freudian id, and the Holocaust. In the present century, then, the gothic and the grotesque mate and become the dominant imagery of our era. (Clarke, 1991, p. 18)

Perhaps the most obvious example of the contemporary Gothic is Jim Crace's novel *Being Dead.* The novel describes the last days and the death and decomposition of a middle-aged couple (Joseph and Celice), whose bodies lie undiscovered for several days following their murder on the south coast of England. The narrative of their final days is interspersed with graphic descriptions of the stages of decomposition. Their final days are also depicted in reverse chronological order so that for the reader, the depiction of Joseph and Celice's lives is haunted with the knowledge that they are already dead. Similarly through the course of the novel the corpses can be seen to become human again as the reader is given access to the characters behind the corpses. In producing a novel that plays with the power of the Gothic both to humanize the dead and reveal the ever-present process of decay, Crace produces a novel that plays an aesthetic game with the gothic elements of the grotesque, never allowing any one image to dominate in the novel. This produces an effect that is closer to Bakhtin's notion of the regenerative force of the carnival-grotesque as the couple are variously figuratively reincarnated and returned to their death within the same sentence:

> It would be comforting, of course, to believe that humans are more durable than other animals, to think that by some miracle (of natural science obviously) his hand and her lower leg remained unspoilt, enfolding and enclosed, that his one fingertip was still amongst her baby hairs, that her ankle skin was firm and pastel-grained, and that her toenails were still berry red and manicured. But death does not discriminate. All flesh is flesh. And Joseph and Celice were sullied everywhere. (Crace, *Being Dead*, 1999, p. 109)

Richard J. Lane notes that in Crace's *Being Dead*: 'life may be reduced to a puddle, the bodies becoming what in some medical and other spheres are called "leakers" but the reduction does *not* represent some kind of literary nihilism' (Lane, 2003, p. 27). Lane's assertion that the novel does not represent a nihilistic standpoint is furthered by the backwards momentum of the narrative; the murder victims end the novel in bed safe and sound at the start of their last day on earth. The text seems to affirm vitality and vigour in the non-religious implication that life goes on even in the presence of death. Left to the natural processes of decomposition the bodies of the murdered couple will of course sustain much life in the form of bacteria and microscopic organisms. *Being Dead* therefore offers an aesthetic use of the grotesque image of decomposition that allies the grotesque with the comforting knowledge that, without a spiritual or religious life after death, Celice and Joseph exist in the memory of their daughter. This memory is essentially rediscovered as Syl investigates her parents' disappearance from their house, her childhood home, allowing her to revisit her relationship with her parents.

The aesthetics of the grotesque are examined in Jenny Disky's *Rainforest* (1989), particularly in the discussion that takes place between central characters Mo and Joe, the two characters who take different sides in a debate concerning the nature of what it is to be part of a human culture which likes to portray itself as being the dominant force acting upon the world. Joe's essay questions man's libertarian desires to 'save the planet', arguing that the desire to 'save the planet' forms another of man's delusions that he can control nature at all. Joe argues that '[. . .] If we touch nature at all, it is through personal catastrophe. Only the death of ourselves or those we feel to be part of ourselves connects us with the planet. The cycle of birth and death and accident is all we have left of nature, and is beyond language and reason . . .' (Diski, 1987, p. 56). Joe represents a post-modern attitude that prioritizes the idea that there are different perspectives rather than instigating a search for a universal truth. In conversation with Mo he explains his ideas thus:

> All I was saying was that human beings need systems, so naturally they find it wherever they happen to look. If drosophila were running the planet they'd come up with an entirely different notion of how the world is organized. No one's right or wrong. It's just a matter of perspective and necessity. (Diski, 1987, p. 61)

Mo is the epitome of a human who needs order. Her research takes the form of categorizing plant and insect species and is opposed to Joe's notion that this does little for the planet itself; she believes that her research will bring enlightenment and in turn conservation.

In *Rainforest* the grotesque becomes a force that although denied continually reinforces itself to challenge perspective after the fashion of Kayser's first principle. It is also similar to Self's depiction in *Great Apes* of the unique propensity of human perspective to be knocked out of kilter:

> The forest embodied in Mo noted the loss of heat and light in the north and added a notion of seasonality to the bank of information it had about its environment. It noted also something more familiar, that it identified as similar to those times when its warm-blooded components lost new life: when a creature whose body had been preparing to give birth produced instead something stillborn, lifeless. When that happened there was incomprehension, confusion. What was to happen had been unknown, yet what did happen was understood as wrong. (Diski, 1987, p. 85)

The grotesque in both *Rainforest* and *Great Apes* serves as a reminder of imperfection:

> For the first few minutes after he emerged from the relative safety of his confinement, Simon was bewildered. Bowen's mask certainly concealed her ghastly simian features, but the trousers she donned to cover her brutish furry legs were made from some diaphanous material, and fur could still be seen through them. This, together with her down-at-heel white coat, made her a clownish figure. (Self, 1998a, p. 189)

Each novel also suggests that more harmful than imperfection is the propensity of any system to deny that imperfection exists. *Rainforest* suggests that unless we undermine dogma with imperfection we are left with Fascism. Mo's mother, Marjorie worries that 'Mo's inability to live with imperfection seemed [. . .] much more dangerous than imperfection itself' (Diski, 1987, p. 101).

Critic Susan Bordo expresses a critical perspective on the fear of a perfection that denies a pluralistic ideal:

> Gradually and surely, a technology that was first aimed at the replacement of malfunctioning parts has generated an industry and an ideology fuelled by fantasies of rearranging, transforming, and correcting, an ideology of limitless improvement and change, defying the historicity, the mortality, and indeed the very materiality of the body. (Bordo, 1993, p. 245)

Like the novelists and texts examined in Chapters 2 and 4 those contemporary novels that deal with the grotesque share a desire to promote a decidedly pluralistic ethical model, suggesting in themselves the pluralistic notion that, 'As no one writer is adequate to all the needs of literature or life, it may be equally appropriate to recommend the satirists as a compliment and correction to the literature of philanthropy' (Bredvold, 1949, p. 16). Many of these novels tread an ideological tightrope, acknowledging that the concept of the ethical in the contemporary era is both complex and problematic, and thus present us with a notion of ethical thought definable only in terms of the personal. A. L. Kennedy elucidates this standpoint when she notes the inherent difficulties of introducing the moral to the modern novel: 'I don't believe I have the right to lecture you . . . with my pet theory on any kind of –ism or –ness. If I tried to, you wouldn't listen to me' (Kennedy, 1995, p. 101).

Despite Kennedy's assertion that there is no audience willing to listen to an author's 'pet theory' Marguerite Alexander identifies a current trend for introducing a polemical agenda and a conscious subversiveness in a more subtle way, operating through the vehicle of post-structuralist theory:

> Post-structuralist theory has had its effect on all the human sciences, questioning priorities which were thought to be unchallengable – the priority of sanity over madness, of culture over nature, of work over play – and to suggest that they might be inverted. It helped to fuel the revolutionary student movements of the late 1960s in France and America; encouraged a revival of Marxist dialectic in the universities; and helped provide

a theoretical basis for the feminist and homosexual rights movements. These developments have all presented a challenge to mainstream culture and have in common with some postmodernist writing a conscious subversiveness. (Alexander, 1990, p. 16)

Similarly Bergson identifies comedy as beginning when the individual solipstically defies society and opts for consciously subversive style. Bergson adds that comedy's task is then corrective (and indeed there is a long and varied tradition of evoking laughter and comedy within the novel to produce a subversive force), but the techniques and the final ends of such comedy have not remained static throughout the history of the novel. As stated in the Introduction, Malcolm Bradbury argues that the prime theme of the kind of novel of manners that forms the benchmark of what has become known as the more 'traditional' form of the nineteenth-century novel is: 'the ethical conduct of man in a society relatively stable and secure' (Bradbury, *Possibilities: Essays on the State of the Novel,* 1973, p. 32). The general ethos of such a text would largely substantiate the notion that the social and moral worlds are both rationally definable and contiguous, notions that during the twentieth century (with its emphasis on the post-modern) came to be ever more questioned. Bradbury goes on to argue however that, despite the presence of such an enlightenment style leaning towards the notion of the rational, this style of novel can be seen to contain a kind of comedic form alongside the more obvious empirical realism, since

[I]t explores dissonances between ethical absolutes or social virtues and the particular individual experience of these, and since it ends with a restoration, that replacement of the social norms, the giving back of sons to fathers and lovers to lovers. (Bradbury, *Possibilities: Essays on the State of the Novel,* 1973, p. 32)

Bradbury describes a text that fulfils an Aristotelian ideal of comedy. Thus within a more traditional form, although a text may contain moments which delve into the comedic, the world of the novel is still, in essence, easily rationalized and finally construed within traditional notions of a 'rationally definable' world.

Thus in an age that was distinctly moving away from religious or moral taboos a new kind of censoring could be said to be taking place, as increasingly the public scene becomes mediated rather than immediate, thus what is 'real' and what is not can sometimes become problematic when the rules of this new system are applied. Angela Carter similarly evokes a world beyond the grasp of the rational conscious mind in *Nights at the Circus*. That Carter uses the fantastic grotesque elements of the character of Fevvers' wings,[12] as a feminist statement concerning the impossibility of fulfilling masculine sexual desire is well documented, but Carter also uses Fevvers on another level, as a 'grotesque'. Fevvers exemplifies the position of the grotesque in the contemporary British novel, in that there is always the possibility that her wings are a cleverly devised 'trick'. Carter constantly alternates between suggesting that Fevver's wings are an elaborate trick that is not 'real', only to then assure us that Fevvers was genuinely born with wings attached to her back. Carter is careful to present a feeling or a sense of something, which can be said to be real but which lies outside of the process of rationalization. Saleem Sinai in Salman Rushdie's *Midnight's Children* espouses a similar position when he insists that:

> Reality is a question of perspective; the further you get from the past, the more concrete and plausible it seems – but as you approach the present, it inevitably seems more and more incredible. Suppose yourself in a large cinema, sitting at first in the back row, and gradually moving up, row by row, until your nose is almost pressed against the screen. Gradually the stars' faces dissolve into dancing grain; tiny details assume grotesque proportions; the illusion dissolves – or rather, it becomes clear that the illusion itself *is* reality. (Rushdie, 1995, pp. 165–6)

The relationship between illusion and reality forms the central conceit of many of the novels under scrutiny in this chapter. Rushdie puts the word grotesque into the mouth of Sinai when describing the process of destabilizing the particular dominant view of the world that has come to represent 'reality', but which is itself constructed of many and various conceits (such that looking too closely causes the illusion to become apparent). The relation between the text that prioritizes the marginal and the carnivalesque is however a complex one, and many texts can be seen to appropriate the carnival only to then finally insist upon a return to normality but not in order to carry on as things were before, but rather to change that 'normal world'. Bakhtin notes that

> [L]aughter and its forms represent, . . . the least scrutinized sphere of the people's creation. The narrow concept of popular character and of folklore was born in the pre-Romantic period and was basically completed by

von Herder and the Romantics. There was no room in this concept for the peculiar culture of the marketplace and of folk laughter with all its wealth of manifestations. (Bakhtin, 1984, p. 24)

In a manner perhaps akin to Bakhtin's urge to look to the folk laughter of the marketplace, to find the purest expression of 'the people's culture', Georges Bataille similarly urges readers to look beyond the system of their existence, into the realm of sensibility, in which Bataille maintains there are 'essential psychological and sociological characteristics which respond not to self-interest but to a principle of pure expenditure and loss' (Richardson, 1994, p. 69). Bataille claims that 'there is a will to give which has priority over the contrasting drive, the will to withhold or retain' (Gibson, 1999, p. 166). Bataille perceives the existence of an 'archaic sensibility' that often resurfaces in protest literature, such as 'the romantic process against the bourgeois world' (Bataille, 1991, p. 29) and was expressed by Bataille thus:

The sun gives without ever receiving. Men were conscious of this long before astrophysics measured that ceaseless prodigality; they saw it ripen the harvests and they associated its splendour with the act of someone who gives without receiving. (Bataille, 1991, p. 29)

This notion that something both subversive and selfless exists at a primal level within 'the people' runs throughout Bataille's work. The same belief can be evidenced again in his assertion that the twentieth century was an era that broke radically from the search for absolute knowledge. Bataille believes that the twentieth century revelled in a baser, material existence, which embodies notions of, 'otherness', obscene laughter and a will to anarchy, and embraces difference rather than running from it as might be expected (Bataille, 1991, p. 29). This was accompanied by a decline in emphasis on the development and evocation of the classical within art and literature, and a rise instead in the eroticized or the grotesque subject. Such evocations of any society's taboos allow in turn for the deconstruction of that society's ideals, since we are made aware of what an ideology lacks through what it excludes as much as we are through what it permits.

The novels under analysis in this chapter represent a new breed of writers who evoke the carnival-grotesque, in order to disrupt the status quo of the novel form itself, hoping it seems to tap into what Bakhtin identified as potential, rather than believing that the novel alone can fulfil the embodiment of a call for change at the societal level. These writers are fully aware that if the power relationship between the margins and the centre is to be truly turned on its head then it will take more than a carnival and it will take more than a carnival-grotesque text to truly disrupt the enshrined power relations expressed in the categorising of literary forms. Yet this knowing evocation of the carnival-grotesque without producing in the end a carnivalesque text incorporates a wider perspective that is closer to Barbara Babcock's definition of the process of symbolic inversion. Babcock notes:

> Far from being a residual category of experience, . . . what is socially peripheral is often symbolically central, and if we ignore or minimize inversion and other forms of cultural negation, we often fail to understand the dynamics of symbolic processes generally. (Babcock, 1978, p. 32)

This literature is not simply about the carnival-grotesque; rather, it is about the symbolic processes of the power relationship between the margin and the centre, something much older and deeper perhaps than even the carnival.

It was against this social backdrop that Fredric Jameson famously declared that post-modern art amounts to little more than 'the cannibalization of all the styles of the past, the play of random stylistic allusion, and in general what Henri Lefebvre has called the increasing primacy of the "neo"' (Jameson, 1991, p. 18). Jameson goes further suggesting that this art of the pastiche has become little more than a type of parody, which he also defines as having undergone a process of negative change.

> Like parody, the imitation of a peculiar or unique, idiosyncratic style, the wearing of a linguistic mask, speech in a dead language. But it is a neutral practice of such mimicry, without any of parody's ulterior motives, amputated of the satiric impulse, devoid of laughter. (Jameson, 1991, p. 17)

Jameson then identifies a crisis in representation since he argues that rather than achieving any critical or political interaction, the art of pastiche and parody in the post-modern context merely form an imitation of an imitation and therefore can have no application outside of its own stylistic concerns.

But if the twentieth century brought with it a new kind of interaction with the notion of parody, pastiche and the grotesque, with increased media coverage of the atrocities of the age, then the twentieth century also ushered in an age in which its authors explicitly sought an association with the type of parodic and grotesque literature that pervaded the pre-Victorian

British scene, perceiving these twin elements to be the very substance of the twentieth century itself. Then as Gilbert Highet suggests:

> Just as the satirist can preach an unconventional and grotesque sermon, just as he can take a traditional literary form, turn it upside down, and grin through it, so he can tell a story which carries his message. The narrative must be interesting and it must be well told. But for the satirist the narrative is not the end: it is the means. (Highet, 1962, p. 148)

In order to remain effective the satirical grotesque must continually adapt and become ever more sophisticated. Linda Hutcheon also offers a different interpretation to Jameson's (Hutcheon, 1989, p. 25). Dismissing Jameson's critique of the demise of a modernist parody with the replacement of a post-modern apolitical pastiche, Hutcheon instead argues that a post-modern version of parody does exist and it is 'a value-problematizing, de-naturalizing form of acknowledging the history (and through irony, the politics) of representations' (Hutcheon, 1989, p. 90). Hutcheon insists, again unlike Jameson, that such an ironic post-modern stance on representation, genre and ideology serves to politicize representation.

> Parody 'de-doxifies'; it unsettles all doxa, all accepted beliefs and ideologies. Rather than see this ironic stance as some infinite regress into textuality. (Hutcheon, 1989, p. 90)

Hutcheon values the resistance in such post-modern works to totalizing solutions to society's contradictions; she applauds post-modernism's willingness to question all ideological positions, all claims to ultimate truth. Hutcheon contends that post-modernity's parody 'is doubly coded in political terms: it both legitimizes and subverts that which it parodies' (Hutcheon, 1989, p. 101), which prevents 'assumptions about its transparency and common-sense naturalness' (Hutcheon, 1989, p. 30). This said, Hutcheon issues a warning: this position does not mean that critique is not effective: post-modern parody 'may indeed be complicitous with the values it inscribes as well as subverts, but the subversion is still there' (Hutcheon, 1989, p. 106).

Indeed through broadening Bakhtin's concept of the societal importance of the renaissance carnival and the carnivalesque in the written word, critics such as Barbara Babcock, Peter Stallybrass and Allon White have identified that the aesthetic trends of artistic humanism can be seen themselves to form a reaction against that same universal self-image which the carnival was said to disrupt with its insistent focus on the 'other', the grotesque, or the human as opposed to the classical. Not least, this can be found in the notion that today, humour is largely born out of an attempt to bring 'back down to earth' any convoluting or euphemistic ideological standpoint that may have gained symbolic significance and come to represent the normalizing cultural code. As Babcock comments:

'Symbolic inversion' may be broadly defined as any act of expressive behaviour which inverts, contradicts, abrogates or in some fashion presents an alternative to commonly held cultural codes, values and norms be they linguistic, literary or artistic, religious, social and political. (Babcock, 1978, p. 14)

Babcock extends the carnival-grotesque to the general act of symbolic inversion and extending the disruptive patterns of the carnival into other spheres of subversion. Satire and the comedy of parody have also come to fulfil this role and to occupy a central place in the public sphere. Thus if Bakhtin is correct when he notes that 'in the world of the carnival the awareness of the people's immortality is combined with the realization that established authority and truth are relative' (Bakhtin, 1984, p. 10), then the carnival must achieve its greatest political potency when that realization 'that established authority and truth are relative' finally exceeds the world of the carnival and enters the realm of the everyday, deconstructing through this act any claims of the dominant ideology towards universality, exposing 'the way that an always recalcitrant reality constrains interpretation' (Gąsiorek, 1995, pp. 191–2). This has particular relevance for the contemporary British novel, as Andrzej Gąsiorek states, 'history and politics lie close to the fore in post-war writers' accounts of reality because they are central to any society's understanding of itself and thus become hotly contested terrains (Gąsiorek, 1995, pp. 191–2).

The truly carnivalesque novel is thought of as having been inspired by a laughing truth (Bakhtin, 1984). Thus in essence such a novel should open out meaning, incorporating, rather than excluding otherwise marginalized voices or perspectives. The high must contain elements that pertain to the classics, whilst the low must reject, subvert or in some way avoid, a solely classical representation of its subject matter, and that subject matter itself will be a determining factor in deciding what status will be given to any particular piece of art. This sets in motion a perpetual and dialogic battle in which the classical and the human, the high and the low and the centre and the periphery must continually mutate in form, but never finally be resolved or concluded.

Indeed when Bakhtin asserts that every serious word in antiquity has its parodic double this does not detract from the potential for serious meaning, rather it adds to the creative process and provides a greater, richer understanding of the world. The parodic double does not simply reduce meaning to the level of cynical pastiche, rather it is "the corrective of reality" (Bakhtin M. M., 'The Prehistory of Novelistic Discourse', 1982, p. 58). Bakhtin insists that the heroic is upheld rather than made impossible within truly parodic literature, and that the triumph of such literature is its ability to complement and make more complex, but not discredit the great ideals, such as heroism and truth. Bradbury similarly notes that 'troubling and grotesque themes: death, perversion, violence, madness, extreme fantasies of adolescent desire' are presented in the same tone as the realism that often sits alongside it in these novels (Bradbury, 2001, p. 390). Thus as Gary Saul and Caryl Emerson note:

> [. . .] parody undermines not authority in principle but only authority with pretensions to be timeless and absolute. Parodic forms enable us to distance ourselves from words, to be *outside* any given utterance and to assume our own unique attitude towards it. (Saul and Emerson, 1990, p. 435)

Conclusion

As Chapter 1 argues, the novel of marginality came to prominence in an era when two linked but at least partly differently motivated groups took to depicting the marginal subject in order to raise awareness about a particular issue, or to give voice to people(s) who traditionally lack representation in the novel form. The first group includes those novelists who maintain that the novel of marginality can fulfil the social function of highlighting through fiction the plight of marginalized peoples; the second group comprises those authors who utilize the marginal as a means of bringing aesthetic newness to the novel. The influence of both groups of authors has resulted in a rise in the number of novels that depict the experiences of minority cultures and taboo subjects. Many of the texts included for discussion in this book explicitly seek to fulfil Brannigan's optimistic wish that literature may be capable of becoming 'available as a voice for the silenced, and as an imaginative space for dissidence, critique and reinvention' (Brannigan, 2003, p. 204).

This type of socially conscious fiction has had to develop both thematically and formally and realign itself almost constantly in order to avoid falling into the 'trap' that Barbara Babcock identifies with literature that simply seeks to extol the virtue of the marginal. Babcock suggests that a literature that does this carries with it an essential problem with regards to truly representing the margins 'in their own terms' since there is an inherent danger in calling for representation, when the means of that representation lies in the hands of others (Babcock, 1978, p. 32).

With specific reference to the British class situation Dan Billany neatly summarizes the problem, suggesting that the marginalized (specifically the working class) risks becoming a literary convention that is almost entirely distanced from the real world:

> Literature had made the working class a convention – literature, which needs leisure, and therefore has been written for the leisured classes, [. . .] One hardly knows how to write simply and straightforwardly, now, about the normal circumstances of ninety per cent of humanity. God, what a decadence. (Billany, 1950, p. 123)

In order to avoid simply becoming a literary convention the novel of marginality has had to constantly maintain its ability to fulfil Caryl Phillip's suggestion that the novel of marginality can create 'communicable' empathy in order to bring the marginal to the centre (Phillips, 1994, p. 77).

The second reason that authors have appropriated the marginal subject within the novel is in an attempt to preserve and maintain a strong literary tradition in the face of continued pessimism regarding the chances of the form's survival. Salman Rushdie, Angela Carter, Ian McEwan and Martin Amis ushered in an age in which the marginal subject was presented alongside the mainstream as a means of making political points but also as an attempt to invigorate the form, allowing for a synthesis of experimental and traditional themes and techniques. Bradbury notes that 'troubling and grotesque themes: death, perversion, violence, madness, extreme fantasies of adolescent desire' (Bradbury, 2001, p. 390) are presented in the same tone as the realism that often sits alongside it in these novels (Bradbury, 2001, p. 390).

Many contemporary novels that concern the relationship between the marginal individual and community and the mainstream do so in a manner that follows the model that Steven Connor identifies:

> [. . .] a sceptical dissatisfaction with the inherited forms in which the condition of England had been represented in novels, combined with a continuing faith in the capacities of narrative to effect kinds of collective symbolic transformation and solidary connections. (Connor, 1996, p. 89)

The resulting furore that these types of texts create mean that before even beginning to read, the reader is made all too aware of whether their chosen title fits into 'mainstream' or 'marginal' culture. Furthermore, the reader is made aware of the status of the book by the way in which texts are arranged and grouped in the bookshop. Headings such as 'popular fiction', 'black' and 'lesbian fiction' and 'new classics' highlight how quick we are to make the distinction between 'high "classical" literature' and novels that concern themselves with 'marginal' interests.

The very observation that this high/low divide is fundamental to Western thought also contains the implicit acceptance that the two ends of the hierarchy; the high and the low, the centre and the marginalized must, at least to some extent, appear together, and are mutually dependent upon one another for their own definition to have any meaning. This interdependent relationship sets in motion a perpetual and dialogic battle in which the high and the low; the centre and the periphery must continually mutate in form, but the battle may never finally be resolved or concluded.

Thus when a novel becomes to all intents and purposes 'unclassifiable', even if this is only for a brief moment, this is when it has the most potential to bring the excluded and the marginalized into the official realm. And further when this occurs in a single text then the concept of public discourse may be altered, and this is most possible in texts which contain elements which both appeal to the vernacular, the ironic, the comedic or the fantastic as well as those elements that can be adequately described as fitting into a more mainstream form of literary realism. As Bakhtin argues it is only through literature that the carnival's power to communicate and foster such rebellion and revolution has the potential to be fulfilled; since the physical act of carnival only contains

[T]he shoots of a new world outlook . . . [but these] could not grow and flower as long as they were enclosed in the popular gaiety of recreation and banqueting, or in the fluid realm of familiar speech. In order to achieve this growth and flowering, laughter has to enter the world of great literature. (Bakhtin, 1984, p. 96)

These novels themselves then form a kind of canon that digresses from those unsatisfactory inherited forms to make the marginal its subject matter. This new 'canon' also raises a problem however in that, if as Levinas states we see ourselves most clearly in the face of the Other, then the question has to be asked who gains the most from the appropriation of marginalized characters into mainstream literature? If the exchange is not equal, or even not at all two-way, it may only succeed in producing a literature that is still most widely read and analysed by those residing not at the margins but at the centre, in terms of class, sexuality, gender and race.

In each case the novel of marginality can be said to fulfil a transitional function. For those seeking a voice, once the novel of marginality has fulfilled its function and highlighted the cause of marginalized groups the hope will always be to gain a place that is more central. Hanif Kureishi's novel *Intimacy* (1998) signals that Kureishi feels that it is now possible to move away from discussing race altogether; he makes it impossible for the reader to identify the race of the narrator. Thus *Intimacy* cannot be read as a comment upon race relations in Britain in the same way that *The Buddha of Suburbia* (1990) and *The Black Album* (1995) can be interpreted. *Intimacy* and Kureishi's next novel *Gabriel's Gift* (2001) are concerned with the internal lives of the characters and seem less polemical (and somehow more traditional) than Kureishi's earlier work.

For those who hope that the novel of marginality can perform an aesthetic function by renewing the form and providing fresh and previously untapped narratives that will re-invigorate the novel there is an obvious 'built in' obsolescence point when using any subject solely because it is 'new'. Authors such as Salman Rushdie, Bernadine Evaristo, Pat Barker, Zadie Smith and Will Self are in fact increasingly combining their innovative styles with an interaction with older narratives and acknowledge within their work the influence of other, more established (canonical) writers and texts, whilst attempting to maintain a 'newer' perspective. These authors allude to other artists at various points in their texts (or when being interviewed) in a manner that indicates an emergent interest in the aesthetic and a willingness to engage with the literary canon, rather than a desire to remain completely exterior to it.

Rushdie's fiction is laden with references to religious texts and to ancient myths and legends. As Chapter 1 argues, Evaristo (in an interview with Alistair Niven) acknowledges the influence of historian Peter Fryer on *The Emperor's Babe: A Verse Novel of Londinium, 211 A.D* (2001) (Evaristo, 2004, p. 280). Barker references Robert Graves, Wilfred Owen and Siegfried Sassoon (amongst other literary figures) in *The Regeneration Trilogy* (1991–95), and in various interviews, Will Self has noted the influence of J. G. Ballard, Jonathan Swift, Franz Kafka, Joseph Heller and Louis-Ferdinand Céline on his own style.

With *Dorian: An Imitation* (2002) Self returns to a text that is now widely regarded as a 'classic' (Oscar Wilde's *A Picture of Dorian Grey* (1890)). Self uses the narrative of this older, more 'canonical' text as a means to discuss the politics of AIDS healthcare and to critique the *zeitgeist* of 1980s Britain. The fact that Self chooses to call the novel 'an imitation' indicates the novel's interest in the aesthetics of the original as well as the 'message'. 'Wildeisms' litter the text, 'Self control is always easier to practice in the country, after all – there's nowhere for the self to escape to.' (Self, 2002, p. 102). The world of *Dorian* is the arty, Bohemian community of London, and Dorian has allowed 'Baz' (an 'up-and-coming' artist friend) to create a video installation, consisting of nine screens showing his naked body, filmed from various angles, as in Wilde's painting it is the instillation (and not the man himself) who will become ravaged by the activities of its subject. Like Wilde's Dorian the protagonist of Self's novel begins as an innocent and is corrupted by the extravagant lifestyle of a group of wealthy heroin addicted, sexually liberated hedonists, most of whom contract AIDS, only Dorian remains, seemingly unaffected.

It is interesting to examine Zadie Smith's treatment of E. M. Forster's *Howards End* (1910) in her novel, *On Beauty* (2005) here. Smith's book also represents a sincere engagement with the traditional 'literary canon' and as such forms a point of divergence for Smith from the conventions of the 'novel of marginality', and perhaps marks something of an end point for the distinctly 'marginal' text. *On Beauty* is strikingly different to *White Teeth* (2000), Smith's earlier groundbreaking debut novel of marginality, in which as argued in Chapter 2 each of the characters' marginalized status is affirmed, re-affirmed and complicated several times within the narrative. Whereas in *White Teeth* Smith employs a light comic tone that ultimately works to bring together the heterogeneous cast of characters, with *On Beauty* the intent is to depict the inner lives of the central protagonists. Instead of reaching outwards to the margins *On Beauty* takes its inspiration from within the literary canon and the model, alluded to throughout, is E. M. Forster.

Smith's homage to *Howards End* announces itself in the opening line of the novel: 'One may as well begin with Jerome's emails to his father.' It would be reductive to call *On Beauty* an updating of Forster's novel – Smith alters some of the configurations of the relationships between the characters and new themes are introduced – but the central concerns of *Howards End*, remain intact in Smith's treatment of the novel; the conflict between two families of opposing political and moral sensibilities, issues of class, behaviour, ambition and opportunity in a society with prescribed rules and roles.

To simulate the stratified society of Forster's turn-of-the-century England, Smith sets the novel in the knowingly archaic and insular landscape of an east coast American university outside Boston, which prides itself on having liberal principles but remains almost wholly estranged from a world in which prejudice, poverty, crime, terror and fear are the forces that move those outside academia. Smith has added an extra dimension to Forster's scrutiny of class by evoking Caryl Phillips' notion of the 'communicable' element between marginalized groups and infuses the issues of class that Forster raises with a discussion of race and nationality. Like Forster, Smith is concerned with creating and conveying beautiful descriptions and gently ironic authorial interjections that frame the novel. Forster resonates in Smith's style as much as Wilde does in Self's. From the stately scene-setting passages (particularly where rooms or houses are being evoked) to the most incidental moments, for example where the lovelorn elder Belsey boy joins his mother and her middle-aged friends at an outdoor festival: 'Jerome, in all his gloomy Jeromeity, had joined them. The ill-pitched greetings that compassionate age sings to mysterious youth rang out; hair was almost tousled then wisely not' (Smith, 2005, p. 21).

More specifically, the plot of Forster's *Howards End*, although slightly manipulated by Smith to allow for a more contemporary setting, underpins much of the storyline of *On Beauty*. The unruly Belseys, like Forster's Schlegels, become embroiled with another family whose conventional household seems the opposite of their own. The Kippses, provide this opposite family, presided over by Sir Monty Kipps, a West Indian intellectual who delights in provoking liberals with his ultra-conservative views on homosexuality, the role of women and affirmative action amongst other issues. Sir Monty has written a popular appreciation of Rembrandt which Howard Belsey, himself an art historian, though of a more highbrow bent, has denounced for its retrogressive stance. Unfortunately his attack was marred by a factual error, which Sir Monty has exploited to maximum humiliating effect, and vague dislike on Howard's part has turned to boiling resentment, exacerbated by the fact that he has been unable to complete his own book, *Against Rembrandt.* To this self-inflicted injury the opening chapters add two choice insults: first Howard's elder son falls in love with Sir Monty's daughter Vee, and then Sir Monty is offered a visiting celebrity appointment at Wellington, the very college at which Howard himself teaches.

The notion of marginality is still present in *On Beauty* and *Dorian: An Imitation* but it is not the central concern of the characters; a student of Howard's is so unfamiliar with the notion that she has to look up the word 'liminal' in the dictionary, despite this allusion to the importance of the marginal or liminal space however there is a much greater emphasis in this text on the pleasure of the vividness with which such scenes have been imagined. *On Beauty* prioritizes the importance of observed details of clothing, weather, cityscapes and the bustling human background of drivers, shoppers and passers-by which are constantly being folded into the central flow of thought, feeling and action, giving even the most mundane moments – Levi riding a bus into Boston, Howard setting up a projector – a dense, pulsing life.

With the self-righteous Kippses thus plumped down on the doorstep of the self-sabotaging Belseys, the situation has the makings of a small-scale campus comedy with scope for all the familiar farcical posturing so dear to the heart of academe. But while Smith does indeed deliver a superbly wicked example of that genre, this is only a small part of her achievement. Forsterian themes are present in Smith's novel. The Belseys' marriage is in crisis following Kiki Belsey's discovery that Howard has been unfaithful; the novel discusses social tension and links this with the tensions between different types of artistic expression (the novel discusses the painter Rembrandt alongside the late American rapper Tupac). These issues are meditated on with an unguarded seriousness that differs from Smith's earlier style, and to some extent the book could be seen as a rather heroic attempt to dignify contemporary life with a mirror held up in the Bloomsbury manner.

The framework of *On Beauty* consciously echoes Forster's seminal *Howards End*, translating Edwardian England to New England and the warring families of the Schlegels and the Wilcoxes into the Belseys and the Kippses. However, unlike Jean Rhys' *The Wide Sargasso Sea* or Fowles' *The French Lieutenant's Woman*, Smith's 'pseudo-postcolonial' updating is intended as homage. Smith's text is offered in flattery's sincerest form – a structural gesture that has as much to say about the conventional themes of beauty and art as it does about the marginal (or otherwise) status of any of the characters. The book represents an engagement with the traditional 'literary canon' that the novel of marginality has previously been excluded from (either for aesthetic or cultural reasons).

Smith, like Self, draws the reader's attention to her homage to Forster in her acknowledgements, and although Forster himself could be regarded as a marginal author because of his sexuality, Smith focuses on highlighting the importance of his seminal text *Howards End* (1910) and not on the man himself. Smith also refers to a philosophical text, Elaine Scarry's *On Beauty and Being Just* (2000) as the inspiration behind the novel's title and its interrogation of the theme of beauty. Smith's acknowledgement of both of these texts is interesting. The acknowledgement of the influence of Forster may suggest that Smith is aligning herself as an author with Forster; and that she wishes to be regarded in similar terms as a figure that has in some respect occupied a marginal status and written novels that deal with this status but whose texts can also be regarded amongst the classics of British fiction. Both *Dorian* and *On Beauty* acknowledge the influence of their parent texts and pay homage to Wilde and Forster respectively, but significantly in attempting a reworking both also position themselves as viable successors. The legacy of both Wilde and Forster suggests that it is possible for an author to move between the margins and the centre of the literary world.

Scarry's text is also an interesting choice as *On Beauty and Being Just* essentially articulates a desire for a return to an emphasis on beauty within art. Scarry suggests that we should no longer regard beauty and political interests as separate within the arts. She notes:

Something beautiful immediately catches attention yet prompts one to judgements that one then continues to scrutinize, and that one not infrequently discovers to be in error.

> Something beautiful fills the mind yet invites the search for something beyond itself, something larger or something of the same scale with which it needs to be brought into relation. (Scarry, 2000, p. 29)

The return to an emphasis on beauty could also suggest that political activism can be achieved within the canon and does not have to be resigned to the margins of artistic expression. Figures such as Self, Barker, Evaristo and Smith have taken this challenge to heart. Through *On Beauty* Smith produces a novel that lacks the comic exaggeration that accompanies her representation of marginal issues in *White Teeth* (2000). In referencing or echoing older, already established texts, these authors state a claim for novels that can be regarded outside of the margins as well as within them. Positioning marginality is thus problematized, and yet avowed as a force for aesthetic and cultural renovation. In the twenty-first century marginality demands and has our attention.

Notes

Chapter 1

[1] Novels that detail the lives of previously marginalized ethnic groups have indeed become popular with Zadie Smith's *White Teeth* (2000) and Monica Ali's *Brick Lane* (2003) becoming bestsellers.

[2] Francois Lyotard claims that 'lamenting the "loss of meaning" in postmodernity boils down to mourning the fact that knowledge is no longer principally [linear] narrative' quoted in Landow, 1992, p. 11.

[3] Leon Golden argues that according to Aristotle 'Literary mimesis represents a complete and unified action with a beginning, middle, and end linked by necessary and probable causes. The art form should also be small enough for the audience to clearly remember it. Arts succeeds when the beginning, middle, and end of an action are clearly and persuasively motivated (i.e. are sufficiently mimetic for learning and inference)'. See Leon Golden's Article on Aristotle (1994) for the *Johns Hopkins Guide to Literary Theory & Criticism*, edited by Michael Groden and Martin Kreiswirth, Baltimore, MD: Johns Hopkins University Press, available online at: http://www.sou.edu/English/Hedges/Sodashop/RCenter/Theory/People/aristotl.htm (last accessed 23 April 2006). Although Phillips' novel would fail the dramatic unities of time and place, the novel does in fact almost adhere to the principle of clearly defined beginning, middle and end, linked by probable causes. The shift in characters perhaps disqualifies Phillips from a complete adherence to Aristotle's model as Golden defines it – but the thematic continuance strongly suggests at least a partial fulfilment of Aristotle's insistence upon a beginning, middle and end.

[4] For a more detailed analysis of liberal humanism see Barry, 1987 and Lodge, 1988.

[5] Evaristo expresses her belief in the socially transformative powers of literature in an interview with *Wasafiri* reprinted in: 'Bernadine Evaristo with Alistair Niven' in Susheila Nasta (ed.) (2004) *Writing Across Worlds: Contemporary Writers Talk*, London: Routledge, p. 280.

[6] Winterson discusses the power of *Oranges are not the only Fruit* in this context in the Virago introduction to the text as I discuss later in this chapter (London: Vintage, 1996).

[7] The name given to the villagers who know how to make tools out of flint and who thus begin the novel as powerful traders and workmen but become redundant upon the discovery of bronze and iron.

Chapter 2

[1] See Barry, 1987.
[2] This process has perhaps been made most prominent by the work of feminists such as bell hooks, Donna Harraway, Mary Eagleton, Julia Kristeva etc.
[3] Wood's term for a text that depicts events that are not technically impossible but are incredibly unlikely. See James Wood, 'Tell me how does it feel?' *The Guardian*, Saturday 6 October 2001 available at http://books.guardian.co.uk/departments/generalfiction/story/0,6000,563868,00.html (last accessed 12 December 2006).

Chapter 3

[1] A story told in the theme park about a woman who was saved from certain death after falling from a cliff top by her skirt bellowing out and slowing her fall as a parachute would. (Barnes, *England, England* (1998) p. 238).
[2] Levinas expresses this exteriority of the 'comfortable self' thus, 'The I is, to be sure, happiness, presence at home with itself. But, as sufficiency in its non-sufficiency, it remains in the non-I; it is enjoyment of "something else," never of itself. Autochthonous, that is, rooted in what it is not, it is nevertheless, within this enrootedness independent and separated.' Levinas, 1991 [1969], p. 152.
[3] FutureMouse is a genetically modified mouse that is programmed so that every stage of its development including the appearance of various cancer cells and its eventual death are supposedly programmed into its genes at the moment of its artificial conception. The mouse is developed by Marcus Chalfen, with one application being in the field of medical research for finding the cure for cancer; however, the presence of the Nazi scientist Perret on the stage reminds the reader also of the ever-present threat of more nefarious applications of such a controlled genetic environment.
[4] See Smith, 2000, pp. 356–64; particularly, the depiction of the relationship between Ambrosia and Captain Durham can be read as a metaphor for the colonial relationship that exists between their respective countries.

Chapter 4

[1] Siegfried Sassoon and William Rivers are both published public figures; Sassoon in the realm of poetry; Rivers wrote a series of ground breaking medical texts that proffered a different, more humane approach to dealing with shock and other neurasthenic conditions and used Freudian psychology to help patients to understand their illnesses – the nod to Freudian analysis being relevant also to the way that some readers will interpret the novel along the lines of psychoanalysis and thus adding to the metafictional tone to the text.
[2] The open letter that Sassoon sent to *The Times*, which is quoted in its entirety on the first page of the novel is just one example of this method of incorporating genuine articles and 'true' stories that were recorded between 1914 and 1918.
[3] Myth and perhaps more specifically the structure and textures of myth and history form an integral and constituent part of much contemporary British fiction; this phenomena perhaps forms part of a rejection of the Victorian realist novel,

although the didactic aims of such novels remain at the very heart of much of the fiction that constitutes the contemporary scene.

Chapter 5

[1] Typical examples of writers who are popularly associated with the use of the grotesque in literature are as many and as varied as; Francois Rabelais, John Webster, Jonathan Swift, Alexander Pope, Lord Byron, E. T. A Hoffmann, Victor Hugo, Edgar Alan Poe, Charles Dickens, Robert Browning, Franz Kafka, Alfred Jarry, Samuel Beckett, Evelyn Waugh, Mervyn Peake and Roald Dahl. The fact that this list contains almost the entire range of form, from poetry to drama to the novel, and spans over half a millennium, is perhaps testimony enough of the enduring popularity of the grotesque form.

[2] See figures such as Mikhail M. Bakhtin, in *Rabelais and His World* (1965), Arthur Clayborough, in *The Grotesque in English Literature* (1965), Philip Thomson, in *The Grotesque* (1972), John R. Clarke, in *The Modern Satiric Grotesque and It's Traditions*, (1991), and Daniel K Danow, in *The Spirit of Carnival, Magical Realism and The Grotesque* (1995).

[3] Tew, 2004, p. 29. Whilst the term grotesque is not directly employed in either of these examples, the sense of otherworldliness that Tew argues is a concern of the evolving British aesthetic, and Phelp's sense that chaos and violence pose an ever present threat can certainly also be read as an indication of the underlying tone of a literature that produces all of the effects that Kayser marks out as belonging to the genre of the grotesque.

[4] Simon becomes the patient of Dr Zack Busner, an eminent celebrity psychologist who attempts to reintroduce Simon into the ape world and to cure him of his psychosis.

[5] This flawed perspective manifests itself for Dykes by the simple fact that the media, and presumably therefore their reading public are more interested in the lifestyle of artists than their work, beginning to be described in terms that seem more akin to descriptions of chimpanzees than humans.

[6] 'Whenever he stopped to contemplate his relationship to this body, this physical idiot twin, it occurred to Simon that something critical must have gone wrong without his noticing. He was bemused to awaken to this insistent reminder of his corporeality. He seemed to recall – within the memory banks of his body itself – those unconstrained, atemporal afternoons of childhood, twilight playing, parental calls to return home like hooting apes in the suburban gloaming; and accompanying that memory, suffusing it like the sunset, a sense of his body as also unconstrained, not as yet inhabited, hemmed-in, by the knowledge of the future, which became like a thermostat, regulating any enjoyment or ease of action, ease of repose.' (Self, 1998, pp. 11–12)

[7] The term is used throughout *Great Apes* to refer to the chimps' version of humanity.

[8] The circus of celebrity psychiatry, the jungle of hospital politics and its resulting effect on patients' care, the Vanity Fair of the London art scene – all are mordantly satirized through their apish reincarnations.

9   This laughing context provides an opportunity to remove the reader from the ideological confines of experiencing fiction *through* their own direct experience allowing instead a more revelatory experience through externalizing the reader, which in turn allows for a greater questioning of the institutions and ideas expressed within the novel, that if portrayed in a more naturalistic setting would be regarded as somehow natural or given, and therefore above the level of ideological interrogation. Bakhtin, 1984 [1965], p. 10.

10   Many of these novels achieved a kind of infamy before they were even widely read due to the reputation that preceded them, and this reputation was a result in large part to the perception of the levels of 'grotesquerie' that their authors had employed.

11   NB: Page 401 occurs twice in the novel, this quote is taken from the second version of p. 401.

12   Fevvers is the protagonist of Carter's novel; she has a pair of working wings sprouting from her back resulting from either a quirk of nature or an elaborate and extremely well maintained trick.

Bibliography

Section 1: primary sources

Note: Where a first edition is not used the original date of publication is indicated in additional parenthesis.

Ackroyd, Peter (1993) [1985] *Hawksmoor*, Harmondsworth: Penguin.

Ali, Monica (2004) [2003] *Brick Lane*, London: Black Swan.

Amis, Kingsley (1992) [1954] *Lucky Jim*, Harmondsworth: Penguin.

Amis, Martin (1981) *Other People: A Mystery Story*, London: Jonathan Cape.

Amis, Martin (1987) *Einstein's Monsters*, London: Athlone.

Amis, Martin (1990) *London Fields*, Harmondsworth: Penguin.

Amis, Martin (1991) *Time's Arrow*, London: Jonathan Cape.

Amis, Martin (1996) *The Information*, London: Flamingo.

Amis, Martin (2000) [1984] *Money: A Suicide Note*, Harmondsworth: Penguin.

Ballard, J. G. (1994) [1973] *Concrete Island*, London: Viking.

Ballard, J. G. (2003) *Millennium People*, London: Flamingo.

Barker, Pat (1991) *Regeneration*, London: Viking.

Barker, Pat (1993) *The Eye in the Door*, London: Viking.

Barker, Pat (1995) *The Ghost Road*, London: Viking.

Barker, Pat (2002) *Border Crossing*, Harmondsworth: Penguin.

Barnes, Julian (1981) *Metroland*, London: Robin Clark.

Barnes, Julian (1985) *Flaubert's Parrot*, London: Picador.

Berendt, John (1995) [1994] *Midnight in the Garden of Good and Evil: A Savannah Story*, London: Vintage.

Bradbury, Malcolm (1975) *The History Man*, London: Secker and Warburg.

Bradbury, Malcolm (1983) *Rates of Exchange*, London: Secker and Warburg.

Brooke-Rose, Christine (1968) *Between*, London: Michael Joseph.

Brooke-Rose, Christine (1984) *Amalgamation*, Manchester: Carcanet.

Brooke-Rose, Christine (1986) *Xorandor*, Manchester: Carcanet.

Brooke-Rose, Christine (1991) *Textermination*, Manchester: Carcanet.

Byatt, A. S. (1990) *Possession*, London: Chatto & Windus.

Carter, Angela (1978) *The Passion of New Eve*, London: Arrow.

Carter, Angela (1981) *The Magic Toyshop*, London: Virago.

Carter, Angela (1985) [1984] *Nights at the Circus*, London: Picador.

Carter, Angela (1992) [1991] *Wise Children*, London: Vintage.

Coe, Jonathan (1995) [1994] *What a Carve Up!*, Harmondsworth: Penguin.

Crace, Jim (1988) *The Gift of Stones*, London: Secker and Warburg.

Crace, Jim (1999) *Being Dead*, London and New York: Viking.

Diski, Jenny (1987) *Rainforest*, London: Methuen.

Diski, Jenny (1992) [1991] *Happily Ever After*, Harmondsworth: Penguin.

Drabble, Margaret (1977) [1979] *The Ice Age*, Harmondsworth: Penguin.

Drabble, Margaret (1980) *The Middle Ground*, London: Weidenfeld and Nicholson.

Drabble, Margaret (1988) [1987] *The Radiant Way*, Harmondsworth: Penguin.

Drabble, Margaret (1991) *The Gates of Ivory*, London: Viking.

Evaristo, Bernardine (1997) *Lara*, Tunbridge Wells: Angela Royal Publishing Ltd.

Evaristo, Bernardine (2001) *The Emperor's Babe*, London: Hamish Hamilton.

Evaristo, Bernardine (2005) *Soul Tourists*, London: Hamish Hamilton.

Fowles, John (1987) [1969] *The French Lieutenant's Woman*, London: Pan.

Fowles, John (1991) [1985] *A Maggot*, London: Picador.

Fowles, John (2000) [1964] *The Magus*, London: Vintage.

Hornby, Nick (1997) *High Fidelity*, London: Victor Gollancz.

Hornby, Nick (2000) [1998] *About a Boy*, Harmondsworth: Penguin.

Hornby, Nick (2005) *A Long Way Down*, London: Viking.

Ishiguro, Kazuo (1987) *An Artist of the Floating World*, London: Faber & Faber.

Ishiguro, Kazuo (1990a) [1989] *The Remains of the Day*, London and Boston, MA: Faber & Faber.

Ishiguro, Kazuo (1990b) *A Pale View of the Hills*, New York: Vintage.

Ishiguro, Kazuo (1996) *The Unconsoled*, London: Faber & Faber.

Ishiguro, Kazuo (2001) *When We Were Orphans*, London: Faber & Faber.

Joyce, Graham (2005) *The Limits of Enchantment*, London: Gollancz.

Kelman, James (1984) *The Bus Conductor Hines*, London and Melbourne: J. M. Dent.

Kureishi, Hanif (1990) *The Buddha of Suburbia*, London and Boston, MA: Faber & Faber.

Kureishi, Hanif (1995) *The Black Album*, London and Boston, MA: Faber & Faber.

Kureishi, Hanif (1998) *Intimacy*, London: Faber & Faber.

Kureishi, Hanif (2001) *Gabriel's Gift*, London: Faber & Faber.

Levy, Andrea (2004) *Small Island*, London: Review.

Litt, Toby (2000) *Corpsing*, London: Hamish Hamilton.

Litt, Toby (2001) *Deadkidssong*, London: Hamish Hamilton.

Lodge, David (1975) *Changing Places: A Tale of Two Campuses*, London: Secker and Warburg.

Lodge, David (1984) *Small World: An Academic Romance*, London: Secker and Warburg.

Lodge, David (1988) *Modern Criticism and Theory*, London: Longman.

Lodge, David (1989) [1988] *Nice Work*, Harmondsworth: Penguin.

McEwan, Ian (1988) [1987] *The Child in Time*, London: Picador.

McEwan, Ian (1997) *The Cement Garden*, London: Vintage.

McEwan, Ian (1998) *Amsterdam*, London: Vintage.

McEwan, Ian (1998) *Enduring Love*, London: Vintage.

McEwan, Ian (2002) [2001] *Atonement*, London: Vintage.

Phillips, Caryl (1986) *A State of Independence*, London: Faber & Faber.

Phillips, Caryl (1991) *Cambridge*, London: Bloomsbury.

Phillips, Caryl (1995) [1985] *The Final Passage*, London: Picador.

Rushdie, Salman (1995) [1981] *Midnight's Children*, London: Vintage.

Rushdie, Salman (1998) [1988] *The Satanic Verses*, London: Vintage.
Rushdie, Salman (2001) *Fury: A Novel*, London: Jonathan Cape.
Sebald, W. G. (2033) [1999] *The Rings of Saturn*, London: Norton.
Self, Will (1998a) [1997] *Great Apes*, Harmondsworth: Penguin.
Self, Will (1998b) *Tough, Tough Toys for Tough, Tough Boys*, London: Bloomsbury.
Self, Will (2002) *Dorian: An Imitation*, London: Viking.
Smith, Zadie (2001) [2000] *White Teeth*, Harmondsworth: Penguin.
Smith, Zadie (2002) *The Autograph Man*, London: Hamish Hamilton.
Smith, Zadie (2005) *On Beauty*, Harmondsworth: Penguin.
Thorpe, Adam (1994) [1992] *Ulverton*, London: Vintage.
Welsh, Irvine (1994) [1993], *Trainspotting*, London: Vintage.
Winterson, Jeanette (1990) *Sexing the Cherry*, London: Vintage.
Winterson, Jeanette (1991) [1985] *Oranges Are Not the Only Fruit*, London: Vintage.
Winterson, Jeanette (1992) *Written On the Body*, London: Cape.
Winterson, Jeanette (1996) *The Passion*, London: Vintage.
Winterson, Jeanette (1998) *Gut Symmetries*, London: Granta.
Winterson, Jeanette (2001) *The PowerBook*, London: Vintage.
Winterson, Jeanette (2004) *Lighthousekeeping*, London: Fourth Estate.

Section 2: secondary sources

Adorno, Theodor (1990) [1973] *Negative Dialects*, trans. E. B. Ashton, London: Routledge and Kegan Paul.
Ahearn, Edward J. (2000) 'The modern English visionary: Peter Ackroyd's *Hawksmoor* and Angela Carter's *The Passion of New Eve*', *Twentieth Century Literature*, Winter, available at http://www.findarticles.com/p/articles/mi_m0403/is_4_46/ai_75141044 (last accessed 11 Feburary 2007).
Ahmad, Ajaz (1992) *In Theory: Classes, Nations, Literature*, London and New York: Verso.
Alexander, Marguerite (1990) *Flights from Realism: Themes and Strategies in Post-modernist British and American Fiction*, London: Routledge.
Alexander, Victoria N (2005) 'Amis in conversation with Victoria N Alexander', available at www.dactyl.org/amis.html (last accessed 5 April 2006).
Amis (1995) 'An interview with James Diedrick from, "A biographical sketch"' in James Diedrick, *Understanding Martin Amis*, Columbia: University of South Carolina Press, available at: http://www.uv.es/~fores/amisbio.html (last accessed 10 March 2005).
Anderson, Benedict (1983) *Imagined Communities: Reflections on Origin and Spread of Nationalism*, London: Verso.
Annan, Gabriele (1989) 'On the high wire: review of Ishiguro's *A Pale View of Hills*, *An Artist of the Floating World* and *The Remains of the Day*', *New York Review of Books* 36 (19): 3–4.
Armitt, Lucy (2000) *Contemporary Women's Fiction and the Fantastic*, Basingstoke: Macmillan.
Arnold, Mathew (1965) 'Preface to the first edition of *Poems* (1853)' in Kenneth Allott (ed.) *The Poems of Mathew Arnold*, London: Faber and Faber.

Ashcroft, Bill, Gareth Griffiths and Helen Tiffin (2002) *The Empire Writes Back: Theory and Practice in Post-Colonial Literature*, 2nd edition, London and New York: Routledge.

Babcock, Barbara (1978) *The Reversible World: Symbolic Inversion in Art and Society*, Ithaca, NY: Cornell University Press.

Baker, Stephen (2003) 'Salman Rushdie: history, self and the fiction of truth', in Richard Lane, Rod Mengham and Philip Tew (eds) *Contemporary British Fiction*, London and New York: Polity, pp. 145–57.

Bakhtin, Mikhail (1981) [1934–41] *The Dialogic Imagination: Four Essays*, ed. and trans. Caryl Emerson and Michael Holquist, Austin, TX: University of Texas Press.

Bakhtin, Mikhail (1984) [1965] *Rabelais and his World*, trans. Helene Iswolsky, Bloomington, IN: Indiana University Press.

Bakhtin, Mikhail M. (1937–38) 'Forms of time and of the chronotope in the novel: notes toward a historical poetics', in M. Holquist (ed.), *The Dialogic Imagination*, Austin, TX: University of Texas, pp. 84–54.

Bakhtin, Mikhail M. (1982) 'The prehistory of novelistic discourse', in *The Dialogic Imagination: Four Essays*, Austin, TX: University of Texas Press, Slavic Series.

Ball, Michael, Fred Gray and Linda McDowell (1989) *The Transformation of Britain: Contemporary Social and Economic Change*, London: Fontana.

Barker, Pat (1996) *The Regeneration Trilogy*, Harmonsdworth: Penguin.

Barnes, Julian (1998) *England, England*, London: Jonathan Cape.

Barry, Peter (1987) *Issues in Contemporary Critical Theory*, London: Macmillan.

Barth, John (1967) 'The literature of exhaustion', in Raymond Federman (ed.) (1975) *Surfiction: Fiction Now ... and Tomorrow*, Chicago, IL: Swallow, pp. 19–33.

Barthes, Roland (1972) [1957] *Mythologies*, trans. Annette Lavers, London: Jonathan Cape.

Bataille, Georges (1929) *Documents 7*, December, p. 382.

Bataille, Georges (1973) *Literature and Evil*, New York: Urizen Books.

Bataille, Georges (1991) [1976] *The Accursed Share: An Essay on General Economy*, Volume II: *The History of Eroticism* and Volume III: *Sovereignty*, trans. Robert Hurley, New York: Zone Books. Originally published in 1976 as *L'Histoire de l'erotisme* and *La Souverainete* in *Ouevres Completes* Volume 8, Paris: Editions Gallimard.

Bataille, Georges (2001) *The Unfinished System of Nonknowledge*, ed. Stuart Kendall trans. Michelle Kendal and Stuart Kendall, Minneapolis, MN and London: University of Minnesota Press.

Baudrillard, Jean (1988) *The Ecstasy of Communication*, trans. Bernard and Caroline Schutze, New York: Semiotext.

Baudrillard, Jean (2002) *The Spirit of Terrorism*, London and New York: Verso.

Benhabib, Seyla (1984) 'Epistemology of Postmodernism: A Rejoinder to Jean-François Lyotard', *New German Critique* 33: 103–26.

Bergonzi, Bernard (1970) *The Situation of the Novel*, London: Macmillan.

Bergson, Henri (1910) *Time and Free Will: Essay on the Immediate Data of Consciousness*, trans. F. L. Pogson, London: George Allen & Unwin.

Bergson, Henri (1913) *An Introduction to Metaphysics*, trans. T. E. Hulme, London: Macmillan.

Berman, Marshall (1983) [1982] *All That Is Solid Melts Into Air: The Experience of Modernity*, London and New York: Verso.

Bhabha, Homi K. (1990) *Nation and Narration*, London: Routledge.

Bhabha, Homi K. (1994) *The Location of Culture*, London and New York: Routledge.

Billany, Dan (1950) *The Trap*, London: Faber & Faber.

Blincoe, Nicholas and Matt Thorne (2000) 'Introduction: the pledge', in Nicholas Blincoe and Matt Thorne (eds) *All Hail the New Puritans*, London: Fourth Estate, pp. vii–xvii.

Bordo, Susan (1993) *Material Girl: The Effacements of Postmodern Culture in Unbearable Women, Western Culture, and the Body*, Berkeley, CA: University of California Press.

Botting, Fred and Scott Wilson (eds) (1998) *The Bataille Reader*, London: Blackwell.

Bourdieu, Pierre (1984) *Distinction: A Social Critique of the Judgement of Taste*, trans. Richard Nice, London and New York: Routledge and Kegan Paul.

Bourdieu, Pierre (1993) *The Field of Cultural Production: Essays on Art and Literature*, trans. Randall Johnson, Cambridge: Polity.

Bradbury, Malcolm (1973) *Possibilities: Essays on the state of the Novel*, Oxford: Oxford University Press.

Bradbury, Malcolm (1977) *The Novel Today: Contemporary Writers on Modern Fiction*, Manchester: Manchester University Press.

Bradbury, Malcolm (2001) *The Modern British Novel 1878–2001*, 2nd edition, Harmondsworth: Penguin.

Bradbury, Malcolm and David Palmer (eds) (1979) *The Contemporary English Novel*, London: Edward Arnold.

Brannigan, John (2003) *Orwell to the Present: Literature in England 1945–2000*, Basingstoke and New York: Palgrave Macmillan.

Bredvold, Louis I. (1949) 'The gloom of the Tory satirists', in James L. Clifford and Louis A. Landa (eds) *Pope and His Contemporaries*, New York: Oxford University Press.

Brennan, Timothy (1989) *Salman Rushdie and the Third World: Myths of the Nation*, Basingstoke: Macmillan.

Briggs, Asa (1991) *A Social History of England*, Harmondsworth: Penguin.

Bristow, Joseph and Trev Lynn Broughton (eds) (1997) *The Infernal Desires of Angela Carter: Fiction, Femininity, Feminism*, London: Longman.

Brooks, Peter (1984) *Reading for the Plot: Design and Intention in Narrative*, Oxford: Oxford University Press.

Buford, Bill (ed.) (1993) *Granta: Best of Young British Novelists*, London: Granta.

Burgess, Anthony (1967) *The Novel Now*, London: Faber & Faber.

Butler, Judith (1990) *Gender Trouble: Feminism and the Subversion of Identity*, London: Routledge.

Carter, Angela (1979) *The Sadeian Woman and the Ideology of Pornography*, London: Virago.

Carter, Angela (1998) *Shaking a Leg: Collected Journalism and Writings*, London: Vintage.

Cassirer, Ernst (1955) *The Philosophy of Symbolic Forms, Vols 1–4: Volume 1: Language*, New Haven, CT and London: Yale University Press; (1955) *Volume 2: Mythical*

Thought, trans. Ralph Manheim, New Haven, CT and London: Yale University Press; (1955) *Volume 3: The Phenomenology of Knowledge*, trans. Ralph Manheim, New Haven, CT and London: Yale University Press; (1955) *Volume 4: The Metaphysics of Symbolic Forms*, John Michael Krois and Donald Phillip Verene (eds), trans. John Michael Krois. New Haven, CT and London: Yale University Press.

Champagne, J (1995) *The Ethics of Marginality: A New Approach to Gay Studies*, Minneapolis, MN: University of Minnesota Press.

Chaudhuri, Una (1990) 'Imaginative maps: excerpts from a conversation with Salman Rushdie', *Turnstile 2*, 1: 36–47.

Childs, Peter (2005) *Contemporary Novelists: British Fiction Since 1970*, Basingstoke and New York: Palgrave Macmillan.

Chow, Rey (1998) *Ethics After Idealism: Theory, Culture, Ethnicity, Reading*, Bloomington, IN: Indiana University Press.

Clarke, John R. (1991) *The Modern Satiric Grotesque And Its Traditions*, Lexington, KY: University of Kentucky Press.

CNN Book News (2000) Interview with Ishiguro, available at http://www.cnn. com/2000/books/news/10/27/kazuo.ishiguro/–cnn.com books (last accessed 10 March 2004).

Connor, Steven (1992) *Theory and Cultural Value*, Oxford: Basil Blackwell.

Connor, Steven (1994) 'Rewriting wrong: on the ethics of literary reversion', in Theo d'Haen and Hans Bertens (eds) *Liminal Postmodernisms: The Postmodern, the (post) Colonial and the (Post)-Feminist*, Amsterdam and Atlanta, GA: Rodopi, pp. 79–97.

Connor, Steven (1996) *The English Novel in History 1950–1995*, London: Routledge.

Connor, Steven (2000) 'Rewriting wrong: on the ethics of literary reversion', in Niall Lucy (ed.) *Postmodern Literary Theory: An Anthology*, Oxford: Blackwell.

Conradi, P. (ed.) (1997) *Iris Murdoch, Existentialists and Mystics*, London: Chatto and Windus.

Cowart, David (1989) *History and the Contemporary Novel*, Carbondale and Edwardsville, IL: Southern Illinois University Press.

Crace, Jim (1997) *Quarantine*, London: Viking.

Cundy, Catherine (1996) *Salman Rushdie*, Manchester: Manchester University Press.

Currie, Mark (ed.) (1995) *Metafiction*, London and New York: Longman.

Curtius, Ernst Robert (1953) *European Literature and the Latin Middle Ages*, London: Pantheon Books.

Dällenbach, Lucien (1989) [1977] *The Mirror in the Text*, trans. Jeremy Whitley with Emma Hughes, Chicago, IL: University of Chicago Press; Cambridge: Polity.

Davison, Carol (1994) 'CrissCrossing the River: An Interview with Caryl Phillips' *Ariel: A Review of International English Literature*, 25 (4).

Day, Aidan (1998) *Angela Carter: The Rational Glass*, Manchester: Manchester University Press.

Debord, Guy (1995) [1967] *The Society of the Spectacle*, trans. Donald Nicholson-Smith, London: Zone Books.

Deleuze, Gilles (1993) *Essays Critical and Clinical*, trans. Daniel W. Smith and Michael A. Green, London and New York: Verso.

Derrida, Jacques (1993) *Spectres of Marx: The State of the Debt, the Work of the Morning, and the New International*, trans. Peggy Kamuf, London: Routledge.

Eagleton, Terry (1988) 'The silences of David Lodge', *New Left Review*, 172: 93–102.

Elaine Yee Lin Ho (2000) *Timothy Mo*, Manchester: Manchester University Press.

Emecheta, Buchi (1986) *Head above Water*, London: Ogwugwu Afo.

Emecheta, Buchi (1988) 'Buchi Emecheta with Susheila Nasta', dir. Fenella Greenfold, ICA Guardian Conversations, London: ICA Video/Trilion.

Evaristo, Bernadine (2004) 'Bernadine Evaristo in conversation with Alastair Niven' in Susheila Nasta (ed.) *Writing Across Worlds: Contemporary Writers Talk*, London: Routledge.

Fanon, Frantz (1967) [1963] *The Wretched of the Earth*, trans. Constance Farrington, Harmondsworth: Penguin.

Faulkner, Peter (ed.) (1992) *A Modernist Reader: Modernism in England 1910–1930*, London: Batsford.

Federman, Raymond, (ed.) (1975) *Surfiction: Fiction Now . . . and Tomorrow*, Chicago, IL: Swallow.

Fish, Stanley (1980) *Is There a Text in this Class? The Authority of Interpretive Communities*, Cambridge, MA: Harvard University Press.

Fishburn, Katherine (1995) *Reading Buchi Emecheta: Cross Cultural Conversations*, Westport, CT: Greenwood Press.

Fleishman, Avrom (1971) *The English Historical Novel*, Baltimore, MD: John Hopkins University Press.

Fletcher, M. D. (1994) *Reading Rushdie: Perspectives on the Fiction of Salman Rushdie*, Amsterdam: Rodopi.

Foucault, Michel (1965) [1961] *Madness and Civilization*, New York: Pantheon.

Foucault, Michel (1966) *The Order of Things*, London: Tavistock.

Foucault, Michel (1971) 'Nietzsche, genealogy, history' in Paul Rainbow (ed.) (1994) *The Foucault Reader*, Harmondsworth: Penguin, pp. 76–100.

Foucault, Michel (1973) [1963] *Birth of the Clinic*, New York: Pantheon.

Foucault, Michel (1980) *Power/Knowledge: Selected Interviews and Other Writings 1972–77*, ed. Colin Gordon, London: Harvester.

Foucault, Michel (1981) 'The order of discourse' trans. R. Young, in R. Young (ed.) *Untying the Text: A Poststructuralist Reader*, London: Routledge.

Foucault, Michel (1991) [1975] *Discipline and Punish*, trans. Alan Sheridan, Harmondsworth: Penguin.

Fowles, John (1977) *The Magus*, Revised edition, London: Jonathan Cape.

Freud, Sigmund (1955) *Beyond the Pleasure Principle*, in *The Standard Edition of the Psychological Works of Sigmund Freud*, trans. James Strachey, Vol. 18, London: Hogarth Press, pp. 1–64.

Frye, Northrop (1957) *Anatomy of Criticism: Four Essays*, Princeton, NJ: Princeton University Press.

Gamble, Sarah (1997) *Angela Carter: Writing from the Front Line*, Edinburgh: Edinburgh University Press.

Gamble, Sarah (ed.) (2001) *The Fiction of Angela Carter*, Basingstoke: Palgrave.

Gąsiorek, Andrej (1995) *Post-War British Fiction: Realism and After*, London: Arnold.

Gates, Henry Louis. Jr (ed.) (1986) *'Race', Writing and Difference*, Chicago, IL: University of Chicago Press.

Georg Lukács, (1967) [1923] *History and Class Consciousness*, trans. Rodney Livingstone, London: Merlin Press.

Gibson, Andrew (1999) *Postmodernity, Ethics and the Novel: From Leavis to Levinas*, London and New York: Routledge.

Gilroy, Paul (2000) *Between Camps: Nations, Cultures and the Allure of Race*, Harmondsworth: Penguin.

Glinga, Werner (1986) *Legacy of Empire: A Journey Through British Society*, trans. Stephan Paul Jost, Manchester: Manchester University Press.

Glover, David and Kora Kaplan, (2000) *Genders*, London: Routledge.

Golden, Leon (1994) Article on Aristotle, in Michael Groden and Martin Kreiswirth (eds) *Johns Hopkins Guide to Literary Theory & Criticism*, Baltimore, MD: Johns Hopkins University Press, available online at http://www.sou.edu/English/Hedges/Sodashop/RCenter/Theory/People/aristotl.htm (last accessed 23 April 2006).

Goonetilleke, D. C. R. A. (1998) *Salman Rushdie*, Basingstoke: Macmillan.

Gorra, Michael (1986) 'Review of Timothy Mo's *Sour Sweet*', *Hudson Review* 38: 671–2.

Grant, Damian (1999) *Salman Rushdie*, Plymouth: Northcote House.

Graves, Benjamin (1998) Homi K. Bhabha: The Liminal Negotiation of Cultural difference available at: http://www.postcolonialweb.org/poldiscourse/bhabha/bhabha2.html (last accessed 15 November 2007).

Grice, Helena and Tim Woods (eds) (1998) *I'm Telling You Stories: Jeanette Winterson and the Politics of Reading*, Amsterdam: Rodopi.

Haffenden, John (1985) *Novelists in Interview*, London: Methuen.

Hagemann, Susanne (ed.) (1996) *Studies in Scottish Fiction: 1945 to the Present*, Frankfurt: Peter Lang.

Hall, Stuart and Tony Jefferson (eds) (1975) *Resistance through Rituals: Youth Subcultures in Post-war Britain*, Birmingham: Centre for Contemporary Cultural Studies, University of Birmingham.

Harraway, Donna (1991) *Simians, Cyborgs and Women: The Reinvention of Nature*, New York: Routledge.

Harvey, David (1989) *The Condition of Postmodernity: An Enquiry into the Origins of Social Change*, Oxford: Blackwell.

Hashimi, Alamgir (1992) 'Hanif Kureishi and the tradition of the novel', *International Fiction Review*, 19: 88–95.

Haywood, Ian (1997) *Working Class Fiction from Chartism to 'Trainspotting'*, Plymouth: Northcote House.

Head, Dominic (2002) *The Cambridge Introduction to Modern British Fiction, 1950–2000*, Cambridge: Cambridge University Press.

Head, Dominic (2003) 'Zadie Smith's *White Teeth*: multiculturalism for the millennium', in Richard Lane, Rod Mengham and Philip Tew (eds) *Contemporary British Fiction*, London and New York: Polity, pp. 106–19.

Heidegger, Martin (1962) [1927] *Being and Time*, trans. John Macquarrie and Edward Robinson, Oxford: Blackwell.

Henstra, Sarah (2005) 'The McReal thing: personal/national identity in Julian Barnes *England, England*', in Nick Bentley (ed.) *British Fiction Of The 1990s*, London: Routledge.

Highet, Gilbert (1962) *The Anatomy of Satire*, Princeton, NJ: Princeton University Press.

Hiro, Dilip (1991) *Black British White British: A History of Race Relations in Britain*, London: Grafton.

Holmes, Frederick M. (1997) *The Historical Imagination: Postmodernism and the Treatment of the Past in Contemporary British Fiction*, ELS Monograph Series no. 73, Victoria, BC: University of Victoria.

Hutcheon, Linda (1984a) *Narcissistic Narrative: The Metafictional Paradox*, London: Methuen.

Hutcheon, Linda (1984b) *The Politics of Postmodernism*, London: Routledge.

Hutcheon, Linda (1988) *A Poetics of Postmodernism: History, Theory, Fiction*, London and New York: Routledge.

Hutcheon, Linda (1989) *The Politics of Postmodernism*, London and New York: Routledge.

Hutcheon, Linda (1994) *Irony's Edge: The Theory and Politics of Irony*, London and New York: Routledge.

Ian McEwan (1978) 'The State of Fiction: A Symposium', *New Review* Summer 5 (1): 14–76, 51.

Ilona, Anthony (2003) 'Hanif Kureishi's *The Buddha of Suburbia*', in Richard J. Lane, Rod Mengham and Philip Tew (eds) *Contemporary British Fiction*, London: Polity.

James, Edward (1994) *Science fiction in the Twentieth Century*, Oxford: Oxford University Press.

Jameson, Frederic (1991) *Postmodernism, Or, The Cultural Logic of Late Capitalism*, London, Verso.

Jennings, Lee Byron (1963) *The Ludicrous Demon: Aspects of the Grotesque in German Post-Romantic Prose*, Berkeley and Los Angeles, CA: University of California Press.

Joyce, James (1993) [1916] *A Portrait of the Artist as a Young Man*, London: Vintage.

Kaleta, Kenneth (1998) *Hanif Kureishi: Postcolonial Storyteller*, Austin, TX: University of Texas Press.

Kant, Immanuel (1960) [1764] *Observations on the Feeling of the Beautiful and Sublime*, trans. John T. Goldthwait, Berkeley, CA: University of California Press.

Kayser, Wolfgang (1963) *The Grotesque in Art and Literature*, trans. Ulrich Weisstein, Indiana, IN: Indiana University Press, pp. 29–47. Originally published in German under the title *Das Groteske: seine Gestaltung in Malerei und Dichtung*, Gerhard Stalling Verlag, Oldenburg, 1957.

Kearney, Richard (2001) *On Stories*, London and New York: Routledge.

Kennedy, A. L (1995) 'Not changing the world', in Ian. A. Bell (ed.) *Peripheral Visions: Images of Nationhood in Contemporary British Fiction*, Cardiff: The University of Wales press.

King, Roger (1979) 'The middle class in revolt?', in Roger King and Neill Nugent (eds) *Respectable Rebels: Middle Class Campaigns in Britain in the 1970s*, London: Hodder & Stoughton, pp. 1–22.

Kristeva, Julia (1991) 'Women's time', in Robyn Warhol and Diane Hernde (eds) *Feminisms*, Brunswick, NJ: Rutgers University Press, pp. 443–62.

Kronfeld, Chana (1996) *On the Margins of Modernism: Decentring Literary Dynamics*, Berkeley, CA: University of California Press.

Kureishi, Hanif (1986) 'The rainbow sign', in Hanif Kureishi (1996) *My Beautiful Launderette and Other Writings*, London: Faber & Faber.

Landow, George P. (1992) *Hypertext: The Convergence of Contemporary Critical Theory and Technology*, Baltimore, MD: John Hopkins University Press.

Lane, Richard J. (2003) 'The fiction of Jim Crace: narrative and recovery', in Richard J. Lane, Rod Mengham and Philip Tew (eds) *Contemporary British Fiction* Cambridge: Polity Press, pp. 27–39.

Lane, Richard, Rod Mengham and Philip Tew (eds) (2003) *Contemporary British Fiction*, Cambridge: Polity Press.

Leader, Zachary (ed.) (2003) [2002] *On Modern British Fiction*, Oxford: Oxford University Press.

Lee, Alison (1990) *Realism and Power: Postmodern British Fiction*, London: Routledge.

Lee, A. Robert (ed.) (1995) *Other Britain, Other British: Contemporary Multicultural Fiction*, London: Pluto Press.

Lefebvre, Henri (1991) [1974] *The Production of Space*, trans. Donald Nicholson-Smith, Oxford and Cambridge, MA: Blackwell.

Levinas, Emmanuel (1961) *Totality and Infinity*, trans. Alphonso Lingis, Pittsburgh, PA: Duquesne University.

Levinas, Emmanuel (1991) *Totality and Infinity: An Essay on Extremity*, trans. Alphonso Lingis, Dordrecht: Kluwer.

Lodge, David (1979) *The Modes of Modern Writing*, London: Edward Arnold.

Lukács, Georg (1938) 'Realism in the balance', in Theador Adorno, Walter Benjamin, Ernst Bloch, Bertolt Brecht and Georg Lukács (1977) [1980] *Aesthetics and Politics*, London: Verso, pp. 28–59.

Lukács, Georg (1950) *Studies in European Realism – a Sociological Survey of the Writings of Balzac, Stendhal, Zola, Tolstoy, Gorki and Others*, London: Hillway.

Lukács, Georg (1962) *The Historical Novel*, trans. Hannah and Stanley Mitchell, London: Merlin.

Lukács, Georg (1980) 'Writer and critic, 1970', in Terry Lovell, *Pictures of Reality*, London: Athlone.

Lyotard, Jean-Francois (1979) *The Postmodern Condition: A Report on Knowledge*, trans. Geoff Bennington and Brian Massumi, Manchester: Manchester University Press.

McDonough, Frank (1997) 'Class and politics', in Mike Storry and Peter Childs (eds) *British Cultural Identities*, London and New York: Routledge, pp. 201–39.

McEwan, Neil (1981) *The Survival of the Novel: British Fiction in the Later Twentieth Century*, London: Macmillan.

McEwan, Neil (1987) *Perspective in British Historical Fiction Today*, London: Macmillan.

McGowan, John (1991) *Postmodernism and Its Critics*, Ithaca, NY: Cornell University Press.

McHale, Brian (1987) *Constructing Postmodernism*, London: Routledge.

McHale, Brian (1987) *Postmodernist Fiction*, New York and London: Methuen.

McLeod, John (2004) *Postcolonial London: Rewriting the Metropolis*, London: Routledge.

McLuhan, Marshall (1967) *Understanding Media*, London: Sphere Books.

Macherey, Pierre (1978) *A Theory of Literary Production*, trans. G. Wall, London: Routledge and Kegan Paul.

Macherey, Pierre (1995) [1990] *The Object of Literature*, trans. David Macey, Cambridge and New York: Cambridge University Press.

Madsen, Deborah (ed.) (1999) *Postcolonial Literatures*, London: Pluto.

Malcolm, David (2002) *Understanding Ian McEwan*, Columbia, SC: University of South Carolina Press.

Mann, Thomas (1968) 'Conrad's "Secret Agent"' in *Past Masters and Other Papers*, trans. H. T. Lowe-Porter, New York: Freeport.

Marcuse, Herbert (1964) *One Dimensional Man: Studies in the Ideology of Advanced Industrial Society*, London: Routledge and Kegan Paul.

Marvel, Mark (1990) 'Winterson: trust me I'm telling you stories', *Interview*, 20: 165–8.

Marwick, Arthur (1991) *Culture in Britain since 1945*, Oxford: Basil Blackwell.

Massie, Alan (1990) *The Novel Today*, London: Longman.

Mengham, Rod (1999) *An Introduction to Contemporary Fiction: International Writing in English Since 1970*, Cambridge: Polity Press.

Middleton, Peter and Tim Woods (2000) *Literatures of Memory, History Time and Space in Postwar Writing*, Manchester: Manchester University Press.

Milne, Drew (2003) 'The fiction of James Kelman and Irvine Welsh: accents, speech and writing', in Richard Lane, Rod Mengham, and Philip Tew (eds) *Contemporary British Fiction*, London and New York: Polity, pp. 158–73.

Meletinsky, Eleazar M. (2000) *The Poetics of Myth*, trans. Guy Lanoue and Alexandre Sadetsky, London: Routledge.

Mo, Timothy (1992) *The Redundancy of Courage*, London: Vintage.

Mo, Timothy (1999) *Sour Sweet*, London: Paddlepress.

Moore-Gilbert, Bart (2001) *Hanif Kureishi*, Manchester: Manchester University Press.

Morrison, Jago (2003) *Contemporary Fiction*, London: Routledge.

Mulhern, Francis (1990) 'English reading', in Homi K. Bhabha (ed.) *Nation and Narration*, London and New York: Routledge, pp. 250–64.

Murdoch, Iris (1967) *The Sovereignty of Good over Other Concepts: The Leslie Stephen Lecture 1967*, Cambridge: Cambridge University Press.

Murdoch, Iris (1977) [1961] 'Against dryness: a polemical sketch', in Malcolm Bradbury (ed.) (1977) *The Novel Today: Contemporary Writers on Modern Fiction*, Manchester: Manchester University Press, pp. 23–31.

Myer, Kim Middleton (2003) 'Jeanette Winterson's evolving subject: "Difficulty into Dream"', in Richard Lane, Rod Mengham and Philip Tew (eds) *Contemporary British Fiction*, London and New York: Polity Press, pp. 210–25.

Nasta, Susheila (ed.) (2004) *Writing Across Worlds: Contemporary Writers Talk*, London: Routledge.

Ngugi wa Thiong'o (1981) *Decolonising the Mind: The Politics of Language in African Literature*, London: James Currey.

Ngugi wa Thiong'o (1993) *Moving the Centre: The Struggle for Cultural Freedoms*, London: James Currey.

Nick Hornby (2001) Interview with Francis Leach, 20 September, available at http://www.abc.net.au/arts/books/stories/s424255.htm (last accessed 10 May 2007)

Nietzsche, Friedrich (1986) [1878] *Human All Too Human: A Book For Free Spirits*, trans. R. J. Hollingdale, introduction by Erich Heller, Cambridge: Cambridge University Press.

Norris, Christopher (1982) *Deconstruction: Theory and Practice*, London and New York: Routledge.

Orwell, George (1970) [1968: 1941] 'The lion and the unicorn: socialism and the English genius – "Part 1: England Your England"', in Sonia Orwell and Ian Angus (eds) *The Collected Essays, Jornalism and Letters of George Orwell*, Volume II *My Country Right or Left 1940–1943*, Harmondsworth: Penguin, pp. 74–99.

Peach, Linden (1998) *Angela Carter*, Basingstoke: Macmillan.

Pearce, Lynne (1994) *Reading Dialogics*, London: Edward Arnold.

Peterson, Alan and Robin Bunton (eds) (1997) *Foucault, Health and Medicine*, London: Routledge.

Peterson, Nancy J. (2001) *Against Amnesia: Contemporary Women Writers and the Crisis of Historical Memory*, Philadelphia, PA: University of Pennsylvania Press.

Phelps, Gilbert (1992) *Cambridge Cultural History of Britain*, Cambridge: Cambridge University Press.

Pressler, Christopher (2000) *So Far So Linear: Responses to the Work of Jeanette Winterson*, Nottingham: Paupers Press.

Pritchett, V. S. (1946) 'The future of fiction', *New Writing and Daylight*, 7: 75–81.

Radhakrishnan, N. (1984) *Indo-Anglican Fiction: Major Trends and Themes*, Madras: Emerald.

Ranaisinha, Ruvani (2001) *Hanif Kureishi*, Plymouth: Northcote House.

Reynolds, M. (1998) *Jeanette Winterson*, Plymouth: Northcote House.

Rhys, Jean (1966) *The Wide Sargasso Sea*, London: Deutsch.

Richardson, Michael (1994) *Georges Bataille*, London: Routledge.

Ricoeur, Paul (1969) [1967] *The Symbolism of Evil*, trans. Emerson Buchanan, Boston, MA: Beacon Press.

Rushdie, Salman (1992) [1991] *Imaginary Homelands: Essays and Criticism, 1981–1991*, rev. edn 1992, London: Granta.

Rushdie, Salman (1999) [interview] 'When life becomes a bad novel', *Salon*, 6, available online at http://www.salon.com/06/features/interview.html (last accessed 10 October 2007).

Ryan, Kiernan (1994) *Ian McEwan*, Plymouth: Northcote House.

Sage, Lorna (1994) *Angela Carter*, Plymouth: Northcote House.

Said, Edward W. (1979) *The World, the Text, and the Critic*, Cambridge, MA: Harvard University Press.

Said, Edward W. (1993) *Culture and Imperialism*, London: Chatto & Windus.

Sandhu, Sukhdev (2003) *London Calling: How Black and Asian Writers Imagined a City*, London: HarperCollins.

San Juan Jr, E. (1998) *Beyond Postcolonial Theory*, London: Macmillan.

Saul, Gary and Caryl Emerson (1990) *Creation of a Prosaics*, Stanford, CA: Stanford University Press.

Scarry, Elaine (2000) [1999] *On Beauty and Being Just*, London: Duckbacks.

Seaboyer, Judith (1997) 'Second death in Venice: romanticism and the compulsion to repeat in Jeanette Winterson's *The Passion*', *Contemporary Literature*, 38 (3) (Fall): 483–509.

Self, Will (1995) *Junk Mail*, London: Bloomsbury.

Shanks, Michael and Christopher Tilley (1987) *Social Theory and Archaeology*, Cambridge: Polity Press.

Sheppard, Richard (2000) *Modernism – Dada – Postmodernism*, Evanston, IL: North-western University Press.

Shields, Carol (2003) The *Guardian*, 26 July.

Sinfield, Alan (1997) *Literature, Politics and Culture in Post-war Britain*, London: Athlone.

Slay, Jack Jr (1996) *Ian McEwan*, New York: Twayne.

Smethurst, Paul (2000) *The Postmodern Chronotope: Reading Space and Time in Contemporary Fiction*, Amsterdam: Rodopi.

Smith, Zadie (2001) 'This is how it feels to me', *The Guardian*, Saturday 13 October, available at http://books.guardian.co.uk/departments/generalfiction/story/0,6000,563868,00.html. (last accessed 5 May 2007).

Smyth, Edmund (ed.) (1991) *Postmodernism and Contemporary Fiction*, London: B. T. Batsford.

Spivak, Gayatri Chakravorty (1990) 'Reading the Satanic Verses', *Third Text* 11 (Summer): 41–69.

Spivak, Gayatri Chakravorty (1999) *A Critique of Postcolonial Reason: Toward a Vanishing History of the Present*, Cambridge, MA and London: Harvard University Press.

Springhall, John (2001) *Decolonisation Since 1945: The Collapse of European Overseas Empires*, Basingstoke: Palgrave.

Stallybrass, Peter and Allon White (1986) *The Politics and Poetics of Transgression*, London: Methuen.

Stevenson, Randall (1986) *The British Novel Since the Thirties*, London: Batsford.

Stevenson, Randall (2000) 'Greenwich meetings: clocks and things in modernist and postmodernist fiction', *Yearbook of English Studies*, 30: 124–36.

Suleiman, Susan Rubin (1990) 'Mothers and the Avant-Garde: a case of mistaken identity?' in Francoise van Rossum Guyon (ed.), *Avant Garde interdisciplinary and International Review: Femmes, Frauen, Women*, Amsterdam: Rodopi, pp. 135–46.

Swift, Graham (1983) *Waterland*, London: Heinemann.

Swift, Graham (1990) *The Agony and the Ego*, ed. C. Boylan, London: Penguin.

Tanner, Tony (1965) *Saul Bellow*, London: Athlone.

Taylor, D. J. (1989) *A Vain Conceit: British Fiction in the 1980s*, London: Bloomsbury.

Tew, Philip (2004) *The Contemporary British Novel*, London: Continuum.

Thieme, John (2001) *Postcolonial Con-Texts: Writing Back to the Canon*, London and New York: Continuum.

Thomson, Philip (1972) *The Grotesque*, London: Methuen and Co.

Wardle, Marc (2002) 'The death of the real', *Forum*, 633, 22 October 2002.

Watkins, Susan (2001) *Twentieth Century Women Novelists: Feminist Theory into Practice*, Basingstoke: Palgrave.

Watt, Ian (2001) [1957] *The Rise of The Novel*, (new edition with afterword by W. B. Carnochan), Berkeley, CA. University of California Press.

Waugh, Patricia (1984) *Metafiction*, London: Methuen.

Waugh, Patricia (1989) *Feminine Fictions: Revisiting the Postmodern*, London: Routledge.

Waugh, Patricia (1995) *Harvest of the Sixties: English Literature and its Background 1960–1990*, Oxford: Oxford University Press.

Weber, Max (1968) [1922] *Economy and Society*, trans. Guenther Roth and Claus Wittich, Berkley, CA: University of California Press.

Wells, Lynn (2003) *Allegories of Telling: Self-Referential Narrative in Contemporary British Fiction*, Amsterdam and New York: Rodopi.

White, Hayden (1985) [1978] *Topics of Discourse: Essays on Cultural Criticism,* Baltimore, MD: The John Hopkins University Press.

Wilson Angus (1983) *Diversity and Depth in Fiction: Selected Critical Writings of Angus Wilson,* ed. Kerry McSweeney, London: Secker and Warburg.

Wilson, Colin (2001) *The Outsider,* London: Phoenix.

Witting, Monique (1992) *The Straight Mind,* New York: Harvester Wheatsheaf.

Wood, James (2001) 'Tell me how does it feel?' in *The Guardian,* Saturday 6 October 2001 available at http://books.guardian.co.uk/departments/generalfiction/ story/0,6000,563868,00.html (last accessed 12 December 2006).

Wood, James (2002) 'V. S. Pritchett and English comedy', in Zachary Leader (ed.) *On Modern British Fiction,* Oxford University Press.

Woolf, Virginia (1925) *Mrs. Dalloway,* London: Hogarth Press.

Wyatt, David (1993) *Out of the Sixties: Storytelling and the Victorian Generation,* Cambridge: Cambridge University Press.

Young, Robert J. C. (1995) *Colonial Desire: Hybridity in Theory, Culture and Race,* London and New York: Routledge.

Youngs, Tim (1997) *Writing and Race,* London: Longman.

Yudice, George (1988) 'Marginality and the ethics of survival', in Andrew Ross. (ed.) *Universal Abandonment? The Politics of Postmodernism,* Minneapolis, MN: University of Minnesota Press, pp. 214–36.

Index

Ackroyd, Peter, *Hawksmoor*, 92, 103–5
Adorno, Theodor, on narrow definition
    of 'realism', 55
aesthetic dimension of marginality, 30
Alexander, Marguerite, 9–10
    *Flights from Realism: Themes and
        Strategies in Postmodern British and
        American Fiction*, 32
    on historical writing, 95
    on modern concept of
        history, 110–11
alienation in contemporary
    literature, 61, 72, 132
Amis, Martin
    Dickens' influence, 133
    Einstein's Monsters, 71
    interview with James Diedrick, 72–3
    Money: A Suicide Note, 44, 83–4
    Other People: A Mystery Story, 62,
        72, 73
    on need to write, 84
anarchist novel, 51, 152
anonymity, in contemporary novels, 12
Aristotelian ideal of comedy, 150
art and negation, 125
artificial barriers, 13
atheist mysticism of Bataille, 11
authority and truth, relativity of,
    (Bakhtin), 29, 155

Bakhtin, Mikhail M.
    'The Prehistory of Novelistic
        Discourse', 134, 156
    on the Chronotope, 95
    on folk laughter, 152
    on 'potential' of
        carnivalesque, 135–6
Balzac, Honoré de, objective reality in
    novels, 17

Barker, Pat, 4, 18
    The Ghost Road, author's note, 111
    The Regeneration Trilogy, 24, 92,
        109–11
    narrative on Great War, 100
Barnes, Julian, *England, England*, 73
Barstow, Stan, *Ask Me Tomorrow*, 52, 53
Bataille, Georges, 3
    deconstruction of language, 40
    'formlessness', 82
    giving without receiving, 152
    knowledge, enslavement by, 134
    Literature and Evil, 11
    notion of unreason, 65
    rationality, 34
    strangers in a novel, 12, 67
    'unknowable', 13, 14
Beckett, Samuel, 56
Bellow, Saul, 'moral artist', 85
Bergonzi, Bernard, realism and
    rationalism, 10
Bhabha, Homi, *The Location of Culture*, 6
Bhaskar, Roy, on exclusion, 26
black experience of Britain, 5, 116
black people as marginalized, 15
Blincoe, Nicholas and Thorne,
    Nicholas eds., 5
    All Hail the New Puritans, 18–19
Booker Prize, founding, 52
boredom and anarchy, 136–7
Botting, Fred, on Bataille, 11
Bourdieu, Pierre, 35
    The Field of Cultural Production, 4
    on control by 'dominant class', 37
Bradbury, Malcolm
    *Possibilities: Ethics on the State of the
        Novel*, 53, 150
    on culture as youth style, 41
    on 'traditional' novel, 5, 7, 8, 50

Brannigan, John, *Orwell to the Present:*
        Literature in
        England,1945–2000, 21
Brecht, Bertolt, 56
Britain as 'racially' pure, 116
British history, lesser known aspects, 5
Bronte, Charlotte, 11
        Jane Eyre, 24
butler's story, in *Remains of the Day,* 113
Byatt, A.S., 5
        evolving British novel, 57

canon of marginal material, 159
capitalist values of Western society,
        critique, 72, 146
carnival grotesque, 152
carnivalesque forms as escape
        routes, 30, 134–5
Carter, Angela, 11, 57
        Dickens' influence, 133
        Nights at the Circus, 10, 133, 151
        The Passion of New Eve, 133
        sexuality and gender politics, 28
        Wise Children, 21
Cassirer, Ernst, on mythical
        consciousness, 121, 122
centre, marginal is excluded from, 31
character as caricature in Dickens, 133
child's perspective, 63–4
Childs, Peter, *Contemporary Novelists,*
        British Fiction Since 1970, 42
chimp versions of famous figures, 128
Chinese community in London, 79
Chow, Rey, *Ethics after Idealism,* 26, 27,
        61, 70
        on contemporary novel, 57
civilization's 'pretence', 66
Clarke, John R. *The Modern Satiric*
        Grotesque and Its Traditions, 131
class, 6
        markers, blurring of 42
        as taboo subject, 42
classical and populist in novel, 42
classical inheritance, 123
clown figure, 135
Coe, Jonathan, *What a Carve up!,* 23, 29,
        36–7
        on dreams in human psyche, 29

colonial rule, 6
'colonizer', and 'colonized', 6
'communicable empathy' (Phillips), 15
Connor, Steven
        The English Novel in History
                1950–1995, 25, 42, 43, 74
        'Rewriting wrong: on the ethics of
                literary reversion', 94, 97
contemporary British fiction, the
        marginal in, 11, 30–57
contemporary critics
        on alienation and violence, 126
        on the marginal, 21
contemporary novel, as social
        critique, 143
continuous narrative, 123
corruption and anarchy, 69, 70
Crace, Jim, 5, 11, 27
        Arcadia, 133
        Being Dead, 133, 146–9
        distancing effect in novels, 57
        The Gift of Stones, 25, 27–8
        Quarantine, story of Christ in, 27
crisis of identity, 32
Cromwell, Oliver, silencing of religious
        past, 114, 115
cultural squalor in capital city, 145

Dahl, Roald, *Charlie and the Chocolate*
        Factory, 62
Dällenbach, Lucien, *The Mirror in the*
        Text, 107
Debord, Guy, *The Society of the*
        Spectacle, 20
deconstruction of history, 112
Defoe, Daniel, *Moll Flanders,*
        heroine, 62
democratizing the novel form, 19
demonic elements, 103
Descartes, René, *cogito ergo sum,*
        ('I think, therefore I am'), 31
Dickens, Charles
        Bleak House, character of
                Hortense, 62
        David Copperfield, Rosa Dartle, 62
        grotesque portraiture, 133
        Little Dorrit, Miss Wade, 62
        Oliver Twist, 62, 75

influence in contemporary British
    fiction, 133
misfits in supporting roles, 62
satiric caricature, 133
difference, representation of, 6
Diski, Jenny, *Rainforest*, 147–9
dislocation from civilized world, 138
dismissive of high culture,
    Trainspotting, 143–5
dominant social formations, 6
Don Quixote, picaresque novel, 75
Dorian (Self), and grotesque art, 141
Dostoevsky, Fyodor, 80
Drabble, Margaret, *The Ice Age*, 52, 53
drug addiction, 145

elitism, 3, 4
Emecheta, Buchi, Nigerian-born
    writer, 45–6
Empire Windrush, 31, 116
England, selling off its history, 73
English and Indian, 13
'ethical conduct of man in society', 7,
    150
ethnicity as selling point, 38
Evaristo, Bernadine, 4
    *The Emperor's Babe: A Verse Novel of
        Londinium*, 5, 31, 116–17
    black history in London, 100
    marginal characters, 42
    novel as socially democratizing
        force, 18
exclusion
    by gender or race, 15
    of marginalized groups, 7

family life, sham sanctity, 81
Fanon, Franz, *The Wretched of the Earth*, 33
fascism and fraudulence, 27
Fascist sympathizers in British
    aristocracy, 112–13
fashions
    in criticism, 57
    dictating taste, 98
fear of unknown, 13
feelings, evocation of, 54
feminist novel, 25, 52
fictions of marginalized peoples, 21

First World War, 109
'fitting in', 65
fool figure, 135
Forster, E. M.
    marginalized by sexuality, 22
Foucault, Michel
    *Birth of the Clinic: An Archaeology of
        Medical Perception*, 65
    Madness and Civilization, 65
    on language and discourse, 66
    on potential of misfit, 65
Fowles, John, 57
    The French Lieutenant's Woman,
        8, 23
    The Magus, 92, 96–100
    and marginality, 8
freedom, 12
Freud, Sigmund, as ape, 128
Frye, Northrop, 9
Fryer, Peter, on black experience of
    Britain, 5

Garnett, Alf, 77
Gąsiorek, Andrzej
    critique of *Midnight's Children*, 20
    on history and politics in novel, 28
gender, 6
genetic science and racism, 18
genre distinctions, 56
global power, 9
God as emotional role model, 81
Goodall, Jane, (as ape studying wild
    humans), 128
Gothic element of grotesque, 146
Gramsci, Antonio, *Avanti!*, 80
Great Apes, (Self), and grotesque
    art, 141, 142
Great War, multiple versions, 112
Green, Renee, African-American
    artist, 7
Greer, Germaine, *The Female Eunuch*, 52
grotesque forms
    in art, 131
    in contemporary British fiction, 125
    as escape routes, 134–5
    in literature, 167
    in *Rainforest* (Diski) 147, 148–9
'ghettoising' of authors and texts, 15

Harraway, Donna, 18
Haywood, Ian, 25
  *Working Class Fiction: From Chartism to
    Trainspotting*, 39, 145
  on contemporary British novel, 38
Head, Dominic, 18
  *The Cambridge Introduction to Modern
    British Fiction*, 40
  on marginal against mainstream, 25,
    26
hedonistic capitalism, 44
Heidegger, Martin, on identity, 32
Hesse, Hans, 'outsider', 80
historical contextualization, 56
historicizing process in novels, 92–124
histories untold, 24
history, role of, 25
homogeneous societies and writing, 4
Hornby, Nick
  About a Boy
    child's perspective, 62–3
    misfit, 62
    marginal characters, 42
human becoming ape, 127–8
humanism, European and North
    American, 5
humanity, spiritual advancement of, 18
Hutcheon, Linda, on parody, 154
hybrid names, 13
'hysterical realism' (James Wood), 53

identity
  authentic, 32
  loss of, 13
  personal and national, 73, 74
illusion and reality, 151
imagination in writing, 3
immigrant experiment, 12
immigrant poor, 46
imperfection, dangerous fear of, 149
Indian and English, 13
individual, decentring of, 19
inner city living, 78
insane, exclusion of, 65
intention to shock, 143, 144
interpretations of novels, 57

Ishiguro, Kazuo, 47
  The Remains of the Day, 62, 81,
    112–13
  misfit protagonists, 61
Islamic fundamentalism, 87–8

James, Edward, on genres, 56
Jameson, Fredric, on pastiche and
    parody, 153
Joyce, Graham, 11
  The Limits of Enchantment, 8
Joyce, James, 135
  *Portrait of the Artist as a Young
    Man*, 75

Kafka, Franz, 11, 56
  'outsider', 80
Kant, Immanuel, on grotesque in
    rituals of religion, 140–41
Kayser, Wolfgang, *The Grotesque in Art
    and Literature*, 125–6
Kearney, Richard, on narrative, 8–9
Kennedy, A. L., on identification, 43–4
knowledge and servitude, 134
Kristeva, Julia, 56
  Revolution in Poetic Language, 56
Kronfeld, Chana
  On the Margins of Modernism, 3
  on literary canon, 22–3
  marginality and rationality, 8
Kureishi, Hanif
  Asians in England, 46
  Black Album, 8, 43–6, 74, 75–6
  The Buddha of Suburbia, 8, 76–7
  Gabriel's Gift, child's perspective, 62,
    67–70, 139
  Intimacy, 12, 159
  misfit protagonists, 61, 62
  self in novels, 32

labour movement, and working-class
    fiction, 36
lack of connection to friends, 12
laughter
  act of, and reality principle, 13, 14
  and sense of survival, 134

Lawrence, D.H., marginalized by
    class, 22
Lee Yin Ho, on second cultural
    heritage as source, 48
Lee, Alison, critic, 19, 20, 25
Levinas, Emmanuel
    philosophy of ethics, 35
    Totality and Infinity, 35
liberal humanism, 9
    attack on, 50
    decline, 39
    ideology of, 17
    and the text, 16–17
linear mimetic narrative, 15
literary canon, engagement with, 160
literary identities, marginal
    position, 22
literary modes, conflicting, 105–6
literary realism, 47, 48
literature
    purpose of, 17
    as safety valve, 11
    as social critique, 21
    as voice for silenced, 21, 22
Litt, Toby, 5, 11, 27
    Deadkidsong, 'graveyard humour', 58,
    136–8
Lodge, David
    The Modes of Modern Writing, 99
    Nice Work, 52, 53
loud names in Dickens, 133
love, 122
Lukács, Georg
    The Historical Novel, 17, 55, 105, 106,
    112
    History and Class Consciousness, 35
    Marxist criticism, 36
    Studies in European Realism, 17
    on political histories, 96
    on social-historical
        transformations, 123–4
Lyotard, Jean François, 56
    on realism and reality, 47

madness and unreason, 65
magical realism, 20, 21, 30, 119

mainstream culture
    challenge to, 149, 150
    and margins, 70, 71
    relativity of, 35
marginal characters, 23, 42
marginal in modernist art, 8
marginal narratives, denial of, 114
marginal novel, recognition of, 3, 7,
    30–31, 157
    as aesthetic device, 3, 157
    as innovator, 43
    problematic term, 30
    as salvation for fiction, 43
    as social purpose, 4
    as 'tourism' for dominant
        class, 37
marginal revisionism, 24
marginalized communities, 15, 157
    voice of, 157
marginalized status, aspects of, 38
marginality
    and narrative, 9
    and social purpose, 18
marginalization by nationality, 22
McEwan, Ian
    The Child in Time, 108–9
    depiction of time, 29
    on sense of identification in
        literature, 48
McLeod, John, on post-colonial
    Britain, 96
McLuhan, Marshall, on demise of
    novel, 50
meaning and external reference, 11
Meletinsky, Eleazar, M.
    The Poetics of Myth, 93
    on process of myth, 54
memory and cultural
    re-shaping, 113–14
middle classes
    critical hegemony, 26
    experience, contradictions, 40, 41
    and the novel, 42
    perspective, 53
migrant figures as anonymous, 12
minority groups or individuals, 30

misfit character in novel, 21, 61, 62, 70,
        80, 86
    'attacking the system', 79
    commentator on fictive world, 71
    in Bohemian London, 81
    versus 'status quo', 80
Mo, Timothy, 47
    The Redundancy of Courage, 12
    Sour, Sweet, 79
modernism, 22
moral bankruptcy, 83
morality, pluralistic, 62
Morrison, Jago, *Contemporary Fiction*, 49
Morrison, Toni, 6
multiculturalism, 90
    Britain, 31
multiple narratives, 118
Murdoch, Iris
    on art, 84–5
    on 'moral truths', 51
Muslim males and 'mainstream' British
        culture, 46
myth and history, 55, 93
mythification in literature, 97, 107
    of post-World war II, 102

Naipaul, V.S., 47, 133
    Dickens' influence, 133
narrative
    importance of, 8
    shared, of the past, 55
narrative form, 19, 49
    introspective, 54
narrative value, 99
narrator switching, 15
national identity in post-war British
        novel, 74
nationalists' fears of unknown in
        immigrants, 13
natives' zones and settlers' zones, 33
nature of human existence, 119
Nazi sympathizer, (Ishiguro) 113
negation 31
'New Labour' government, 39
Nietzsche, Friedrich
    *Human, All Too Human: A Book For
        Free Spirits*, 131
    an 'outsider', 80

nostalgia and national consciousness, 107
novel
    as history, 25
    as humanizer of characters, 12
    of ideas, 4
    of manners, 7, 53
    survival of, 49
    as voice for silent, 90
novel form, renewal of, 160
novelistic literary tradition, invigorated
        by marginal, 158

objectification, 35–6
Orwell, George, *Down and Out in Paris
        and London*, 145
Ovid's Metamorphoses,
        grotesquerie, 141

parody and pastiche, 153, 154
peasant villagers, untold histories, 114,
        115
phenomenology, 31
Phillips, Caryl, 4
    Crossing the River, 14–16
    marginal characters, 42
picaresque novels, 75
political 'messages' in novels, 18
politicization of literature, 5, 17, 21, 106
'post', an ambiguous prefix, 7
post-colonial text, 25, 32
post-modernism, 9, 56, 57
post-modernist aesthetic, 19, 20
poverty, 73
Powell, Enoch, 'rivers of blood'
        speech, 77
power relations, 4, 153
proletariat and intellectual power, 80
Puritanism silencing Catholicism, 115

race, 6, 7
    as marginalized status, 38
racism, 15, 87
radicalization of novel, 4
Ramidin, Ron, on black experience of
        Britain, 5
rationality
    challenges to, 3
    dominance of, 50

homogeneity of, 14
knowledge, limits of 120
meanings, 9, 150
'rationally definable' world, 8
realism, 20
    critical, 36
    decline of, 39
    in literature, 20, 54, 55, 56
reality in terms of binary
        oppositions, 31, 130
reification, 130
relationship between classes, 139
religion and culture in Britain and
        world, 14
religious fundamentalism, 44
revisionism
    of contemporary novel, 18, 25
    of historical novel, 106
revisionist rewriting of past, 94
rewriting the myths, 29
Rhys, Jean, *The Wide Sargasso Sea*, 24
Rivers, William, 166
rogue figure, 135
Roman London, black woman in, 117
Romantic vision, 98
Rowling, J.K. *Harry Potter* series, 62
Roy, Arundhati, 47
Rushdie, Salman, 57
    Dickens' influence, 133
    Midnight's Children, 151
    Satanic Verses, 10, 33, 105–7
        laughter and parody in, 14
    on Eden myth, 107
    on imagination, 33–4
    on 'newness' in novel form, 28
    politics of race and religion, 28
    self in novels, 32
Sade, Marquis de, literature as release
        of repression by culture, 11
Said, Edward
    Culture and Imperialism, 3
    *The World, the Text and the
        Critic*, 32
Sandhu, Sukhdev
    *London Calling: How Black and
        Asian Writers Imagined
        a City*, 75
    on Hanif Kureishi, 46

sanity over madness, priority, 149
Sartre, Jean-Paul, literature as
        innocence, 11
Sassoon, Siegfried, 166
    letter to *The Times*, 109
satire and grotesque, 126–56
scapegoat targets in Britain, 39
Sebald, W.G., 4
Second World War and sense of
        history, 107–8
Self, Will, 4, 8, 11, 27
    Cock and Bull, 133
    distancing effect in novels, 57
    Dorian: An Imitation, 27, 133 160
    Great Apes, alternate
        universe, 127–33
self-awareness, 31, 32
self-determination, 65
Selvon, Sam, 47
servants represented in novels, 8
sexual orientation, 110
shepherd's pipe music, 116
Shields, Carol, on *The Girls of Slender
        Means*, 125
Sillitoe, Alan
    *The Loneliness of the Long Distance
        Runner*, 36
    *Saturday Night and Sunday
        Morning*, 36, 52, 53
Simpson, O.J., 128, 132
Sinfield, Alan, 5
    on subcultural novel, 45
'single-issue' writing, 75
Smith, Zadie, 13, 18, 27
    On Beauty, 43
    White Teeth, 8, 12, 85–90
        homage to *Howard's End*
            (Forster), 161–2
        misfit role in, 62
        promotion of it, 38
snobbishness and elitism in Britain, 25
social
    division, 39
    norms, replacement, 7
    realism, Soviet doctrine, 36
    relevance of novel, 43
    situations of writers, 17
    transformation, 4

socially conscious modes, 53
Spark, Muriel, *The Girls of Slender
    Means*, 125
  Dickens' influence, 133
spiritual guidance, lack of, in
    Britain, 140
Stallybrass, Peter, *The Politics and Poetics
    of Transgression*, 67
states of mind, representation of, 48
Stevens, butler, in *The Remains of
    the Day*, 81–2
Storey, David, *Saville*, 52, 53
storytelling
  direct, 19
  on man's existence, 118
suburbia, racism in, 77
subversion and selflessness, 152
subversiveness, conscious, 149
Swift, Graham, 3
  Waterland, 25
Swift, Jonathan, 57
  Gulliver's Travels, 129
'symbolic inversion' of cultural codes,
    (Babcock), 153, 155

Tanner, Tony, *Saul Bellow*, 125
technological world, making misfits, 12
television age, and isolated
    individuals, 83
terrorism and war, and the novel, 53–4
Tew, Philip
  The Contemporary British Novel, 11
  on marginal against
    mainstream, 25–7
  on middle-class identity, 41
  on myth and history, 93
  on postcolonialism, 37
  on postmodernism, 10–11
text facilitating change, 4
Thackeray, William, *Vanity Fair*, Becky
    Sharpe, 62
Thatcher, Margaret, politics and
    history, 93
the Other, 35
theatre of the absurd, 56
Thomson, Philip, on properties of
    grotesque, 126

Thorne, Matt, *All Hail the
    New Puritans*, 18–19
Thorpe, Adam, 27
  distancing effect in novels, 57
  Ulverton, 57, 114
threat of violence, 13
Tolstoy, Leo, objective reality in
    novels, 17
tradition, 6
truth
  and falsity in novel, 23–4
  in proletariat's literature, 51–2
  as relative, 29
  search for, 146

universal principles, shared, 3, 49, 51
unknowable state, 13
untold histories, 111–16
upper and lower, class, 7
urban life, 78

value-judgement, 9
Van Gogh, Vincent, 'outsider', 80
violence
  and the grotesque, 138–9
  and marginalization in
    Trainspotting, 143
voice of the silenced, 157

Wardle, Marc, on man and the
    'spectacle', 21
welfare capitalism, 5
Wells, Lynn
  *Allegories of Telling: Self-Referential
    Narrative in Contemporary British
    Fiction*, 47
  on British novel, 57
Welsh, Irvine, 11
  Trainspotting, 133, 146
  and grotesqe art, 141, 142–5
White, Allon, *The Politics and Poetics of
    Transgression*, 67
Wilde, Oscar
  A Picture of Dorian Gray, 27, 160
  on re-writing history, 117
Wilson, Angus, Dickens'
    influence, 133

Wilson, Colin, *The Outsider*, 79–80
  on 'truth', 66
Wilson, Scott, 11
Winterson, Jeanette, 4, 11, 27, 57
  Lighthousekeeping, 118–21
  misfit protagonists, 61
  novel as socially democratising
    force, 18
  Old Testament, 27
  Oranges Are Not The Only Fruit, 25,
    27–8, 74, 81, 100–103
women as marginalized, 15
Wood, James, 'V.S.Naipaul and English
  comedy', 133

Woolf, Virginia
  Mrs Dalloway, 8
  and marginality, 8
  marginalized by sex, 22
working-class fiction, 25, 36,
  39, 52
working classes in Dickens, 133
working classes in literature, 157
World Trade Center, attacks, and
  writers, 53–4
worship of holy bones, 141

Yee Lin Ho, Elaine, 'literary landmarks'
  in British fiction, 47